250 BEST
meals
in a mug

250 BEST meals in a mug

Camilla V. Saulsbury

Robert
ROSE

For complete cataloguing information, see page 312.

Disclaimer
The recipes in this book have been carefully tested by our kitchen and our tasters. To the
best of our knowledge, they are safe and nutritious for ordinary use and users. For those
people with food or other allergies, or who have special food requirements or health
issues, please read the suggested contents of each recipe carefully and determine whether
or not they may create a problem for you. All recipes are used at the risk of the consumer.

We cannot be responsible for any hazards, loss or damage that may occur as a result of
any recipe use.

For those with special needs, allergies, requirements or health problems, in the event
of any doubt, please contact your medical adviser prior to the use of any recipe.

Design and Production: Martina Hwang/PageWave Graphics Inc.
Editor: Sue Sumeraj
Recipe editor: Jennifer MacKenzie
Proofreader: Sheila Wawanash
Indexer: Gillian Watts
Photographer: Colin Ericson
Associate Photographer: Matt Johannsson
Food Stylist: Kathryn Robertson
Prop Stylist: Charlene Ericson

Cover image: Shrimp, Sausage and Brown Rice Jambalaya, page 216.

Published by Robert Rose Inc.
120 Eglinton Avenue East, Suite 800, Toronto, Ontario, Canada M4P 1E2
Tel: (416) 322-6552 Fax: (416) 322-6936
www.robertrose.ca

Printed and bound in Canada

4 5 6 7 8 9 10 MI 23 22 21 20 19 18 17

Contents

Introduction

Microwave mug recipes first made their appearance a few years ago in a handful of small cookbooks and gift books marketed as fun novelties. The intended audience was home cooks who used their microwave ovens to cook (as opposed to mere heating and reheating), as well as individuals interested in creating simple homemade crafts and gifts. Recipes from these early collections fit into two main categories: 1) simple, sugary cakes and brownies, many of which began with commercially prepared mixes; and 2) make-ahead dry mixes for cakes, soups and dips that could be packaged, given as a gift with a coffee mug and prepared at a later date.

Microwave mug cooking quickly achieved web stardom on food blogs, Pinterest, Instagram and the websites of a host of leading North American newspapers and magazines. An October 2013 Google search of the phrase "mug recipes" yielded more than 40,900,000 hits. Although the majority of recipes in this new wave of microwave mug cooking are for mug cakes and muffins, the range of offerings extends to one-serving cookies, egg dishes, French toast, meatloaf and macaroni and cheese.

Why the fast fame for such a humble way to make food? One explanation is that people feel more time-strapped than ever and want (make that *demand*) food in an instant. Microwave meals and treats fit the bill, providing hot, tasty, fast, easy mini meals in minutes for workers on their lunch break, college students in their dorm rooms, RV enthusiasts, kids and teens looking for an after-school snack, single adults (from first-time apartment dwellers to senior citizens and everyone in between), busy moms and dads on the go, individuals watching their portion sizes, and, in general, anyone who is hungry, is short on time and has access to a microwave and a mug.

Beyond the obvious convenience factor, mug cooking is also an economical alternative to fast food. Even with their abundance of cheap menu offerings, fast-food restaurant costs can mount quickly, especially if they become routine. Excess calories, high fat content and too much sodium and sugar are additional incentives for passing up the drive-through window in favor of a wholesome meal in a mug. Moreover, no matter how short the line, mug cooking is still swifter than any burger, taco or fried chicken joint.

But most of all, meals and treats made in a mug are delicious fun. No cooking prowess is required, nor is any fancy equipment. Mug cooking can be done in the middle of the day at work, in the middle of the night when everyone else is fast asleep, at the end of a hectic day or anytime the desire for a homemade meal strikes.

With *250 Best Meals in a Mug* in hand, your options are extensive, and the results are sure to satisfy. Your choices include healthy breakfasts, snacks, grain and pasta dishes, entrées, and desserts, and the opportunities for kitchen fun, creativity and spontaneity are vast. So grab a mug, get set and go!

Microwave Know-How

Chances are you have used a microwave oven countless times already, even if you never cook in any other capacity. The great news is that mug cooking requires no more cooking prowess than that needed to reheat a cup of coffee, prepare a bag of popcorn or zap a frozen dinner. With the exceptions of a bit of whisking and stirring, the ability to push a few buttons is the only skill required. Following are some microwave guidelines to ensure a foolproof mug meal experience every time.

How Microwave Ovens Work

Despite their ubiquity, microwaves maintain something of a magical aura because many consumers — including those who have owned microwave ovens for years — don't know how the familiar metal box in the kitchen actually works. Dispelling the mysteries of the microwave begins with an understanding of its energy source: microwaves.

Microwaves are a form of electromagnetic energy, or radiation. Microwaves fall between infrared rays and radio waves on the electromagnetic spectrum. They are a form of non-ionizing energy, which means they do not have sufficient strength to dislodge electrons from atoms. This makes them far safer than ionizing energy, which can damage the cells of living tissue. They are used for an array of modern functions, including broadcasting, surveillance, cell phones and airport scanners.

But mention "microwave" in most circumstances and the connotation is the oven. A microwave oven reflects the beams of microwaves, which bounce around inside the oven until they hit, and are then absorbed by, the food inside. This causes the moisture molecules in the food to vibrate rapidly — specifically, at the rate of two and a half billion times each second. This friction creates heat that then cooks the food. In effect, then, the food is cooking itself.

A particular advantage of the microwave oven is that very little heat is wasted in heating up the oven or the air inside of it. The same holds true for the container holding the food: rather than absorbing or reflecting heat, the container in a microwave

A Bit of Microwave Oven History

The microwave oven had an accidental beginning. It all began in 1946 when an engineer named Percy Spencer, an employee of the Raytheon Corporation, was working on magnetrons (vacuum tubes that produce microwave radiation). One day at work, he discovered that a candy bar he was carrying in his pocket had melted. He soon realized that the microwaves he was working with had caused it to melt. After some additional experimentation with popcorn and eggs, he concluded that microwaves have the potential to cook foods in record time.

Spencer set about fashioning a metal box with an opening into which he provided microwave power. Energy entering the box could not escape, thereby creating a higher-density electromagnetic field. When food was placed in the box and microwave energy supplied, the temperature of the food rose very rapidly. The first microwave oven was born.

Within a year, Raytheon introduced the first commercial microwave, called the Radarange, a 6-foot-tall monster of a machine that weighed 750 pounds and cost $5000. Perhaps unsurprisingly, it garnered little attention and few sales. It took several more years before the first domestic models were developed and released. Tappan introduced a home microwave oven in the early 1950s, but the $1295 price was still prohibitive. It wasn't until Raytheon acquired Amana Refrigeration Inc. that affordable home microwaves started to become a reality. They launched a small, reliable countertop oven in 1967 for just under $500. It took time for it to gain popularity and acceptance, but by 1975, microwave oven sales surpassed those for gas ranges. Within two more decades, microwave ovens were no longer a luxury, but an affordable feature of more than 90% of North American homes.

oven allows the microwaves to pass right through it. The result is drastically shorter cooking times than with conventional ovens.

Microwave Wattage and Settings

The recipes in *250 Best Meals in a Mug* were tested in a contemporary, 1000-watt oven; additional testing was done in both older and newer models ranging from 800 to 1200 watts. In addition to having less power, older ovens tend to cook less evenly than models made in the past five years.

Regardless of the size, age and wattage of your oven, you can have success with all of the recipes in this collection. Each recipe has a range of cooking times to account for the variance across different oven makes and models. After completing a few recipes, you will get a sense of whether, for example, your oven tends to need the minimum or maximum times or somewhere in between. The most important rule is to check at the minimum time first; since microwave ovens cook so quickly, it does not take long for foods to overcook, especially more delicate items such as cakes and egg dishes.

The majority of the recipes are prepared using High (100%) power: simply set the time and go. The small number of recipes

Are Microwave Ovens Safe to Use? Science Says "Yes!"

Type "microwaves" and "danger" into any search engine and you will generate countless links to sites proclaiming that microwave ovens are profoundly harmful to human health. The claims, however, are unsupported by science, as noted by countless scientists, science journalists and consumer advocacy groups, including notable physicist Louis A. Bloomfield of Stanford University, nutritionist Marion Nestle of New York University, *Consumer Reports* and the food safety group Center for Science in the Public Interest.

In the literature claiming that microwaved food is depleted of nutrients and/or is full of carcinogenic chemicals, a study from the December 9, 1989, issue of *The Lancet* is repeatedly cited. However, the piece, entitled "Aminoacid Isomerisation and Microwave Exposure," is not a formal peer-reviewed article, but rather a brief letter to the editor. According to the letter, the authors microwaved milk and found that one of the proteins changed shape from L-proline to D-proline. This was a worry because D-proline, in large concentrations, is toxic to the kidney and liver. This letter was followed up by health authorities around the world, who concluded that this was irrelevant to home heating of milk because the scientists had exposed the milk to much greater levels of microwaves than are ever used in the home.

A slew of articles and chain emails also claim that microwaves change the molecular structure and composition of food. According to Dr. Bloomfield, as well as the technicians and scientists at Consumers Union, the organization that publishes *Consumer Reports*, microwaves do *not* affect the molecular structure of food, except through the thermal effects we associate with normal cooking (e.g., denaturing of proteins with heat and caramelizing of sugars). Like all electromagnetic waves, microwaves are emitted and absorbed as tiny photons that cannot cause any chemical rearrangement in a molecule. Instead, they only add a tiny amount of heat to a water molecule. During the microwave cooking process, microwave photons stream into the food and heat it up.

An article written by David Schardt, entitled "Microwave Myths" and published in 2005 by the Center for Science in the Public Interest, dispels two additional pieces of "research" still being posted and reposted today. One is the unsubstantiated research of Swiss food chemist Hans Hertel. In 1989, Hertel and seven fellow vegetarians confined themselves to a hotel room and consumed only milk and vegetables, prepared in different ways, for two months. When he emerged, he announced his findings: that microwave ovens cause cancer and degenerative diseases, despite a complete and utter lack of evidence. His "research" was never peer reviewed or published in any reputable journal, yet it has become the cornerstone of the anti-microwave advocates' arguments.

Schardt's piece further refutes claims by U.S. researcher William Kopp, who wrote in 1996 that Cold War research in the Soviet Union had proven the dangers of microwave ovens. Although the Soviet Union may have banned the ovens for a short period, no countries ban them today. The "evidence" that microwaved foods cause cancer boils down to Hertel's and Kopp's claims, and both are unsupported by science.

Nutrition and cancer risks aside, many still worry about microwaves leaking radiation. Physics professor Dr. Bloomfield notes that, yes, microwaves do in fact leak radiation, but it is a non-ionizing form of radiation found in many devices, including computer screens, radios, televisions and infrared lights. The frequency is extremely low and cannot damage the DNA in our cells.

In sum, the overwhelming evidence indicates that microwave cooking is indeed safe, so heat, eat and be merry.

prepared at a lower wattage are equally simple: you just need to adjust the power setting. Many of the latest microwave ovens can be set by entering a power percentage from 10% to 100%. Other models have wattage settings ranging from Low to High, which correspond to the percentages as follows:

Power Setting	Power Percentage
High	100%
Medium-High	70%
Medium	50%
Medium-Low	30%
Low	10%

How to Determine the Wattage of Your Microwave Oven

If you don't know your microwave's wattage, it can be determined in several ways. The simplest is to check the inside of the oven's door, on the serial number plate on the back of the oven, in the owner's manual or on the manufacturer's website. If you can't find the information from one of these sources, you can estimate wattage with a boiling water test. Measure 1 cup (250 mL) of water into a 2-cup (500 mL) glass measure. Add ice cubes and stir until the water is ice cold. Discard the ice cubes and pour out any water more than 1 cup (250 mL). Place the ice water in the oven and microwave on High for 4 minutes. Watch through the window to see when the water boils. Water that boils in:

- Fewer than 2 minutes = a very high wattage oven (1000 watts or more).
- 2 to $2^1/_2$ minutes = a high wattage oven (800 watts or more).
- $2^1/_2$ to 3 minutes = an average wattage oven (600–700 watts).
- 3 to 4 minutes = a slow wattage oven (300–500 watts).

If your microwave's wattage is in the average or slow range, it will generally take a bit longer than the recipe specifies to cook or heat the dish.

Mug Smarts

Part of the fun of mug meals is just that: they are made and eaten right out of a mug. With the bounty of mugs available for purchase or already in your cupboard, it's a certainty that you will find one (or two, or three) that suits your fancy. Here are some guidelines that will help you select the right mug for the job.

Microwave Mug Safety

Food safety comes first and foremost, so first check the mug to be sure it is microwave-safe. Ceramic and glass are the most common mug materials, but not all glass and ceramic mugs are made for microwave ovens. Your best bet is to look on the bottom of the mug for a "microwave-safe" imprint. Contact the manufacturer if you are uncertain. Avoid using hand-thrown ceramic mugs, as they are unlikely to be microwave-safe and may contain trace amounts of metal.

Mug Size and Shape

Many of the recipes in this collection call for a 16-ounce (500 mL) mug; others can be made in a smaller mug that holds between 12 and 16 ounces (375 and 500 mL). While you can use any shape of mug that fits the volume criteria, keep in mind that mugs with straight sides allow for more even penetration of microwaves than those with sloping sides. I prefer to use straight-sided mugs for making cakes, custards, muffins, breads, egg dishes and cookies, because the recipe cooks more evenly. In addition, choose mugs that have circular bottoms, as opposed to square bottoms, especially when making egg dishes, cakes, breads and muffins. The ingredients in the corners of square mugs tend to overcook.

Mug Thickness

The thickness of the mug will make a difference in the amount of time it takes to cook or heat a recipe. It takes longer for microwaves to pass through thick mugs, resulting in longer cooking times; conversely, the thinner the mug, the shorter the cooking time.

Mugs with Metal Decoration

Never use a mug — or any other dish — that has any gold or silver decoration on it in the microwave. It can cause arcing, an electrical current that flows from the microwave wall to the metal in the oven. It will cause a light flash and a popping sound and can damage the oven. Look closely at mugs with intricate design patterns; the design may include a small amount of metal decoration that may not be noticeable at first glance.

Mug Alternatives

No mug? No problem. Microwave-safe bowls, ramekins or Mason jars that match the volume capacity specified in the recipe can be used with equal success. Be sure to keep a potholder or oven mitt nearby for removing the vessel from the oven, to make up for the absence of a handle.

The Mug Meals Pantry

Most of the recipes in this collection can be made with ingredients you already have in your pantry. My focus in developing the recipes was to use a small number of readily available ingredients, to maximize both taste and convenience in one fell swoop. In this section, you'll find information on some of the most commonly used ingredients in my recipes. With these ingredients on hand, you'll always be ready to prepare a variety of mug meals.

Eggs, Dairy Products and Non-Dairy Milks

Eggs
All of the recipes in this book were tested with large eggs. Select clean, fresh eggs that have been handled properly and refrigerated. Do not use dirty, cracked or leaking eggs, or eggs that have a bad odor or unnatural color when cracked open; they may have become contaminated with harmful bacteria, such as salmonella.

Milk
The recipes that call for milk were tested with 2% milk, but any fat level of milk can be used in its place, as can any of the non-dairy milk options below.

Non-Dairy Milks
Non-dairy milks are essential for vegans, as well as those who are lactose intolerant or allergic to dairy. They are also extremely convenient for mug cooking because they are sold in shelf-stable Tetra Paks. The variety and availability of non-dairy milks is greater than ever: soy milk, rice milk, hemp milk and almond milk are readily available options in most well-stocked grocery stores. Opt for plain non-dairy milk when substituting for milk in any of these recipes.

Yogurt
Many of the recipes call for plain yogurt or plain Greek yogurt. Greek yogurt is a thick, creamy yogurt similar in texture to sour cream.

Preshredded and Grated Cheeses
Ready-to-use cheeses are a boon to mug meals, saving the steps of shredding or grating cheese and subsequently cleaning a grater. Preshredded and grated cheeses are also easy to freeze. The varieties used most often in this book are shredded Cheddar cheese, shredded Italian-blend cheese and grated Parmesan cheese.

Ricotta Cheese
Ricotta is a rich, fresh cheese with a texture that is slightly grainy but still far smoother than cottage cheese. For the best texture in mug cakes and other mug desserts, opt for regular or lower-fat (not nonfat) varieties.

Cottage Cheese
Cottage cheese is used in a number of recipes throughout this collection, from muffins to main dishes. In addition to its versatility, it has significant nutritional value (most notably in protein and calcium).

Frozen and Canned Meats, Chicken and Seafood

Keeping small amounts of fresh meat, chicken and seafood on hand is inconvenient for quick mug meals. The solution is simple: ready-to-use, fully cooked frozen or canned options. Here are my top picks for a wide range of fast meals:

- Frozen cooked meatballs (beef, pork or a mix of the two)
- Frozen cooked breakfast sausages
- Water-packed canned chicken (any variety)
- Water-packed canned tuna (any variety)
- Canned boneless salmon
- Canned lump crabmeat
- Canned shrimp

Soybean Products

Just a short while back, soybean products — tofu, soy milk, tempeh, soy cheese and soy yogurt — were considered health food oddities. Now, most of these items have gone mainstream and are commonly available in well-stocked grocery stores.

Tofu

Tofu, or bean curd, is made from soybeans that have been cooked, made into milk and then coagulated. The soy milk curdles when heated, and the curds are skimmed off and pressed into blocks. Tofu can be found in extra-firm, firm and soft varieties in the refrigerated section of the supermarket. Be sure to use the variety specified in the recipe for optimal results.

All of the recipes in this collection were tested with refrigerated tofu. While shelf-stable tofu is convenient, the flavor and texture are markedly inferior.

Tempeh

Tempeh (pronounced *TEM-pay*) is a traditional Indonesian food. It is made from fully cooked soybeans that have been fermented with a mold called rhizopus and formed into cakes. Some varieties have whole grains added to the mix, creating a particularly meaty, satisfying texture. Tempeh, like tofu, takes on the flavor of whatever it is marinated with, and also needs to be stored in the refrigerator.

Legumes

Canned Beans and Lentils

With their high protein content, wide availability, low cost and convenience, canned beans and lentils are ideal for a wide variety of hearty mug meals. Here are some great choices to keep on hand:

- Black beans
- White beans (e.g., cannellini, great Northern beans, white navy beans)
- Pinto beans (plain or chili-seasoned)
- Red kidney beans
- Chickpeas
- Lentils

Nuts, Seeds and Nut/Seed Butters

In addition to being excellent sources of protein, nuts and seeds contain vitamins, minerals, fiber and essential fatty acids (such as omega-3 and omega-6).

Nuts

A wide variety of nuts are used in this collection, including walnuts, cashews, pecans, almonds and peanuts. Many of the recipes call for the nuts to be toasted before they are used. Toasting nuts deepens their flavor and makes them crisp. To toast whole nuts, spread the amount needed for the recipe on a rimmed baking sheet. Bake in a preheated 350°F (180°C) oven for 8 to 10 minutes or until golden and fragrant. Alternatively, toast the nuts in a dry skillet over low heat, stirring constantly for 2 to 4 minutes or until golden and fragrant. Transfer the toasted nuts to a plate and let them cool before chopping.

Ground Flax Seeds (Flaxseed Meal)
Ground flax seeds are highly nutritious, tiny seeds from the flax plant that have been ground into meal to reap the most nutritional benefits. Store ground flax seeds in an airtight container in the refrigerator for up to 5 months or in the freezer for up to 8 months.

Green Pumpkin Seeds (Pepitas)
Pepitas are pumpkin seeds with the white hull removed, leaving the flat, dark green inner seed.

Sesame Seeds
Tiny and delicate, the flavor of sesame seeds increases exponentially when they are toasted. Look for toasted sesame seeds where Asian foods are shelved in the supermarket.

Shelled Sunflower Seeds
Sunflower seeds are highly nutritious and have a mild, nutty flavor and texture.

Nut and Seed Butters
Delicious, nutritious, ultra-convenient nut and seed butters are a boon for any meal of the day, as well as for snacks, desserts and quick breads. They can also impart instant richness to a wide range of sauces and dressings. Use your favorite creamy nut or seed butters interchangeably in any of the recipes calling for peanut butter or nut/seed butter.

Flours and Grains

All-Purpose Flour
Made from a blend of high-gluten hard wheat and low-gluten soft wheat, all-purpose flour is fine-textured flour milled from the inner part of the wheat kernel and contains neither the germ nor the bran. All-purpose flour comes either bleached or unbleached; they can be used interchangeably.

Bulgur
Bulgur is wheat kernels that have been steamed, dried and crushed. The outer layers of the bran are removed, and the grains are cracked. It is generally available in coarse, medium and fine

grinds. It has a nutty taste and, when rehydrated, a tender, chewy texture. For best results in microwave mug cooking, opt for a medium or fine grind.

Cornmeal

Cornmeal is simply ground dried corn kernels. There are two methods of grinding. The first is the modern method, in which milling is done by huge steel rollers, which remove the husk and germ almost entirely; this creates the most common variety of cornmeal found in supermarkets. The second is the stone-ground method, in which some of the hull and germ of the corn is retained; this type of cornmeal is available at health food stores and in the health food sections of most supermarkets. The two varieties can be used interchangeably, but I recommend sticking with the stone-ground variety where specified, as it has a much deeper corn flavor and is also more nutritious.

Instant Brown Rice

Instant brown rice is precooked (parboiled) whole-grain brown rice that cooks in a fraction of the time of regular brown rice. Unlike instant white rice, which has little nutritional value, instant brown rice is considered a whole grain and is a good source of manganese, magnesium, selenium and fiber.

Pancake Mix

Ingredients vary slightly by manufacturer, but ready-to-use pancake mixes are typically made of all-purpose flour, milk or buttermilk powder, vegetable oil, baking powder and salt. It is important to select a mix that requires the addition of eggs and milk, as opposed to those that only require the addition of water. Once opened, the mix will keep in an airtight container for up to 6 months. You can also refrigerate or freeze the mix in an airtight container for up to 1 year.

Quick-Cooking Barley

Unlike instant brown rice, quick-cooking barley is not parboiled. Rather, it is pearl barley that has been thinly rolled (it looks like rolled oats before cooking), which cuts the cooking time down to a few minutes. Look for it in one of two places in the supermarket: where rice and grains are shelved or where soups and broths are shelved.

Quinoa

Quinoa is actually a seed, not a true grain, and resembles couscous when uncooked. White (or pale golden) quinoa is the most commonly available variety, but red and black varieties are also available in North America. Any color can be used in these recipes. To keep quinoa as fresh as possible, store it in an airtight container in the refrigerator for up to 6 months or in the freezer for up to 1 year.

Rolled Oats

Two types of rolled oats are called for in these recipes. Large-flake (old-fashioned) rolled oats are oat groats (hulled and cleaned whole oats) that have been steamed and flattened with huge rollers. Quick-cooking rolled oats are groats that have been cut into several pieces before being steamed and rolled into thinner flakes. For the best results, it is important to use the type of rolled oats specified in the recipe.

Wheat Germ

Wheat germ is the most nutritious portion of the wheat kernel. It is usually separated from the bran and starch during the milling of flour because the germ's perishable oil content limits the storage time of the flour. It looks like very finely ground nuts and has a nutty flavor. Due to its high oil content, wheat germ is best stored in the refrigerator or freezer in an airtight container to keep it from turning rancid. Either toasted or untoasted wheat germ can be used in the recipes.

Pasta

Pasta cooks remarkably well in a mug, with a texture akin to traditionally cooked stovetop pasta. As a bonus, only a small amount of liquid is required, which means that draining is unnecessary. It is essential, however, to use small shapes to achieve the best results. The following types of pasta are used most frequently in this collection:

- Cut spaghetti (or regular spaghetti broken into 1-inch/5 cm pieces)
- Small elbow macaroni
- Ditalini (small short tubes)
- Orzo (rice-shaped pasta)
- Couscous (regular or whole wheat)

Shelf-Stable Tomato Products

Diced Tomatoes

Canned diced tomatoes are an easy way to add tremendous flavor to a wide variety of mug recipes, especially soups and stews. For an extra boost of flavor with zero added effort, stock up on diced tomatoes with green chiles and diced tomatoes with Italian seasoning, too.

Tomato Sauce

Tomato sauce can be used to make delicious sauces, stews and soups when you want to give them a distinct tomato flavor. For the best tomato flavor, opt for tomato sauce that is low in sodium and has no added seasonings.

Marinara Sauce

Jarred marinara sauce — a highly seasoned Italian tomato sauce made with onions, garlic, basil and oregano — is typically used on pasta and meat, but it is also a great pantry staple for creating a range of mug meals in minutes.

Chunky Tomato Salsa

Ready-made chunky salsa is rich with tomatoes, peppers, onions and spices, and low in calories — a great way to perk up a mug meal in an instant.

Frozen Fruits and Vegetables

In addition to its convenience, frozen produce can sometimes be more nutritious than fresh. When fresh fruits and vegetables are shipped long distances, they rapidly lose vitamins and minerals thanks to exposure to heat and light; by contrast, frozen fruits and vegetables are frozen immediately after being picked, ensuring that all of the vitamins and minerals are preserved.

Having a selection of frozen chopped fruits and vegetables on hand will give you maximum flexibility in preparing your mug meals. Here are the ones I use most often:

- Berries (blueberries, blackberries, raspberries, strawberries)
- Broccoli florets
- Chopped bell pepper and onion blend
- Chopped greens (spinach, Swiss chard, mustard greens)
- Chopped onions
- Corn
- Petite peas
- Shelled edamame
- Snow peas
- Sugar snap peas
- Vegetable stir-fry blends (including sliced bell peppers and onions)
- Winter squash purée (typically a blend of acorn and butternut squash)

Fats and Oils

Fats and oils are used sparingly in this collection, largely because they simply aren't needed in many microwave recipes, especially these extra-quick mug ones.

Butter

Butter is used most in the desserts chapter, and sparingly through the rest of the book. Butter quickly picks up off-flavors during storage and when exposed to oxygen, so once the carton or wrap is opened, place it in a sealable plastic food bag or other airtight container. Store it away from foods with strong odors, especially items such as onions or garlic.

If you only use butter occasionally, I recommend storing it in the freezer. Cut it into 1-tbsp (15 mL) pats and place them on a baking sheet lined with plastic wrap. Freeze for 30 to 60 minutes, until frozen, then place the frozen pats in an airtight container. Butter can be frozen for up to 6 months. Remove pats as needed and thaw in the refrigerator or at room temperature.

Vegetable Oil

Vegetable oil is a generic term used to describe any neutral, plant-based oil that is liquid at room temperature. You can use a vegetable oil blend, canola oil, light olive oil, grapeseed oil, safflower oil, sunflower oil, peanut oil or corn oil.

Olive Oil

Olive oil is monounsaturated oil that is prized for a wide range of cooking preparations. I recommend using plain olive oil (simply labeled "olive oil"), which contains a combination of refined olive oil and virgin or extra virgin oil. The subtle nuances of extra virgin olive oil are not very noticeable after cooking in the microwave.

Unrefined Virgin Coconut Oil

Virgin coconut oil, which is semi-solid at room temperature, is used in a few recipes or variations in this collection, often as an alternative to butter.

Toasted Sesame Oil

Toasted sesame oil has a dark brown color and a rich, nutty flavor. It is used sparingly, mostly in Asian recipes, to add a tremendous amount of flavor.

Nonstick Cooking Spray

A number of recipes in this collection call for the use of nonstick cooking spray, which helps keep foods from sticking to the mug. It may seem odd to spray a mug before mixing cake or muffin batter in it, but it really works: the cooked food is much easier to remove and cleanup is far simpler.

Sweeteners

Granulated Sugar
Granulated sugar (also called white sugar) is refined cane or beet sugar, and is the most common sweetener used in this book. Once opened, store granulated sugar in an airtight container in a cool, dry place.

Brown Sugar
Brown sugar is granulated sugar with some molasses added to it. The molasses gives the sugar a soft texture. Light brown sugar (also known as golden yellow sugar) has less molasses and a more delicate flavor than dark brown sugar. Once opened, store brown sugar in an airtight container or a sealable plastic food bag to prevent clumping.

Confectioners' (Icing) Sugar
Confectioners' (icing) sugar (also called powdered sugar) is granulated sugar that has been ground to a fine powder. Cornstarch is added to prevent the sugar from clumping together. It is used in recipes where regular sugar would be too grainy.

Honey
Honey is plant nectar that has been gathered and concentrated by honeybees. Any variety of honey may be used in the recipes in this collection. Unopened containers of honey may be stored at room temperature. After opening, store honey in the refrigerator to protect against mold. Honey will keep indefinitely when stored properly.

Maple Syrup
Maple syrup is a thick liquid sweetener made by boiling the sap from maple trees. It has a strong, pure maple flavor. Maple-flavored pancake syrup is just corn syrup with coloring and artificial maple flavoring added, and it is not recommended as a substitute for pure maple syrup. Unopened containers of maple syrup may be stored at room temperature. After opening, store maple syrup in the refrigerator to protect against mold. Maple syrup will keep indefinitely when stored properly.

Stevia
Stevia is derived from the leaves of a South American shrub, *Stevia rebaudiana*. It is about 300 times sweeter than

cane sugar. Stevia is not absorbed through the digestive tract, and therefore has no calories. Stevia comes in several forms: dried leaf, liquid extract and powdered extract. The few recipes in this collection that call for stevia use it in powdered form.

Flavorings and Leavening Agents

Elevating the flavor of mug meals can be as easy as creating a delicious balance of flavorings from the pantry. Here are my top recommendations for ingredients that will make your mug meals shine.

Salt
Unless otherwise specified, the recipes in this collection were tested using common table salt. An equal amount of fine sea salt can be used in its place.

Black Pepper
Black pepper is made by grinding black peppercorns, which have been picked when the berry is not quite ripe, and then dried until it shrivels and the skin turns dark brown to black. Black pepper has a strong, slightly hot flavor, with a hint of sweetness.

Baking Powder
Baking powder is a chemical leavening agent made from a blend of alkali (sodium bicarbonate, known commonly as baking soda) and acid (most commonly calcium acid phosphate, sodium aluminum sulfate or cream of tartar), plus some form of starch to absorb any moisture so a reaction does not take place until a liquid is added.

Fresh Herbs
Fresh herbs add both flavor and color to mug meals. Parsley, cilantro and chives are readily available and inexpensive, and they store well in the produce bin of the refrigerator, so keep them on hand year-round. Basil, mint and thyme are best in the spring and summer, when they are in season in your own garden or at the farmers' market.

Spices and Dried Herbs
Spices and dried herbs can turn the simplest of meals into masterpieces. They should be stored in light- and airproof containers, away from direct sunlight and heat, to preserve their flavors.

Co-ops, health food stores and mail order sources that sell herbs and spices in bulk are all excellent options for purchasing very fresh, organic spices and dried herbs, often at a low cost.

With ground spices and dried herbs, freshness is everything. To determine whether a ground spice or dried herb is fresh, open the container and sniff. A strong fragrance means it is still acceptable for use.

Note that ground spices, not whole, are used throughout this collection. Here are my top picks for a wide variety of mug meals:

◆ Cayenne pepper (also labeled "ground red pepper")
◆ Cinnamon
◆ Cumin
◆ Curry powder (any heat level, but mild is the most versatile)
◆ Ginger
◆ Italian seasoning
◆ Nutmeg
◆ Pumpkin pie spice
◆ Rubbed sage

Hot Pepper Sauce

Hot pepper sauce is a spicy condiment made from chili peppers and other common ingredients such as vinegar and spices. It comes in countless heat levels and flavors, so pick the multipurpose sauce that best suits your taste buds.

Citrus Zest

"Zest" is the name for the colored outer layer of citrus peel. The oils in zest are intense in flavor. Use a zester, a Microplane-style grater or the small holes of a box grater to grate zest. Avoid grating the white layer (pith) just below the zest; it is very bitter.

Cocoa Powder

Select natural cocoa powder rather than Dutch process for these recipes. Natural cocoa powder has a deep, true chocolate flavor and tends to be less expensive. The packaging should state whether it is Dutch process, but you can also tell the difference by sight: if it is dark to almost black, it is Dutch process; natural cocoa powder is much lighter and is typically brownish red.

Vanilla Extract

Vanilla extract adds a sweet, fragrant flavor to dishes, especially baked goods. It is produced by combining an extraction from dried vanilla beans with an alcohol and water mixture. It is then aged for several months.

Almond Extract

Almond extract is a flavoring manufactured by combining bitter almond oil with ethyl alcohol. It is used in much the same way as vanilla extract. Almond extract has a highly concentrated, intense flavor, so measure with care.

Miso
Miso is a sweet, fermented soybean paste usually made with some sort of grain. It comes unpasteurized and in several varieties, from golden yellow to deep red to sweet white. It can be made into a soup or a sauce or used as a salt substitute.

Thai Curry Paste
Available in small jars, Thai curry paste is a blend of Thai chiles, garlic, lemongrass, galangal, ginger and wild lime leaves. It is a fast and delicious way to add Southeast Asian flavor to a broad spectrum of recipes in a single step. Panang and yellow curry pastes tend to be the mildest. Red curry paste is medium hot, and green curry paste is typically the hottest.

Mustard
Mustard adds depth of flavor to a wide range of dishes. Dijon mustard and brown mustard have the most versatility.

Vinegars
Vinegars are flavor powerhouses. When used at the end of cooking, they enhance and balance the natural flavors of dishes. Cider vinegar, red wine vinegar and white wine vinegar are excellent multi-purpose options. Store vinegars in a dark place, away from heat or light.

Ready-to-Use Broths
Ready-to-use chicken, beef and vegetable broths are an essential component of many of these recipes. Select broths that are all-natural, reduced-sodium (you can always add more salt) and MSG-free. For chicken and beef broths, choose brands that are made from chicken or cattle raised without hormones or antibiotics.

For convenience, look for broths in Tetra Paks, which typically come in 32-oz (1 L), 48-oz (1.5 L) and occasionally 16-oz (500 mL) sizes. Once opened, these can be stored in the refrigerator for up to 1 week. You can also freeze small amounts (2 to 4 tbsp/30 to 60 mL) in ice cube trays. Once frozen, simply pop out the cubes and store in a freezer bag for up to 6 months. Thaw in the microwave or the refrigerator.

Prepared Basil Pesto
Basil pesto is an Italian sauce that is traditionally made from basil, garlic, pine nuts, olive oil and cheese. It adds a huge amount of flavor in one simple step. Look for it where pasta and marinara sauce are shelved, or in the refrigerated section, near fresh pastas.

Measuring Ingredients

Accurate measurements are important for mug meals, to achieve the right balance of flavors and avoid mug overflows. So take both time and care as you measure.

Measuring Dry Ingredients

When measuring a dry ingredient, such as flour, cocoa powder, sugar, spices or salt, spoon it into the appropriate-size dry measuring cup or measuring spoon, heaping it up over the top. Slide a straight-edged utensil, such as a knife, across the top to level off the extra. Be careful not to shake or tap the cup or spoon to settle the ingredient, or you will have more than you need.

Measuring Moist Ingredients

Moist ingredients, such as brown sugar, coconut and dried fruit, must be firmly packed in a measuring cup or spoon to be measured accurately. Use a dry measuring cup for these ingredients. Fill the measuring cup to slightly overflowing, then pack down the ingredient firmly with the back of a spoon. Add more of the ingredient and pack down again until the cup is full and even with the top of the measure.

Measuring Liquid Ingredients

Use a clear plastic or glass measuring cup or container with lines up the sides to measure liquid ingredients. Set the container on the counter and pour the liquid to the appropriate mark. Lower your head to read the measurement at eye level.

Super-Fast, Cheap and Easy Recipes

with 4 Ingredients (or Less)

Apple Pancake Puff

This puffy creation is a quick and easy take on a "Dutch baby." Gussy it up with a drizzle of syrup, a sprinkle of confectioners' sugar, a bit of butter or all of the above for an extra-special weekday breakfast on the go.

Tips

One medium apple will yield about $3/4$ cup (175 mL) shredded apple.

For even more flavor, add $1/8$ tsp (0.5 mL) vanilla extract and/or $1/4$ tsp (1 mL) ground cinnamon to the batter.

An equal amount of liquid honey or maple syrup can be used in place of the brown sugar.

♦ **12- to 16-oz (375 to 500 mL) mug, sprayed with nonstick cooking spray**

$3/4$ cup	shredded apple (preferably tart or tart-sweet)	175 mL
2 tbsp	dry buttermilk pancake mix	30 mL
1 tbsp	packed brown sugar or granulated sugar	15 mL
1	large egg	1

Suggested Accompaniments

Cinnamon sugar or confectioners' (icing) sugar; pure maple syrup or liquid honey; pat of butter

1. In the mug, whisk apple, pancake mix, brown sugar and egg until blended.
2. Microwave on High for $1^1/2$ to 2 minutes (checking at $1^1/2$) or until puffed and set at the center. Serve with any of the suggested accompaniments, as desired.

Variations

- **Maple Pear Puff:** Use shredded firm-ripe pear in place of the apple and pure maple syrup in place of the brown sugar. Add a pinch of ground nutmeg, if desired.
- **Cheddar Apple Puff:** Add $1/4$ cup (60 mL) shredded sharp (old) Cheddar cheese with the apple.

> **Prep Ahead Option**
> Place the shredded apple in a small airtight container; cover and refrigerate. (If desired, add a few drops of lemon juice to prevent browning.) Whisk the egg and brown sugar in the mug; cover and refrigerate until ready to use. Keep the pancake mix separate in an airtight container.

Egg Mug-Muffin Sandwich

You'll never wait in a fast-food drive-through again once you try this super-speedy breakfast sandwich. It's endlessly customizable, too (think bits of bacon or ham, vegetables, herbs and cheeses).

Tip

For a lighter mug-muffin, replace one of the eggs with 2 large egg whites.

♦ **12- to 16-oz (375 to 500 mL) mug**

2	large eggs	2
2 tbsp	shredded Cheddar cheese (or cheese of choice)	30 mL
	Salt and ground black pepper	
1	English muffin, split (toast, if desired)	1

1. In the mug, whisk eggs until blended. Stir in cheese and season with salt and pepper.

2. Microwave on High for 30 seconds. Stir with a fork. Microwave for 30 seconds, then stir again. Microwave for 15 to 45 seconds or until eggs are just set.

3. Transfer egg mixture to one muffin half. Top with second muffin half and eat immediately.

Variations

- **Bacon Mug-Muffin:** Add 1 tbsp (15 mL) ready-to-eat real bacon bits with the eggs.

- **Sausage and Peppers Mug-Muffin:** Before preparing the egg, microwave 1 frozen cooked breakfast sausage link and $\frac{1}{4}$ cup (60 mL) frozen or fresh chopped bell pepper and onion blend in the mug on High for 60 to 70 seconds or until warmed through. Break up sausage with a fork. Whisk in eggs and proceed as directed.

- **Veggie Lover's Mug-Muffin:** Before preparing the egg, microwave 2 tbsp (30 mL) thick and chunky salsa, 2 tbsp (30 mL) shredded carrot and 1 tbsp (15 mL) chopped green onions in the mug on High for 30 seconds. Whisk in eggs and proceed as directed.

Prep Ahead Option

Whisk the eggs in the mug and stir in cheese; cover and refrigerate until ready to use.

Mug Frittata

Weekday mornings often feel rushed, especially when it comes to breakfast. Who has time to make a brunch-worthy egg dish like a frittata? You do, that's who! This streamlined mug frittata clocks in well under 5 minutes from start to finish, giving you the chance to nourish body, mind and soul before stepping out the door.

Tips

An equal amount of regular, reduced-fat or nonfat ricotta cheese may be used in place of the cottage cheese.

You can eat the frittata straight out of the mug or serve it atop a toasted English muffin or piece of toast. Alternatively, cut it in half and roll it up into a tortilla or tuck it inside a pita half.

♦ **12- to 16-oz (375 to 500 mL) mug**

2	large eggs	2
2 tbsp	chopped green onions	30 mL
2 tbsp	nonfat or reduced-fat cottage cheese	30 mL
2 tsp	freshly grated Parmesan cheese	10 mL
	Salt and ground black pepper	

1. In the mug, whisk eggs until blended. Whisk in green onions, cottage cheese and Parmesan. Season with salt and pepper.
2. Microwave on High for 30 seconds. Stir with a fork. Microwave for 30 seconds, then stir again. Microwave for 60 to 90 seconds or until eggs are just set.

Variations

- **Basil Pesto Frittata:** Omit the green onions and Parmesan. Add 1 tbsp (15 mL) basil pesto with the eggs.
- **Bacon Frittata:** Add 1 tbsp (15 mL) ready-to-eat real bacon bits with the eggs.
- **Smoked Sausage Frittata:** Add 2 tbsp (30 mL) diced cooked smoked sausage (regular or reduced-fat) with the eggs.
- **Greek Frittata:** Add 1/2 tsp (2 mL) dried dillweed or 1/4 tsp (1 mL) dried oregano with the eggs. Replace the Parmesan with 1 tbsp (15 mL) crumbled feta cheese and add 2 tbsp (30 mL) chopped drained roasted red bell peppers (from a jar) with the green onions.

Prep Ahead Option

Whisk the eggs in the mug. Whisk in green onions, cottage cheese and Parmesan; cover and refrigerate until ready to use.

Tofu Scramble

To give the tofu a golden hue akin to scrambled eggs, add a pinch of ground turmeric (or curry powder, if you like the taste). Delicious straight from the mug, this egg-free scramble is also great tucked inside a tortilla or pita.

Tips

Add $\frac{1}{4}$ tsp (1 mL) of your favorite dried herbs (such as basil or oregano) or herb blend (such as Italian seasoning) with the tofu.

Store the remaining drained tofu in small airtight containers or freezer bags in $\frac{3}{4}$-cup (175 mL) amounts.

If a frozen pepper and onion blend isn't available, use $\frac{1}{2}$ cup (125 mL) mixed chopped fresh bell peppers and onions and, in step 1, cook for about 2 minutes or until vegetables are tender-crisp.

◆ 12- to 16-oz (375 to 500 mL) mug

$\frac{1}{2}$ cup	frozen chopped bell pepper and onion blend	125 mL
$\frac{3}{4}$ cup	crumbled drained extra-firm or firm tofu	175 mL
2 tsp	soy sauce	10 mL
1 tsp	olive oil	5 mL
	Salt and ground black pepper	

1. In the mug, microwave peppers and onions on High for $1\frac{1}{2}$ to 2 minutes or until heated through. Using the tines of a fork, press down firmly on the vegetables and drain off excess liquid.

2. Stir in tofu, soy sauce and oil. Microwave on High for 45 to 75 seconds or until heated through. Season to taste with salt and pepper.

Variations

- **Southwest Scramble:** Add $\frac{1}{4}$ cup (60 mL) canned or fresh diced tomatoes and $\frac{1}{8}$ tsp (0.5 mL) ground cumin or chili powder with the tofu. When seasoning, sprinkle with chopped fresh cilantro, if desired.

- **Mushroom Herb Scramble:** Add 3 tbsp (45 mL) drained canned mushroom pieces, 1 tbsp (15 mL) chopped chives or green onions and a pinch of dried thyme with the tofu.

Prep Ahead Option

Place the frozen peppers and onions in the mug; cover and refrigerate (decrease the cooking time in step 1 by 30 seconds). Measure the tofu, soy sauce and oil into a small airtight container; cover and refrigerate until ready to use.

Bacon Cheddar Grits

Grits aren't just for rich breakfasts from the American South; they are a quick, easy and delicious dish (akin to polenta) that makes a satisfying snack or meal at any time of day.

♦ **12- to 16-oz (375 to 500 mL) mug**

3 tbsp	quick-cooking grits	45 mL
1/2 cup	milk	125 mL
1/4 cup	water	60 mL
2 tbsp	shredded Cheddar or Monterey Jack cheese	30 mL
1 tbsp	ready-to-eat real bacon bits	15 mL
	Salt and ground black pepper	

1. In the mug, combine grits, milk and water. Microwave on High for 1 minute. Stir. Microwave on High for 1 to 2 minutes (checking at 1) or until thickened and creamy.

2. Stir in cheese and bacon. Let stand for 30 seconds. Season to taste with salt and pepper.

Variations

- **Cheesy Grits and Greens:** Omit the bacon. In a separate mug, microwave 1 cup (250 mL) frozen chopped spinach on High for 1 to 2 minutes or until thawed and warm. Using the tines of a fork, press down firmly on the spinach and drain off excess liquid. Add 1 tsp (5 mL) butter or olive oil, and salt and hot sauce to taste; spoon on top of grits.

- **Parmesan Grits with Marinara Sauce:** Omit the bacon and replace the Cheddar cheese with an equal amount of grated Parmesan cheese. After seasoning grits, spoon 2 tbsp (30 mL) prepared marinara sauce over grits. Microwave on High for 25 to 30 seconds or until warmed through. Sprinkle with additional Parmesan, if desired.

> **Prep Ahead Option**
> In the mug, combine grits, milk and water; cover and refrigerate for up to 1 day.

Hearty Hash Brown Mug

Diced frozen hash browns, with the onions and peppers included, are the shortcut secret to this hearty mug meal.

Tips

Frozen hash browns with onions and peppers are often labeled "O'Brien" potatoes.

An equal amount of shredded hash browns can be used in place of the diced hash browns with onions and peppers.

♦ **12- to 16-oz (375 to 500 mL) mug**

$3/4$ cup	frozen diced hash brown potatoes with onions and peppers	175 mL
1	large egg	1
2 tbsp	shredded Cheddar cheese (or cheese of choice)	30 mL
	Salt and ground black pepper	

Suggested Add-Ins

Chopped green onions; ready-to-eat real bacon bits; chopped ham; chopped cooked smoked sausage; chopped tomato; hot sauce

1. In the mug, microwave hash browns on High for $1^1/_2$ to 2 minutes or until warmed through.

2. Using a fork, beat in egg, cheese and any add-ins, as desired. Season with salt and pepper. Microwave on High for 45 to 75 seconds (checking at 45) or until egg is just set.

> **Prep Ahead Option**
>
> Place the hash browns in the mug; cover and refrigerate (decrease the cooking time in step 1 by 30 seconds). Break egg into a small airtight container and, using a fork, beat in cheese and any add-ins; cover and refrigerate until ready to use.

"Baked" Banana Oatmeal

Enriched with sweet banana and a protein-packed egg, this hearty take on basic oatmeal will power you through any morning with ease.

Tips

For even more flavor, add $\frac{1}{8}$ tsp (0.5 mL) vanilla extract and a pinch of ground nutmeg or cinnamon.

To make this dish gluten-free, be sure to use oats that are certified gluten-free.

♦ **16-oz (500 mL) mug**

$\frac{2}{3}$ cup	quick-cooking or large-flake (old-fashioned) rolled oats	150 mL
1	large egg	1
$\frac{1}{2}$ cup	milk	125 mL
$\frac{1}{2}$ cup	mashed very ripe banana	125 mL
Pinch	salt	Pinch

Suggested Accompaniments

Milk or light cream; sliced or diced firm-ripe banana; brown sugar, honey or pure maple syrup; chocolate chips

1. In the mug, whisk oats, egg, milk, banana and salt until blended.
2. Microwave on High for $1\frac{1}{2}$ to $2\frac{1}{2}$ minutes (checking at $1\frac{1}{2}$) or until just set. Let stand for 1 minute. Serve with any of the suggested accompaniments, as desired.

Variations

- **Apple Cinnamon Baked Oatmeal:** Replace the banana with an equal amount of sweetened cinnamon applesauce.
- **Peanut Butter Banana Baked Oatmeal:** Add 1 tbsp (15 mL) peanut butter with the banana in step 1.
- **Chocolate Baked Oatmeal:** Add 1 tbsp (15 mL) unsweetened cocoa powder and 1 tbsp (15 mL) granulated sugar or packed brown sugar with the banana in step 1.
- **Pumpkin Pie Baked Oatmeal:** Replace the banana with an equal amount of pumpkin purée (not pie filling). Add 1 tbsp (15 mL) packed brown sugar and $\frac{1}{4}$ tsp (1 mL) pumpkin pie spice or ground cinnamon.

> **Prep Ahead Option**
> Prepare through step 1; cover and refrigerate for up to 1 day. Continue with step 2.

Creamy Tomato Soup

Prepared marinara sauces can vary in their acidity and sweetness, so taste the finished soup — you may want to add a pinch of sugar to balance the acidity or a few drops of vinegar to balance the sweetness.

Tip

For even more flavor, add $1/4$ tsp (1 mL) dried oregano, basil or Italian seasoning with the broth.

◆ **16-oz (500 mL) mug**

$3/4$ cup	marinara sauce	175 mL
$1/4$ cup	ready-to-use chicken broth, vegetable broth or water	60 mL
$1/4$ cup	milk or half-and-half (10%) cream	60 mL
	Salt and ground black pepper	
1 tbsp	grated Parmesan cheese	15 mL

1. In the mug, stir marinara sauce and broth until blended. Microwave on High for 1 to 2 minutes (checking at 1) or until hot but not boiling.

2. Stir in milk. Microwave for 30 to 60 seconds or until hot but not boiling. Season with salt and pepper and sprinkle with Parmesan.

Variations

- **Tomato Pesto Soup:** Omit the Parmesan and stir in 1 tbsp (15 mL) prepared basil pesto with the milk.

- **Tomato and Chickpea Soup:** Add $1/2$ cup (125 mL) drained rinsed canned chickpeas or white beans (such as cannellini or great Northern) with the broth and marinara in step 1.

> **Prep Ahead Option**
>
> Combine the marinara sauce and broth in the mug; cover and refrigerate. Measure the milk into a small airtight container; cover and refrigerate until ready to use.

Creamy Broccoli Soup

A quick whirl in the blender makes this simple soup rich and thick, like cream-based varieties.

Tips

Opt for bags, as opposed to boxes, of frozen chopped broccoli, as it is easier to remove small amounts at a time.

If you only have frozen broccoli florets, use 1¼ cups (300 mL) and increase the cooking time in step 1 by up to 30 seconds, if needed.

For a richer soup, use an equal amount of light Alfredo sauce in place of the milk.

♦ **16-oz (500 mL) mug**

♦ **Blender**

1 cup	frozen chopped broccoli	250 mL
⅔ cup	ready-to-use chicken or vegetable broth	150 mL
¼ cup	milk	60 mL
1 tbsp	grated Parmesan cheese	15 mL

1. In the mug, microwave broccoli and broth on High for 1½ to 2½ minutes or until very hot.
2. Transfer to the blender and add milk. Let stand for 2 minutes, then blend until partially or completely smooth.
3. Return to mug and Microwave on High for 1 to 2 minutes (checking at 1) or until hot but not boiling. Stir in Parmesan cheese.

Variations

- **Broccoli Cheddar Soup:** Omit the Parmesan cheese and add 2 tbsp (30 mL) shredded sharp (old) Cheddar cheese with the milk.

- **Creamy Cauliflower Soup:** Replace the broccoli with frozen cauliflower florets. If desired, add a pinch of ground nutmeg.

> **Prep Ahead Option**
>
> Prepare the soup through step 2. Return to mug, cover and refrigerate until ready to heat. Microwave on High for 1½ to 2 minutes or until hot but not boiling.

Pumpkin Sage Soup

Bright and beautiful, this velvety pumpkin soup is autumn in a mug. Its rich flavor belies the minimal prep time.

Tips

Canned pumpkin purée can vary in sweetness. If needed, add a pinch of brown sugar or a drizzle of maple syrup to enhance the flavor of the soup.

Consider topping with seasoned croutons or toasted pumpkin seeds.

Freeze the remaining pumpkin in a small sealable freezer bag. You can freeze the entire amount in one bag, or portion out $2/3$ cup (150 mL) per bag so that the pumpkin is recipe-ready. Be sure to label the bag with the contents. Store for up to 3 months. Defrost in the refrigerator or microwave before using.

♦ **16-oz (500 mL) mug**

$3/4$ cup	ready-to-use chicken or vegetable broth	175 mL
$2/3$ cup	pumpkin purée (not pie filling)	150 mL
$1/4$ tsp	dried rubbed sage	1 mL
3 tbsp	half-and-half (10%) cream or milk	45 mL
	Salt and ground black pepper	

1. In the mug, stir broth, pumpkin and sage until blended. Microwave on High for $1^1/_2$ to $2^1/_2$ minutes (checking at $1^1/_2$) or until hot but not boiling.

2. Stir in cream. Microwave on High for 30 to 60 seconds (checking at 30) or until hot but not boiling. Season to taste with salt and pepper.

Variation

• **Winter Squash Soup:** Use an equal amount of thawed frozen winter squash purée in place of the pumpkin.

Prep Ahead Option

Combine the broth, pumpkin and sage in the mug; cover and refrigerate. Measure the cream into a small airtight container; cover and refrigerate until ready to use.

Black Bean Soup

This easy soup gets its Southwestern kick from green chiles and smoky cumin. Adjust the heat by choosing a spicier or milder can of tomatoes with chiles (they are available in mild, medium and hot).

Tips

For a smooth soup, purée all of the ingredients in a blender before heating in the microwave.

If you prefer, you can use ½ cup (125 mL) salsa in place of the canned tomatoes with chiles.

Freeze the remaining beans and tomatoes separately in small sealable freezer bags. Be sure to label the bags with the contents. Store for up to 3 months. Defrost in the refrigerator or microwave before using.

♦ **16-oz (500 mL) mug**

½	can (14 oz/398 mL) black beans, drained and rinsed	½
½	can (10 oz/284 mL) diced tomatoes with green chiles, with juice	½
½ cup	ready-to-use chicken or vegetable broth or water	125 mL
¼ tsp	ground cumin or chili powder Ground black pepper	1 mL

Suggested Accompaniments

Sour cream or plain Greek yogurt; chopped fresh cilantro; chopped green onions; seasoned croutons or crumbled tortilla chips

1. In the mug, coarsely mash beans with a fork. Stir in tomatoes, broth and cumin.
2. Microwave on High for 2 to 3 minutes or until hot but not boiling. Let stand for 1 minute, then season to taste with pepper. Serve with any of the suggested accompaniments, as desired.

Variations

- **Pumpkin Black Bean Soup:** Add 2 tbsp (30 mL) canned pumpkin purée (not pie filling) with the tomatoes. Increase the broth to ⅔ cup (150 mL).
- **Italian White Bean and Tomato Soup:** Replace the black beans with white beans (such as cannellini or great Northern). Instead of the tomatoes with chiles, use canned diced tomatoes with Italian seasoning. Replace the cumin with 1 tbsp (15 mL) grated Parmesan cheese. Serve with additional Parmesan cheese and chopped fresh parsley, if desired.

> **Prep Ahead Option**
> Prepare through step 1; cover and refrigerate until ready to heat.

Speedy Minestrone

Coarsely mashing the vegetables thickens the texture, resulting in a soup that tastes like it has been simmering for hours.

Tips

Canned vegetable blends are typically a mixture of many vegetables, including peas, carrots, potatoes, green beans, corn and celery.

An equal amount of quick-cooking brown rice may be used in place of the pasta.

If desired, sprinkle the finished soup with grated Parmesan cheese.

Freeze the remaining mixed vegetables in a small sealable freezer bag. You can freeze the entire amount in one bag, or portion out $\frac{1}{2}$ cup (125 mL) per bag so that the vegetables are recipe-ready. Be sure to label the bag with the contents. Store for up to 3 months. Defrost in the refrigerator or microwave before using.

◆ **16-oz (500 mL) mug**

3 tbsp	orzo or other small pasta	45 mL
1 cup	ready-to-use chicken or vegetable broth	250 mL
$\frac{1}{2}$ cup	drained canned mixed vegetables	125 mL
$\frac{1}{4}$ cup	thick and chunky marinara sauce	60 mL
	Salt and ground black pepper	

1. In the mug, combine orzo and broth. Place in the microwave atop a doubled paper towel. Microwave on High for 2 minutes. Stir. Microwave on High for 4 to 5 minutes or until orzo is tender.

2. Stir in vegetables and marinara sauce, coarsely mashing the vegetables against the side of the mug with a fork. Microwave on High for 60 to 90 seconds or until heated through. Season to taste with salt and pepper.

Variation

- **Hearty Minestrone:** Add $\frac{1}{3}$ cup (75 mL) drained rinsed canned white beans (such as great Northern or cannellini), red beans or chickpeas with the marinara sauce.

Prep Ahead Option
Measure the orzo and broth into the mug; cover and refrigerate. Measure the vegetables and marinara into a small airtight container; cover and refrigerate until ready to use.

Egg Drop Soup

Egg drop soup, also known as egg flower soup, is one of the easiest (and most frugal) soups to prepare. Plus, it's a snap to make in the microwave. For ribbons of egg throughout the soup, lightly beat the egg so that no bubbles form, then pour it into the hot soup in a very slow stream, stirring — in one direction only — as soon as you start pouring.

Tips

An equal amount of hot pepper sauce may be used in place of the chili-garlic sauce.

For a deeper flavor, add $\frac{1}{4}$ tsp (1 mL) toasted sesame oil with the chili-garlic sauce.

Opt for bags, as opposed to boxes, of frozen chopped spinach, as it is easier to remove small amounts at a time.

♦ **16-oz (500 mL) mug**

1$\frac{1}{4}$ cups	ready-to-use chicken or vegetable broth	300 mL
$\frac{1}{4}$ tsp	Asian chili-garlic sauce	1 mL
$\frac{1}{2}$ cup	frozen chopped spinach	125 mL
1	large egg	1

1. In the mug, combine broth and chili-garlic sauce. Microwave on High for 1$\frac{1}{2}$ to 2 minutes (checking at 1$\frac{1}{2}$) or until starting to boil.
2. Stir in spinach. Microwave on High for 1 to 2 minutes (checking at 1) or until mixture is very hot.
3. In a small bowl or cup, lightly beat egg with a fork until blended. Slowly pour into soup, swirling in one direction with a fork to create long strands.

Variations

- **Scallion Egg Drop Soup:** Replace the spinach with 3 tbsp (45 mL) chopped green onions (scallions).
- **Hearty Egg Drop Soup:** Add $\frac{1}{4}$ cup (60 mL) chopped ham, chopped cooked smoked sausage, drained canned tiny shrimp or chopped cooked chicken with the spinach.

Prep Ahead Option

Combine the broth and chili-garlic sauce in the mug; cover and refrigerate. Measure the spinach into a small airtight container; cover and refrigerate until ready to use.

Bacon and Corn Chowder

Naturally sweet corn and peppers, enhanced with salty-smoky bacon, make this creamy soup deliciously rich.

Tips

Look for ready-to-eat real bacon bits where salad dressings and croutons are shelved in the grocery store, or near the regular bacon in the packaged meat or deli department.

If you prefer, you can use 2 tbsp (30 mL) chopped ham or cooked smoked sausage in place of the bacon.

♦ **16-oz (500 mL) mug**

♦ **Blender**

1	can (11 oz/311 mL) Mexican-style corn (with peppers and onions), with juice	1
$\frac{1}{3}$ cup	milk or half-and-half (10%) cream (approx.)	75 mL
$\frac{1}{8}$ tsp	dried thyme or Italian seasoning	0.5 mL
1 tbsp	ready-to-eat real bacon bits	15 mL
	Ground black pepper	

1. In the blender, pulse corn, milk and thyme until almost smooth. If mixture is too thick, add 1 to 2 tbsp (15 to 30 mL) more milk. Transfer to the mug and stir in bacon.

2. Microwave on High for $1\frac{1}{2}$ to $2\frac{1}{2}$ minutes (checking at $1\frac{1}{2}$) or until hot but not boiling. Let stand for 1 minute, then season to taste with pepper.

Variations

- **Farmers' Market Chowder:** Replace the bacon with $\frac{1}{3}$ cup (75 mL) drained canned mixed vegetables. Sprinkle the finished soup with 1 tbsp (15 mL) minced chives or green onions.

- **Potato Corn Chowder:** Add $\frac{2}{3}$ cup (150 mL) canned drained potatoes, diced, with the bacon.

Prep Ahead Option

Prepare through step 1; cover and refrigerate until ready to heat.

Quinoa Chili

This simple, speedy chili gets loads of spice and flavor — despite its abbreviated list of ingredients — thanks to green chile tomatoes and seasoned chili beans. Quinoa adds extra protein, making this vegetarian chili hearty as well as homey.

Tips

An equal amount of quick-cooking brown rice or quick-cooking barley can be used in place of the quinoa. Reduce the cooking time in step 1 to 5 minutes total, stopping to stir halfway through.

For even more flavor, add $\frac{1}{4}$ tsp (1 mL) ground cumin with the tomatoes.

Freeze the remaining tomatoes in a small sealable freezer bag for future use. Be sure to label the bag with the contents. Store for up to 3 months. Defrost in the refrigerator or microwave before using.

Freeze the remaining chili beans in a small sealable freezer bag. You can freeze the entire amount in one bag, or portion out $\frac{1}{2}$ cup (125 mL) per bag so that the beans are recipe-ready. Be sure to label the bag with the contents. Store for up to 3 months. Defrost in the refrigerator or microwave before using.

♦ **16-oz (500 mL) mug**

3 tbsp	quinoa, rinsed	45 mL
$\frac{1}{2}$ cup	water	125 mL
$\frac{1}{2}$	can (10 oz/284 mL) diced tomatoes with green chiles, with juice	$\frac{1}{2}$
$\frac{1}{2}$ cup	canned seasoned chili beans, with juice	125 mL
	Salt and ground black pepper	

Suggested Accompaniments

Nonfat plain Greek yogurt; fresh cilantro leaves; chopped green onions; chopped radishes; crumbled queso fresco or shredded Cheddar cheese; lime wedges

1. In the mug, combine quinoa and water. Microwave on High for 4 minutes. Stir. Microwave on High for 3 to 5 minutes (checking at 3) or until water is absorbed and quinoa is tender.

2. Stir in tomatoes and beans. Microwave on High for $1\frac{1}{2}$ to $2\frac{1}{2}$ minutes (checking at $1\frac{1}{2}$) or until heated through. Cover mug with a small plate or saucer and let stand for 1 minute. Season to taste with salt and pepper. Serve with any of the suggested accompaniments, as desired.

Variation

- **Beef and Quinoa Chili:** Thaw 2 frozen cooked beef meatballs according to package directions and crumble. Add with the beans.

> **Prep Ahead Option**
> Measure the quinoa into the mug; cover and store at room temperature. Measure the tomatoes and beans into a small airtight container; cover and refrigerate until ready to use.

Mug Enchilada

I love enchiladas, but my favorite recipe takes well over an hour to assemble. Here I've captured the flavors I long for in record time, with only four ingredients. Hurrah!

Tips

An equal amount of taco sauce, picante sauce or thin salsa can be used in place of the enchilada sauce.

Freeze the remaining enchilada sauce in a small sealable freezer bag for future use. Be sure to label the bag with the contents. Store for up to 3 months. Defrost in the refrigerator or microwave before using.

Freeze the remaining chili beans in a small sealable freezer bag. You can freeze the entire amount in one bag, or portion out ½ cup (125 mL) per bag so that the beans are recipe-ready. Be sure to label the bag with the contents. Store for up to 3 months. Defrost in the refrigerator or microwave before using.

♦ 12- to 16-oz (375 to 500 mL) mug

½ cup	red or green enchilada sauce	125 mL
2	6-inch (15 cm) corn tortillas, quartered	2
½ cup	canned seasoned chili beans, drained (but not rinsed)	125 mL
½ cup	shredded sharp (old) Cheddar or Monterey Jack cheese	125 mL

Suggested Accompaniments

Chopped green onions; chopped fresh cilantro; sour cream or plain Greek yogurt; salsa; sliced ripe olives

1. Place the enchilada sauce in a small plate or saucer. Dip one of the tortilla quarters in sauce, coating both sides. Shake off excess, place in the mug and top with 2 tbsp (30 mL) beans. Dip another tortilla quarter, coating both sides, and place in mug; top with 2 tbsp (30 mL) cheese. Repeat layers, finishing with cheese. Drizzle with any sauce remaining on the plate.

2. Microwave on High for $1\frac{1}{2}$ to $2\frac{1}{2}$ minutes (checking at $1\frac{1}{2}$) or until cheese is melted and layers are heated through. Let stand for 1 minute. Serve with any of the suggested accompaniments, as desired.

Variation

- **Chicken Enchilada Mug:** Replace the beans with an equal amount of diced cooked chicken breast. Toss the chicken with an additional 1 tbsp (15 mL) enchilada sauce before using.

> **Prep Ahead Option**
> Prepare through step 1; cover and refrigerate until ready to heat.

Red Beans and Rice

New Orleans fare gets a speedy and healthy makeover in this quick mugful of deliciousness. Instant brown rice stands in for traditional white rice, and a quick trip to the microwave omits hours of stovetop simmering.

Tips

For even more flavor, add $\frac{1}{8}$ tsp (0.5 mL) dried thyme with the salsa.

Freeze the remaining beans in a small sealable freezer bag. You can freeze the entire amount in one bag or portion out $\frac{1}{3}$ cup (75 mL) per bag so that the beans are recipe-ready. Be sure to label the bag with the contents. Store for up to 3 months. Defrost in the refrigerator or microwave before using.

♦ **16-oz (500 mL) mug**

$\frac{1}{4}$ cup	instant brown rice	60 mL
Pinch	salt	Pinch
$\frac{1}{2}$ cup	water	125 mL
$\frac{1}{3}$ cup	drained rinsed canned red beans or kidney beans	75 mL
$\frac{1}{4}$ cup	diced cooked smoked sausage or ham	60 mL
3 tbsp	salsa	45 mL

1. In the mug, combine rice, salt and water. Cover with a small plate or saucer. Microwave on High for 5 to 6 minutes or until almost all of the water is absorbed. Remove from oven and let stand, covered, for 1 minute to absorb the remaining water.

2. Stir in beans, sausage and salsa. Microwave on High for 1 to $1\frac{1}{2}$ minutes or until heated through. Cover with a small plate or saucer and let stand for 1 minute.

Variations

- **Red Beans and Quinoa:** Replace the rice with an equal amount of quinoa, rinsed. Stir the quinoa and water in the mug. Microwave, uncovered, on High for 4 minutes. Stir. Microwave on High for 3 to 4 minutes (checking at 3) or until water is absorbed and quinoa is tender. Continue with step 2.

- **Red Beans and Barley:** Replace the brown rice with an equal amount of quick-cooking barley.

Prep Ahead Option

Measure the rice and salt into the mug; cover and store at room temperature. Measure the beans, sausage and salsa into a small airtight container; cover and refrigerate until ready to use.

Mediterranean Lentil Mug

This is a mug full of both health and deliciousness. Lentils, like beans, are part of the legume family and are a great source of protein and soluble fiber. They are also a significant source of iron, B vitamins and folate.

Tips

If canned lentils are not available, look for vacuum-packed lentils, typically available in the produce section, near the tofu products. Use ³⁄₄ cup (175 mL) of the lentils and add 3 tbsp (45 mL) water or ready-to-use chicken or vegetable broth in place of the canned lentils.

Balsamic vinegar, white wine vinegar or cider vinegar may be used in place of the red wine vinegar.

Freeze the remaining lentils and tomatoes separately in small sealable freezer bags. Be sure to label the bags with the contents. Store for up to 3 months. Defrost in the refrigerator or microwave before using.

♦ **16-oz (500 mL) mug**

¹⁄₂	can (14 oz/398 mL) lentils, with liquid	¹⁄₂
¹⁄₂	can (14 oz/ 398 mL) diced tomatoes with Italian seasoning, with juice	¹⁄₂
¹⁄₈ tsp	dried thyme (optional)	0.5 mL
¹⁄₈ tsp	red wine vinegar	0.5 mL
	Ground black pepper	

1. In the mug, coarsely mash lentils with a fork. Stir in tomatoes and thyme (if using).
2. Microwave on High for 2 to 3 minutes or until hot. Let stand for 1 minute, then stir in vinegar. Season to taste with pepper.

Variations

- **Lentil and Kale Mug:** Add ²⁄₃ cup (150 mL) frozen chopped kale or spinach with the tomatoes. Increase the cooking time by 30 to 45 seconds, if needed.
- **Curried Lentil Mug:** Use ²⁄₃ cup (150 mL) diced tomatoes with green chiles in place of the tomatoes with Italian seasoning, and replace the thyme with 1 tsp (5 mL) curry powder. Serve with a dollop of plain Greek or regular yogurt and chopped fresh cilantro, if desired.

> **Prep Ahead Option**
> Prepare through step 1; cover and refrigerate until ready to heat.

Spinach and Pesto Casserole

Here, earthy spinach is matched with vibrant basil pesto and creamy cottage cheese. Assembled together in an instant casserole, the ingredients mingle to create a simple yet bold mini casserole.

Tips

Opt for bags, as opposed to boxes, of frozen chopped spinach, as it is easier to remove small amounts at a time.

You can use an equal amount of reduced-fat ricotta cheese in place of the regular cottage cheese.

For even more flavor, add $\frac{1}{4}$ tsp (1 mL) dried dill, basil, oregano or Italian seasoning.

♦ 16-oz (500 mL) mug

$1\frac{1}{2}$ cups	frozen chopped spinach	375 mL
1	large egg	1
$\frac{3}{4}$ cup	cottage cheese	175 mL
$1\frac{1}{2}$ tbsp	basil pesto	22 mL

1. In the mug, microwave spinach on High for 1 to 2 minutes or until thawed and warm. Using the tines of a fork, press down firmly on the spinach and drain off excess liquid.

2. Using the fork, beat in egg, cottage cheese and pesto until blended. Microwave on High for $1\frac{1}{2}$ to $2\frac{1}{2}$ minutes (checking at $1\frac{1}{2}$) or until center is just set. Let cool slightly or entirely in mug. Eat directly from mug or gently remove onto a small plate.

Variations

- **Spinach and Tapenade Casserole:** Replace the pesto with an equal amount of prepared olive tapenade.

- **Feta and Spinach Casserole:** Replace the pesto with an equal amount of crumbled feta cheese.

- **Spinach and Red Pepper Casserole:** Add 3 tbsp (45 mL) chopped drained roasted red bell peppers (from a jar) with the cottage cheese.

> **Prep Ahead Option**
>
> Measure the spinach into the mug; cover and refrigerate (decrease the cooking time in step 1 to 30 seconds). Whisk the egg, cottage cheese and pesto into a small airtight container; cover and refrigerate until ready to use.

Beef and Broccoli Takeout Mug

Hoisin sauce is a Chinese dipping sauce made from fermented soybeans, garlic, chiles and spices. Here, it makes quick work of this flavorful "takeout" meal.

Tips

Opt for bags, as opposed to boxes, of frozen broccoli florets, as it is easier to remove small amounts at a time.

If a frozen pepper and onion stir-fry blend isn't available, use 1/2 cup (125 mL) mixed sliced fresh bell peppers and onions and, in step 1, cook for about 2 minutes or until vegetables are tender-crisp.

An equal amount of teriyaki sauce can be used in place of the hoisin sauce.

Once opened, hoisin sauce should be stored in the fridge, where it will keep for months.

♦ 16-oz (500 mL) mug

1 cup	frozen broccoli florets	250 mL
1/2 cup	frozen sliced bell pepper and onion stir-fry blend	125 mL
2 tbsp	hoisin sauce	30 mL
1/4 cup	diced deli roast beef	60 mL
	Salt and ground black pepper	

Suggested Accompaniments

Toasted sesame seeds; sliced green onions; chopped roasted almonds or cashews; prepared instant brown rice

1. In the mug, microwave broccoli and stir-fry blend on High for $1^{1}/_{2}$ to 2 minutes or until thawed and warm. Drain off excess liquid.

2. Stir in hoisin sauce and roast beef. Microwave on High for 1 to $1^{1}/_{2}$ minutes or until heated through. Serve with any of the suggested accompaniments, as desired.

Variations

- **Chicken and Broccoli Takeout Mug:** Use 1/2 can (5 oz/142 g) water-packed chunk chicken, drained and flaked, or tiny shrimp, drained, in place of the beef.
- **Tempeh and Broccoli Takeout Mug:** Use an equal amount of diced tempeh in place of the beef.
- **Veggie Takeout Mug:** Use an equal amount of another frozen chopped vegetable blend in place of the broccoli.

> **Prep Ahead Option**
> Measure the broccoli and stir-fry blend into the mug; cover and refrigerate (decrease the cooking time in step 1 by 30 seconds). Measure the hoisin sauce and roast beef into a small airtight container; cover and refrigerate until ready to use.

Pesto Chicken Couscous

Keep a jar of basil pesto in the refrigerator — it will guarantee a multitude of tasty meals in minutes, 24/7. Need proof? Try this delicious couscous and chicken mug.

Tips

Either regular or whole wheat couscous can be used.

Freeze the remaining chicken in a small sealable freezer bag. Be sure to label the bag with the contents. Store for up to 3 months. Defrost in the refrigerator or microwave before using.

You can replace the canned chicken with $1/2$ cup (125 mL) diced cooked or deli chicken or turkey.

♦ **16-oz (375 to 500 mL) mug**

$1/2$ cup	water	125 mL
$1/2$ cup	couscous	125 mL
$1/2$	can (5 oz/142 g) water-packed chunk chicken, drained and flaked	$1/2$
3 tbsp	basil pesto	45 mL
	Salt and ground black pepper	
1 tbsp	grated Parmesan cheese	15 mL

1. In the mug, microwave water on High for $1^1/2$ to $2^1/2$ minutes or until water is boiling. Stir in couscous. Cover with a plate and let stand for 5 minutes.

2. Fluff couscous with a fork. Stir in chicken and pesto. Microwave on High for 1 to $1^1/2$ minutes or until heated through. Season to taste with salt and pepper, and sprinkle with Parmesan.

Variations

- **Pesto Chickpea Couscous:** Replace the chicken with $1/2$ cup (125 mL) drained rinsed canned chickpeas.
- **Red Pepper and Pesto Chicken Couscous:** Add $1/4$ cup (60 mL) chopped drained roasted red bell peppers (from a jar) with the chicken.

> **Prep Ahead Option**
> Measure the couscous into a small airtight container; store at room temperature. Measure the chicken and pesto into a small airtight container; cover and refrigerate until ready to use.

Thanksgiving in a Mug

All of the flavors of Thanksgiving with only four ingredients and one dish, and in less than 5 minutes? Yes, yes and yes!

Tips

You can replace the canned chicken with ½ cup (125 mL) diced cooked or deli chicken or turkey.

Look for bags of stuffing mix in the supermarket, where breads or bread crumbs are shelved.

For deeper flavor, use an equal amount of ready-to-use chicken broth in place of the water.

For even more flavor, add ⅛ tsp (0.5 mL) dried rubbed sage, dried thyme or poultry seasoning with the cranberries.

♦ 16-oz (500 mL) mug

1	can (5 oz/142 g) water-packed chunk chicken, drained and flaked	1
⅔ cup	dry herbed cornbread stuffing mix	150 mL
½ cup	drained canned mixed vegetables	125 mL
1 tbsp	dried cranberries	15 mL
1 tbsp	water	15 mL
	Salt and ground black pepper	

Suggested Accompaniments

Prepared turkey or chicken gravy; chopped fresh parsley

1. In the mug, combine chicken, stuffing mix, vegetables, cranberries and water.
2. Microwave on High for 1½ to 2½ minutes (checking at 1½) or until stuffing feels dry and mixture is hot. Cover with a small plate or saucer and let stand for 1 minute. Season to taste with salt and pepper. Serve with any of the suggested accompaniments, as desired.

> **Prep Ahead Option**
> Prepare through step 1; cover and refrigerate until ready to heat.

Spaghetti and Meatballs

When it comes to comfort food, spaghetti and meatballs is hard to beat. Now you can have that homemade comfort at a moment's notice.

Tip

If using broken spaghetti, break into 1- to 1½-inch (2.5 to 4 cm) pieces for best results.

♦ **16-oz (500 mL) mug**

2 to 3	frozen cooked beef meatballs	2 to 3
½ cup	cut or broken spaghetti	125 mL
⅛ tsp	salt	0.5 mL
⅔ cup	water	150 mL
4 tbsp	marinara sauce, divided	60 mL
1 tbsp	grated Parmesan cheese	15 mL

1. In the mug, microwave meatballs on High for 1 to 2 minutes or until completely warmed through. Transfer to a small plate or bowl.

2. In the mug, combine spaghetti, salt and water. Place in the microwave atop a doubled paper towel. Microwave on High for 2 minutes. Stir. Microwave on High for 3 minutes. If the mixture appears dry, add 1 tbsp (15 mL) water to the mug. Microwave for 1½ to 2 minutes or until spaghetti is tender.

3. Stir in 3 tbsp (45 mL) marinara sauce. Add meatballs and top with remaining sauce. Microwave on High for 45 to 60 seconds or until heated through. Sprinkle with Parmesan.

Variations

- **Vegan Spaghetti and Meatballs:** Use frozen or refrigerated vegan meatballs in place of the beef meatballs and omit the Parmesan cheese. If using refrigerated vegan meatballs, skip step 1.

- **Gluten-Free Spaghetti and Meatballs:** Use quinoa spaghetti, broken into 1-inch (2.5 cm) lengths, in place of the regular spaghetti and decrease the second cooking time in step 2 to 4 minutes. Check the packaging to make sure the meatballs and sauce are gluten-free.

Prep Ahead Option

Place the meatballs in a small airtight container; cover and refrigerate (decrease the cooking time in step 1 to 30 to 45 seconds). Measure the spaghetti and salt into the mug; cover and store at room temperature. Measure the marinara sauce into a small airtight container; cover and refrigerate until ready to use.

Creamy Blue Cheese Pasta

Restaurant versions of blue cheese pasta can be lethal with fat and calories. Not so here. Calcium-rich cottage cheese plus a small amount of decadent-tasting blue cheese melt into creamy sauce in seconds, delivering the rich flavor you crave.

Tips

For even more flavor, add 1 tbsp (15 mL) chopped fresh parsley just before serving.

An equal amount of ricotta cheese can be used in place of the cottage cheese.

♦ **16-oz (500 mL) mug**

$1/2$ cup	ditalini or elbow macaroni	125 mL
$1/8$ tsp	salt	0.5 mL
$2/3$ cup	water	150 mL
$1/3$ cup	cottage cheese	75 mL
2 tbsp	crumbled blue cheese	30 mL
Pinch	ground nutmeg (optional)	Pinch
	Salt and ground black pepper	

1. In the mug, combine ditalini, salt and water. Place in the microwave atop a doubled paper towel. Microwave on High for 2 minutes. Stir. Microwave on High for 3 minutes. If the mixture appears dry, add 1 tbsp (15 mL) water to the mug. Microwave for $1^1/_2$ to 2 minutes or until pasta is tender.

2. Stir in cottage cheese, blue cheese and nutmeg (if using) until cheeses melt. Microwave on High for 30 to 60 seconds or until warmed through. Let stand for 1 minute, then stir. Season to taste with salt and pepper.

Variation

- **Creamy Goat Cheese Pasta:** Use crumbled goat cheese in place of the blue cheese.

Prep Ahead Option

Measure the ditalini and salt into the mug; cover and store at room temperature. Measure the cottage cheese, blue cheese and nutmeg (if using) into a small airtight container; cover and refrigerate until ready to use.

Peanut Noodles

This easy noodle dish is equally good hot or cold, so you can make it ahead and chill it for a later meal. You can use up all sorts of leftovers — bits of meat, tofu, herbs, vegetables — to enrich the noodles.

Tips

If using broken spaghetti, break into 1- to $1\frac{1}{2}$-inch (2.5 to 4 cm) pieces for best results.

For a higher-protein meal, add up to $\frac{1}{3}$ cup (75 mL) diced cooked chicken, chopped deli roast beef, diced tempeh or drained canned tiny shrimp with the teriyaki sauce.

If you do not have teriyaki sauce, mix 2 tsp (10 mL) soy sauce, 1 tsp (5 mL) packed brown sugar or granulated sugar, $\frac{1}{8}$ tsp (0.5 mL) white, cider or rice vinegar, a pinch of ground ginger and a pinch of garlic powder in a small bowl or cup for every 1 tbsp (15 mL) teriyaki sauce.

♦ **16-oz (500 mL) mug**

$\frac{1}{2}$ cup	cut or broken spaghetti	125 mL
Pinch	salt	Pinch
$\frac{2}{3}$ cup	water	150 mL
2 tbsp	thinly sliced green onions	30 mL
1 tbsp	creamy peanut butter	15 mL
1 tbsp	teriyaki sauce	15 mL

Suggested Accompaniments

Thinly sliced red pepper strips; chopped lightly salted roasted peanuts; toasted sesame seeds; chopped fresh cilantro

1. In the mug, combine spaghetti, salt and water. Place in the microwave atop a doubled paper towel. Microwave on High for 2 minutes. Stir. Microwave on High for 3 minutes. If the mixture appears dry, add 1 tbsp (15 mL) water to the mug. Microwave for $1\frac{1}{2}$ to 2 minutes or until spaghetti is tender.

2. Stir in green onions, peanut butter and teriyaki sauce. Let stand for 1 minute, then stir again. Serve with any of the suggested accompaniments, as desired.

Variation

- **Sesame Noodles:** Reduce peanut butter to 1 tsp (5 mL) and add 2 tsp (10 mL) toasted sesame oil. Sprinkle with 2 tsp (10 mL) toasted sesame seeds, if desired.

> ### Prep Ahead Option
> Measure the spaghetti and salt into the mug; cover and store at room temperature. Measure the peanut butter and teriyaki sauce into a small airtight container; cover and refrigerate until ready to use.

Vegetable Lo Mein

With essentially three ingredients (spaghetti, teriyaki sauce and frozen stir-fry vegetables) and a just a few minutes, you'll have a satisfying, healthy, wallet-friendly rival to Chinese takeout.

Tips

If using broken spaghetti, break into 1- to 1$\frac{1}{2}$-inch (2.5 to 4 cm) pieces for best results.

For a more substantial meal, add up to $\frac{1}{3}$ cup (75 mL) diced cooked chicken, chopped deli roast beef, diced tempeh or drained canned tiny shrimp with the teriyaki sauce.

If you do not have teriyaki sauce, mix 2 tsp (10 mL) soy sauce, 1 tsp (5 mL) packed brown sugar or granulated sugar, $\frac{1}{8}$ tsp (0.5 mL) white, cider or rice vinegar, a pinch of ground ginger and a pinch of garlic powder in a small bowl or cup for every 1 tbsp (15 mL) teriyaki sauce.

♦ **16-oz (500 mL) mug**

$\frac{1}{2}$ cup	cut or broken spaghetti	125 mL
Pinch	salt	Pinch
$\frac{2}{3}$ cup	water	150 mL
$\frac{1}{2}$ cup	frozen stir-fry vegetable blend	125 mL
2 tbsp	teriyaki sauce	30 mL

Suggested Accompaniments

Chopped green onions; chopped lightly salted roasted peanuts; toasted sesame seeds

1. In the mug, combine spaghetti, salt and water. Place in the microwave atop a doubled paper towel. Microwave on High for 2 minutes. Stir. Microwave on High for 3 minutes. If the mixture appears dry, add 1 tbsp (15 mL) water to the mug. Microwave for 1$\frac{1}{2}$ to 2 minutes or until spaghetti is tender.

2. Stir in vegetables and teriyaki sauce. Microwave on High for 60 to 90 seconds or until warmed through. Let stand for 1 minute, then stir again. Serve with any of the suggested accompaniments, as desired.

> **Prep Ahead Option**
>
> Measure the spaghetti and salt into the mug; cover and store at room temperature. Measure the frozen vegetables and teriyaki sauce into a small airtight container; cover and refrigerate until ready to use (decrease the cooking time in step 2 by 20 to 30 seconds).

Vegetable Un-Fried Rice

Nutty brown rice is a terrific vehicle for flavors, like the gingery, salty-sweet teriyaki sauce and crunchy vegetables in this "un-fried" rice. The result is a fragrant and satisfying meal at a moment's notice.

Tips

For a higher-protein meal, add up to $\frac{1}{3}$ cup (75 mL) diced cooked chicken, chopped deli roast beef, diced tempeh or drained canned tiny shrimp with the teriyaki sauce.

You can use another frozen chopped vegetable blend in place of the stir-fry vegetables.

If you do not have teriyaki sauce, mix 2 tsp (10 mL) soy sauce, 1 tsp (5 mL) packed brown sugar or granulated sugar, $\frac{1}{8}$ tsp (0.5 mL) white, cider or rice vinegar, a pinch of ground ginger and a pinch of garlic powder in a small bowl or cup for every 1 tbsp (15 mL) teriyaki sauce.

◆ **16-oz (500 mL) mug**

$\frac{1}{2}$ cup	instant brown rice	125 mL
$\frac{1}{2}$ cup	water	125 mL
$\frac{2}{3}$ cup	frozen stir-fry vegetable blend	150 mL
1 tbsp	teriyaki sauce	15 mL
1	large egg	1
	Salt and ground black pepper	

Suggested Accompaniments

Toasted sesame seeds; sliced green onions; chopped roasted almonds, peanuts or cashews

1. In the mug, combine rice and water. Place vegetables on top. Cover with a small plate or saucer. Microwave on High for 5 to 6 minutes or until almost all the water has been absorbed. Remove from oven and let stand, covered, for 1 minute to absorb remaining water. Stir in teriyaki sauce.

2. In a small bowl or cup, lightly beat egg. Season with salt and pepper.

3. Push rice mixture to one side of the mug and pour beaten egg onto other side. Microwave on High for 20 to 40 seconds or until egg is just set. Break up egg with fork, mixing it in with the rice mixture. Let stand for 30 seconds. Serve with any of the suggested accompaniments, as desired.

Variation

- **Vegetable Un-Fried Quinoa:** Replace the brown rice with $\frac{1}{3}$ cup (75 mL) quinoa, rinsed. Combine quinoa and $\frac{2}{3}$ cup (150 mL) water in the mug. Microwave on High for 4 minutes. Stir. Place vegetables on top. Microwave on High for 3 to 4 minutes (checking at 3) or until water is absorbed and quinoa is tender. Continue with step 2.

> **Prep Ahead Option**
> Measure the rice into the mug; cover and store at room temperature. Measure the vegetable blend into a small airtight container; cover and refrigerate until ready to use.

Cheese Fondue

Melted cheese, enriched with apple juice and a touch of mustard, becomes an indulgent dip for everything from vegetables to sausage to breadsticks.

Tips

You can use prepared yellow or brown mustard in place of the Dijon mustard.

An equal amount of beer or dry white wine can be used in place of the apple juice.

♦ **16-oz (500 mL) mug**

¼ cup	unsweetened apple juice	60 mL
½ cup	shredded Cheddar, Monterey Jack or Swiss cheese	125 mL
2 tsp	all-purpose flour	10 mL
½ tsp	Dijon mustard	2 mL
	Ground black pepper	

Suggested Accompaniments

Pita wedges; breadsticks; crusty bread cubes or large croutons; raw or microwave-cooked vegetables (carrots, broccoli florets, bell pepper strips); microwaved sausage (sliced smoked sausage, breakfast sausage links)

1. In the mug, microwave apple juice on High for 45 to 75 seconds (checking at 45) or until just beginning to boil.
2. Stir in cheese, flour and mustard until blended. Microwave on High for 30 to 45 seconds or until bubbly. Season to taste with pepper. Let cool slightly in mug. Serve with any of the suggested accompaniments, as desired.

Variations

- **Mushroom Swiss Fondue:** Replace the Cheddar cheese with Swiss or Gruyère cheese. Stir in 2 tbsp (30 mL) drained chopped canned or jarred mushrooms. Add a pinch of ground nutmeg or dried thyme, if desired.

- **Pepper Jack Fondue:** Omit the mustard and use pepper Jack cheese in place of the Cheddar. Use an equal amount of beer in place of the apple juice. Add a pinch of chili powder or ground cumin, if desired.

Prep Ahead Option

Measure the apple juice into the mug; cover and refrigerate. Measure the cheese, flour and mustard into a small airtight container; cover and refrigerate until ready to use.

Warm Parmesan Spinach Dip

Party-goers love this warm and creamy dip, but now you can have it anytime as a satisfying snack, spread or mini meal.

Tips

Opt for bags, as opposed to boxes, of frozen chopped spinach, as it is easier to remove small amounts at a time.

Add $\frac{1}{4}$ tsp (1 mL) of your favorite dried herb (such as basil or dill) or herb blend (such as Italian seasoning) with the cheese.

You can use 3 tbsp (45 mL) soft, tub-style cream cheese in place of the brick cream cheese.

You can use either regular or light mayonnaise in this recipe. For best results, do not use nonfat mayonnaise.

♦ **12- to 16-oz (375 to 500 mL) mug**

$\frac{3}{4}$ cup	frozen chopped spinach	175 mL
3 tbsp	brick-style cream cheese ($1\frac{1}{2}$ oz/45 g)	45 mL
2 tbsp	mayonnaise	30 mL
1 tbsp	grated Parmesan cheese	15 mL
	Ground black pepper	

Suggested Accompaniments

Pita wedges or crusty French bread; breadsticks; raw or microwave-cooked vegetables (carrots, broccoli florets, bell pepper strips)

1. In the mug, microwave spinach on High for 1 to 2 minutes or until thawed and warm. Using the tines of a fork, press down firmly on the spinach and drain off excess liquid.

2. Add cream cheese to the mug. Microwave on High for 15 to 20 seconds or until softened. Stir until blended. Stir in mayonnaise and Parmesan. Microwave on High for 30 to 45 seconds or until warmed through. Season to taste with black pepper. Serve with any of the suggested accompaniments, as desired.

Variation

• **Artichoke and Spinach Dip:** Add 3 tbsp (45 mL) drained chopped marinated artichoke hearts (from a jar) with the mayonnaise.

> **Prep Ahead Option**
> Measure the spinach into the mug; cover and refrigerate (decrease the cooking time in step 1 to 30 seconds). Place the cream cheese in a small airtight container; cover and refrigerate. Measure the mayonnaise and Parmesan cheese into a small airtight container; cover and refrigerate until ready to use.

Layered Southwestern Dip

Layers of beans, yogurt, tomatoes and cheese mean this delicious dip can easily double as a healthy mini meal.

Tips

For a higher-protein dip that can double as a meal, add up to $1/3$ cup (75 mL) drained rinsed canned black beans with the salsa.

For even more flavor, add $1/4$ tsp (1 mL) ground cumin or chili powder with the salsa.

Freeze the remaining beans in a small sealable freezer bag. You can freeze the entire amount in one bag or portion out $1/2$ cup (125 mL) per bag so that the beans are recipe-ready. Be sure to label the bag with the contents. Store for up to 3 months. Defrost in the refrigerator or microwave before using.

♦ **16-oz (500 mL) mug**

$1/2$ cup	nonfat refried beans (preferably "spicy")	125 mL
5 tbsp	chunky salsa, divided	75 mL
2 tbsp	shredded Cheddar cheese	30 mL
2 tbsp	plain Greek yogurt	30 mL

Suggested Accompaniments

Baked or regular tortilla chips; chopped or shredded lettuce; diced avocado; canned sliced black olives; chopped green onions; fresh cilantro leaves

1. In the mug, combine refried beans and 3 tbsp (45 mL) salsa until blended. Sprinkle with cheese. Microwave on High for 45 to 75 seconds (checking at 45) or until cheese is melted and beans are hot.

2. Spread yogurt evenly over hot bean mixture. Top with remaining salsa. Serve with any of the suggested accompaniments, as desired.

Variation

• **Layered Chicken Southwestern Dip:** Add $1/2$ can (5 oz/142 g) water-packed chunk chicken, drained and flaked, on top of the bean mixture before sprinkling with cheese.

> **Prep Ahead Option**
> Prepare through step 1; cover and refrigerate for up to 1 day. Continue with step 2.

Pepperoni Pizza Dip

Why wait for delivery? Satisfy your pizza craving in a matter of minutes — for a fraction of the cost and calories — with this delicious dip.

Tips

Turkey pepperoni is much lower in fat and calories than regular pepperoni, but you can use either variety in this recipe. Look for packages of sliced pepperoni in the deli section of the supermarket.

Chopped salami can be used in place of the pepperoni.

♦ 12- to 16-oz (375 to 500 mL) mug

½ cup	thick and chunky marinara sauce	125 mL
2 tbsp	chopped turkey pepperoni	30 mL
¼ cup	shredded mozzarella or Italian-blend cheese	60 mL

Suggested Accompaniments

Breadsticks, pita wedges or crusty French bread

1. In the mug, microwave marinara sauce on High for 45 to 75 seconds (checking at 45) or until beginning to bubble.
2. Stir in pepperoni and sprinkle with cheese. Microwave on High for 30 to 45 seconds or until cheese is bubbly. Let stand for 1 minute. Serve with any of the suggested accompaniments, as desired.

Variations

- **Veggie Pizza Dip:** Before heating the marinara sauce, microwave ½ cup (125 mL) frozen sliced bell pepper and onion stir-fry blend or Italian mixed vegetables in the mug on High for 45 seconds; drain off excess liquid. Stir in the marinara sauce and proceed as directed, omitting the pepperoni.

- **Deluxe Pizza Dip:** Before heating the marinara sauce, microwave 1 or 2 cooked breakfast sausages in the mug for 1 minute. Break apart with a fork. Stir in the marinara sauce and proceed as directed, adding 2 tbsp (30 mL) drained canned or jarred mushroom pieces with the pepperoni.

> **Prep Ahead Option**
> Measure the marinara sauce into the mug; cover and refrigerate. Measure the pepperoni and cheese into a small airtight container; cover and refrigerate until ready to use.

Mug Popcorn

Skip the big bags of chips, pretzels and crackers; this perfectly portioned popcorn will satisfy your cravings — for pennies!

Tip

The mug will be particularly hot once the popcorn is popped (hotter than when the mug is filled with food). Use a towel or oven mitt to remove the mug from the microwave.

♦ **16-oz (500 mL) mug**

½ tsp	vegetable oil	2 mL
1 tbsp	popcorn kernels	15 mL
	Salt	

1. In the mug, swirl the oil to coat bottom. Add popcorn and cover mug with a clean dish towel or paper towel, tucking the towel underneath the mug to secure.
2. Microwave on High for 1 to 2 minutes or until you can count 4 to 5 seconds between pops. Using the towel as an oven mitt, remove mug from oven. Season to taste with salt.

Variations

- **Buttered Popcorn:** Add 1 to 2 tsp (5 to 10 mL) butter along the inside of the mug immediately after removing it from the oven (the hot mug will melt it). Stir the popcorn to coat, then season with salt.
- **Cinnamon Sugar Popcorn:** Add 1 to 2 tsp (5 to 10 mL) butter along the inside of the mug immediately after removing it from the oven (the hot mug will melt it); sprinkle with 2 tsp (10 mL) granulated sugar and a generous pinch of ground cinnamon. Stir the popcorn to coat, then season with salt.
- **Chili Lime Popcorn:** Add ½ tsp (2 mL) finely grated lime zest and a generous pinch of chili powder with the salt.

> **Prep Ahead Option**
> Place the oil and popcorn in the mug as directed in step 1; cover and store at room temperature until ready to use.

Chocolate Peanut Butter Crunch Mix

Chocolate chips, peanut butter and a smidge of butter transform crispy cereal from breakfast fare to an indulgent treat. Vary the chips and nut butter and mix in a few extra goodies for a multitude of yummy possibilities.

Tips

Any other type of creamy nut or seed butter (such as cashew, almond, sesame seed or sunflower seed) can be used in place of the peanut butter.

Any other variety of chocolate chips or baking chips (such as white chocolate, milk chocolate or butterscotch) can be used in place of the semisweet chocolate chips.

♦ **16-oz (500 mL) mug**

♦ **Dinner plate or pie plate, lined with waxed paper or foil**

1/4 cup	semisweet chocolate chips	60 mL
1 tbsp	creamy peanut butter	15 mL
1 tbsp	butter	15 mL
1 cup	corn, rice or wheat cereal squares, such as Chex	250 mL

1. In the mug, microwave chocolate chips, peanut butter and butter on High for 45 seconds. Stir. Microwave on High for 15 to 45 seconds (checking at 15) or until mixture can be stirred smooth.

2. Immediately stir in cereal until coated. Spread mixture evenly on prepared plate. Refrigerate for 20 minutes, until coating is firm, then break into bite-size pieces.

Variations

- **White Chocolate Cranberry Crunch:** Use white chocolate chips in place of the semisweet chocolate chips and add 2 tbsp (30 mL) dried cranberries with the cereal.
- **Chocolate Raisin Crunch:** Add 2 tbsp (30 mL) raisins with the cereal.
- **Peanut Butterscotch Crunch:** Use butterscotch baking chips in place of the chocolate chips.
- **Chocolate Hazelnut Crunch:** Use chocolate hazelnut spread in place of the peanut butter.

Prep Ahead Option

Combine the chocolate chips, peanut butter and butter in the mug; cover and store at room temperature. Measure the cereal into a small airtight container; cover and store at room temperature until ready to use.

Granola Puck

Forget the over-priced granola and energy bars at the supermarket; now you can make your own all-natural puck-shaped version in minutes. The possibilities for variation are extensive, which means you'll never grow tired of this healthy, scrumptious, portable snack.

Tips

For a gluten-free granola puck, make sure to use certified gluten-free oats.

Any other type of creamy nut or seed butter (such as cashew, almond, sesame seed or sunflower seed) can be used in place of the peanut butter.

An equal amount of pure maple syrup, agave nectar, brown rice syrup or dark (cooking) molasses may be used in place of the honey.

Add up to $1/4$ tsp (1 mL) of your favorite ground spice or spice blend (such as cinnamon or pumpkin pie spice) at the end of step 1.

Add $1/4$ tsp (1 mL) vanilla extract or finely grated citrus zest (lemon, orange, lime) at the end of step 1.

If you leave the granola puck in the freezer for more than 10 minutes it will become difficult to remove from the mug. If that happens, allow the puck to thaw at room temperature for 10 to 15 minutes before removing.

For ease of preparation, choose a mug that is not especially narrow.

♦ **12- to 16-oz (375 to 500 mL) mug, sprayed with nonstick cooking spray**

$1^1/2$ tbsp	creamy peanut butter	22 mL
1 tbsp	honey	15 mL
$1/3$ cup	large-flake (old-fashioned) or quick-cooking rolled oats	75 mL
1 tbsp	chopped dried fruit (apricots, raisins, cranberries)	15 mL

1. In the mug, combine peanut butter and honey. Microwave on High for 20 to 40 seconds or until melted and just beginning to bubble.

2. Stir in oats and dried fruit until thoroughly blended. Using the back of the spoon, firmly press and compact mixture into the mug. Place in the refrigerator for 20 minutes or in the freezer for 10 minutes, until firm. Remove puck using the tip of the spoon.

Variations

- **Chocolate Chip Granola Puck:** Let the peanut butter mixture cool for 2 minutes at the end of step 1 (to prevent the chocolate chips from melting). Add 2 tsp (10 mL) miniature semisweet chocolate chips after mixing in the oats and fruit in step 2.

- **Granola Protein Puck:** Decrease the oats to $1/4$ cup (60 mL) and add 1 tbsp (15 mL) vanilla whey protein powder, vanilla vegan protein powder or nonfat instant milk powder with the oats.

Prep Ahead Option

Measure the peanut butter and honey into the mug; cover and store at room temperature. Measure the oats and dried fruit into a small airtight container or sealable plastic bag; cover and store at room temperature until ready to use.

Storage Tip

The granola puck can be made in advance. Tightly wrap in plastic wrap, parchment paper or foil, or store in an airtight container. Store at room temperature for up to 3 days or in the refrigerator for up to 1 week.

Crispy Rice Treat

The very best crispy rice treat is one you can have exactly when you want it. It's best if left to cool in the refrigerator for 10 to 15 minutes, but I can testify that it's mighty fine while still warm in the mug, too.

Tips

Be sure to use crisp rice cereal, not puffed rice, for the best results.

The warm crispy treat can be turned out of the mug onto a piece of waxed paper or parchment paper. Use wet fingertips to gently press it into a bar or square shape. Refrigerate as directed.

♦ **16-oz (500 mL) mug, sprayed with nonstick cooking spray**

1 cup	miniature marshmallows	250 mL
2 tsp	butter	10 mL
1/8 tsp	vanilla extract (optional)	0.5 mL
1 cup	crisp rice cereal	250 mL

1. In the mug, microwave marshmallows and butter on High for 20 to 40 seconds (checking at 20) or until marshmallows are puffed and butter is melted. Add vanilla (if using) and stir until blended.

2. Stir in cereal until coated, then gently press mixture down into the mug. Refrigerate for 10 to 15 minutes or until cooled and firm. Eat directly from the mug or gently remove onto a small plate.

Variations

- **Peanut Butter Crispy Treat:** Add 1 tbsp (15 mL) creamy peanut butter with the butter.

- **Chocolate Crispy Treat:** Add 2 tbsp (15 mL) chocolate chips (any variety) with the butter.

- **Coconut Crispy Treat:** Add 2 tbsp (30 mL) sweetened flaked or shredded coconut with the cereal. If desired, use an equal amount of coconut extract in place of the vanilla.

- **Chocolate Hazelnut Crispy Treat:** Add 1 tbsp (15 mL) chocolate hazelnut spread with the butter.

> **Prep Ahead Option**
>
> Measure the marshmallows and butter into the mug; cover and refrigerate. Measure the cereal into a small airtight container; cover and store at room temperature until ready to use.

Mug Brownie

This two-minute treat is everything you could hope for in a brownie: rich, chocolaty and slightly fudgy. Be sure to check for doneness at the minimum time to avoid overcooking. And in case you're wondering, yes, this is extra-wonderful with a scoop of vanilla ice cream on top.

Tips

Consider sprinkling 1 to 2 tbsp (15 to 30 mL) miniature semisweet chocolate chips on top of the batter before cooking.

For even more flavor, add $\frac{1}{4}$ tsp (1 mL) vanilla extract.

Try topping the brownie with a dollop of vanilla yogurt or whipped cream, or a small scoop of vanilla ice cream.

♦ **16-oz (500 mL) mug, sprayed with nonstick cooking spray**

$\frac{1}{4}$ cup	all-purpose flour	60 mL
$\frac{1}{4}$ cup	granulated sugar	60 mL
2 tbsp	unsweetened cocoa powder	30 mL
Pinch	salt	Pinch
$\frac{1}{4}$ cup	water	60 mL
2 tbsp	vegetable oil or melted butter	30 mL

1. In the mug, use a fork to combine flour, sugar, cocoa powder and salt, breaking up any clumps in the cocoa powder. Stir in water and oil until blended and smooth.
2. Microwave on High for 60 to 75 seconds (checking at 60) or until center is just barely set (be careful not to overcook). Let stand for at least 1 minute. Eat directly from mug.

Variations

- **Mocha Chip Brownie:** Dissolve 1 tsp (5 mL) instant espresso powder in the water before adding. Stir 1 tbsp (15 mL) miniature semisweet chocolate chips into the batter.
- **Spicy Mexican Brownie:** Add $\frac{1}{4}$ tsp (1 mL) vanilla extract, $\frac{1}{4}$ tsp (1 mL) ground cinnamon and a pinch of cayenne pepper to the batter.

> **Prep Ahead Option**
> Combine the flour, sugar, cocoa powder and salt in the mug; cover and store at room temperature. Combine the water and oil in a small airtight container; cover and store at room temperature until ready to use.

1-2-3 Mug Cake

Making a cake doesn't get any easier than this — literally. Angel food cake mix contains egg whites, and regular cake mix contains vegetable oil, which means all you need to add is a few tablespoons of water.

Tip

Try adding 2 to 3 tsp (10 to 15 mL) of any of the following add-ins to the cake batter before cooking: miniature semisweet chocolate chips, finely chopped dried fruit (such as raisins, cranberries or apricots), finely chopped nuts, sprinkles.

♦ **16-oz (500 mL) mug, sprayed with nonstick cooking spray**

For the 1-2-3 Mix

1 box	(16 oz/454 g) angel food cake mix	1
1 box	(15.25 to 18.25 oz/440 to 525 g) cake mix (any flavor)	1

For 1 Mug Cake

3 tbsp	1-2-3 cake mix	45 mL
2 tbsp	water	30 mL

Suggested Accompaniments

Prepared frosting; confectioners' (icing) sugar; ice cream or frozen yogurt; whipped cream

1. *Mix:* In a large airtight container or sealable plastic bag, whisk the two cake mixes until blended and free of any large lumps. Store at room temperature for up to 1 month or in the refrigerator or freezer for up to 6 months.

2. *Cake:* In the mug, use a fork to combine 1-2-3 cake mix and water until blended and smooth. Microwave on High for 60 to 90 seconds (checking at 60) or until center is just set. Let cool slightly or entirely in mug. Eat directly from mug or gently remove onto a small plate. Serve with any of the suggested accompaniments, as desired.

> **Prep Ahead Option**
> Measure 3 tbsp (45 mL) 1-2-3 cake mix into the mug; cover and store at room temperature until ready to use.

Cocoa Banana Pudding Cake

Moist, forgiving and easy, this is the perfect cake for initial ventures into microwave baking. The banana and cocoa combination is always in season, so keep bananas on hand for spur-of-the-moment cravings.

Tips

Mash the banana until it is almost a liquid before measuring.

One medium-large banana will yield about ½ cup (125 mL) mashed. Make sure it is a very soft, squishy banana; the peel should be covered partly or entirely with brown spots.

Try sprinkling the batter with 1 tbsp (15 mL) miniature semisweet chocolate chips before cooking.

♦ **12- to 16-oz (375 to 500 mL) mug, sprayed with nonstick cooking spray**

2 tbsp	unsweetened cocoa powder	30 mL
2 tsp	granulated sugar	10 mL
Pinch	salt	Pinch
1	large egg	1
½ cup	mashed very ripe banana	125 mL

1. In the mug, use a fork to combine cocoa powder, sugar, salt, egg and banana until blended and smooth.
2. Microwave on High for 60 to 90 seconds (checking at 60) or until puffed and center is just set. Let cool slightly or entirely in mug. Eat directly from mug.

Variation

- **Mocha Pudding Cake:** Replace the banana with an equal amount of applesauce and increase the sugar to 3½ tsp (17 mL). Add ½ tsp (2 mL) instant coffee powder in step 1.

> **Prep Ahead Option**
> Prepare through step 1; cover and refrigerate until ready to heat.

Cheesecake in a Mug

For cheesecake lovers like me, this dessert is a dream come true. Forget the springform pans, hours of baking and chilling, and the temptation to eat more than one piece: this mug version is fast, luscious and just enough for one person.

Tips

Try adding $\frac{1}{4}$ tsp (1 mL) vanilla extract to the cream cheese mixture.

An equal amount of crushed crisp cookies (any variety) can be used in place of the crushed graham cracker.

You can use $\frac{1}{2}$ cup (125 mL) ricotta cheese in place of the cream cheese.

♦ **12- to 16-oz (375 to 500 mL) mug, sprayed with nonstick cooking spray**

3 oz	brick-style cream cheese, softened	90 g
1½ tbsp	granulated sugar	22 mL
2 tbsp	beaten egg	30 mL
1	square graham cracker, coarsely crushed (about 1½ tbsp/22 mL)	1

1. In a small bowl, use a fork to beat cream cheese, sugar and egg until blended and smooth.

2. Sprinkle crushed graham cracker in the bottom of the mug. Top with cream cheese mixture, smoothing the top. Microwave on High for 75 to 90 seconds or until filling is slightly puffed at the center.

3. Refrigerate the mug, uncovered, for 45 to 60 minutes or until chilled.

> **Prep Ahead Option**
> Prepare through step 1; cover and refrigerate. Microwave on High for 10 to 15 seconds to soften the cream cheese when ready to use. Place the crushed graham cracker in the mug; cover and store at room temperature until ready to use.

Tip

To measure the egg, whisk 1 large egg in a small airtight container. Measure 2 tbsp (30 mL) into the bowl as directed. Cover and refrigerate the remaining egg (about 2 tbsp/30 mL) for up to 2 days.

Variations

- **Berry Cheesecake:** Add 2 tbsp (30 mL) raspberries, blackberries or blueberries to the cream cheese mixture.
- **Jam, Lemon Curd or Chocolate Hazelnut Swirl Cheesecake:** After adding the cream cheese mixture to the mug, top with 1 tbsp (15 mL) jam (any variety), lemon curd or chocolate hazelnut spread. Swirl into cream cheese with the end of a fork or spoon.
- **Chocolate Chip Cheesecake:** Add 1 tbsp (15 mL) miniature semisweet chocolate chips to the cream cheese mixture.
- **Peanut Butter Cheesecake:** Stir $1\frac{1}{2}$ tbsp (22 mL) creamy or chunky peanut butter into the cream cheese mixture. If desired, replace the granulated sugar with an equal amount of packed brown sugar.
- **Pumpkin Cheesecake:** Stir 2 tbsp (30 mL) canned pumpkin purée (not pie filling) and $\frac{1}{2}$ tsp (2 mL) pumpkin pie spice or ground cinnamon into the cream cheese mixture.

Baked Apple

Baked apples are a cozy finish to almost any fall or winter meal. They make a heart-warming breakfast, too, especially when topped with a dollop of yogurt and a sprinkle of granola or chopped walnuts.

Tip

Sweet-tart apples are the best option here, but in a pinch, any variety will do.

♦ **16-oz (500 mL) mug**

1	medium sweet-tart apple (such as Braeburn, Gala or Golden Delicious)	1
1 tbsp	packed brown sugar	15 mL
1/8 tsp	ground cinnamon	0.5 mL
1 tsp	butter	5 mL
2 tbsp	water	30 mL

Suggested Accompaniments

Vanilla-flavored or plain Greek yogurt; vanilla ice cream; ricotta cheese

1. Peel the apple and quarter it lengthwise, then trim the core and stem off each quarter.

2. In the mug, microwave brown sugar, cinnamon and butter for 25 to 30 seconds or until butter is melted. Stir to combine.

3. Place the apple quarters in the mug and spoon butter mixture over top. Add water and cover mug with a small plate or saucer. Microwave on High for 4 to 6 minutes (checking at 4) or until apple is very tender. Remove plate and let stand for 2 minutes. Spoon juices over apple. Serve with any of the suggested accompaniments, as desired.

Variation

• **Cranberry Spice Apple:** Replace the cinnamon with an equal amount of pumpkin pie spice and add 1 tbsp (15 mL) dried cranberries with the apple.

Prep Ahead Option

Prepare the apple as directed in step 1. Place in a small airtight container, cover and refrigerate. (If desired, add a few drops of lemon juice to prevent browning.) In the mug, combine brown sugar, cinnamon and butter; cover and refrigerate until ready to use.

Breakfast

Mug Granola

You can buy a tiny pouch of granola for an exorbitant price, or you can make a single serving any time, any way you like it, for a few cents at home. You can tweak this basic recipe with whatever nuts, seeds or dried fruit suit your fancy. It's pretty forgiving, so adjust the sweetener and salt — a bit more, a touch less — or add a pinch of a favorite spice.

Tips

To make this granola gluten-free, be sure to use oats that are certified gluten-free.

Add $1/4$ to $3/4$ tsp (1 to 3 mL) of any sweet ground spice (cinnamon, ginger, pumpkin pie spice, allspice) with the salt.

For even more flavor, add a few drops of vanilla or almond extract to the syrup mixture, or add $1/2$ tsp (2 mL) finely grated citrus zest (lemon, orange, lime).

♦ **12- to 16-oz (375 to 500 mL) mug, sprayed with nonstick cooking spray**

1 tbsp	pure maple syrup, liquid honey or agave nectar	15 mL
2 tsp	water	10 mL
1 tsp	vegetable oil	5 mL
Pinch	salt	Pinch
$1/3$ cup	quick-cooking or large-flake (old-fashioned) rolled oats	75 mL
1 tbsp	chopped nuts or seeds	15 mL
1 tbsp	chopped dried fruit (optional)	15 mL

1. In the mug, combine maple syrup, water, oil and salt until blended. Stir in oats and nuts until coated.

2. Microwave on Medium (50%) for 2 minutes. Stir, making sure to stir up any syrup on the bottom of the mug. Microwave on Medium (50%) for $1^1/2$ to $2^1/2$ minutes or until mixture appears somewhat dry. Stir in dried fruit (if using). Let cool for 2 to 3 minutes (or completely) before eating.

Variation

- **Coconut Lover's Granola:** Use honey or agave nectar for the sweetener and replace the dried fruit with 2 tbsp (30 mL) flaked or shredded coconut. If desired, replace the vegetable oil with virgin coconut oil.

Prep Ahead Option

Combine the maple syrup, water, oil and salt in the mug; cover and store at room temperature. Measure the oats and nuts into a small airtight container; cover and store at room temperature until ready to use.

Multigrain Cereal Mug

It's hard to argue against eating more whole grains when you're savoring spoonfuls of this warm, nutty multigrain cereal. The fact that it is ready in a flash clinches the debate.

Tips

For the dried fruit, try raisins, cranberries or chopped apricots, or a combination.

Any variety of dairy or non-dairy (almond, hemp, soy, rice) milk can be used in this recipe.

◆ 12- to 16-oz (375 to 500 mL) mug

¼ cup	wheat and barley nugget cereal (such as Grape-Nuts or Kashi 7 Whole Grain Nuggets)	60 mL
2 tbsp	quick-cooking rolled oats	30 mL
1 tbsp	dried fruit (optional)	15 mL
½ cup	milk	125 mL

1. In the mug, combine cereal, oats, dried fruit (if using) and milk.
2. Microwave on High for 90 seconds. Stir. Microwave on High for 2 to 3 minutes or until cereal is tender (not all of the milk will be absorbed).

Variation

- **Pumpkin Cranberry Multigrain Cereal:** Add 2 tbsp (30 mL) pumpkin purée (not pie filling), 1 tsp (5 mL) packed brown sugar and ¼ tsp (1 mL) pumpkin pie spice or ground cinnamon with the milk. Use dried cranberries for the dried fruit.

> **Prep Ahead Option**
> Prepare through step 1; cover and refrigerate until ready to use.

Quinoa Breakfast Porridge

Sweet and nutty quinoa boasts great taste as well as great nutrition. It is packed with vitamins, minerals and all of the essential amino acids, making it a supercharged way to start your day.

Tips

Instead of adding the dried fruit, try topping the porridge with 1/4 cup (60 mL) diced fresh fruit (peaches, apples, pears) or berries (raspberries, strawberries, blackberries).

Add extra protein and crunch by topping the porridge with 1 to 2 tbsp (15 to 30 mL) chopped raw or toasted nuts or seeds (walnuts, pecans, almonds, green pumpkin seeds, sunflower seeds, chia seeds).

For even more flavor, add 1/4 tsp (1 mL) vanilla extract or finely grated citrus zest (lemon, orange, lime) with the milk.

♦ **16-oz (500 mL) mug**

1/4 cup	quinoa, rinsed	60 mL
Pinch	salt	Pinch
2/3 cup	water	150 mL
1 1/2 tbsp	dried fruit (raisins, cranberries, chopped dates)	22 mL
1/8 tsp	ground cinnamon	0.5 mL
2 tbsp	milk or non-dairy milk (soy, hemp, almond, rice)	30 mL
	Liquid honey, agave nectar, pure maple syrup, brown sugar or stevia (optional)	

1. In the mug, combine quinoa, salt and water. Microwave on High for 4 minutes. Stir. Microwave on High for 3 to 4 minutes or until quinoa is tender and most (but not all) of the liquid is absorbed.
2. Stir in dried fruit, cinnamon and milk. Cover tightly with foil and let stand for 2 minutes. If desired, sweeten to taste.

Variations

- **Apple Maple Quinoa:** Omit the dried fruit. Add 1/3 cup (75 mL) chopped peeled apple (about 1/2 small) to the quinoa for the final 3 minutes of cooking time. Sweeten with maple syrup.
- **Pumpkin Pie Breakfast Quinoa:** Add 2 tbsp (30 mL) canned pumpkin purée (not pie filling) with the milk. Use dried cranberries for the fruit and increase the cinnamon to 1/4 tsp (1 mL).
- **PB&J Quinoa Porridge:** Omit the dried fruit. Add 1 1/2 tbsp (22 mL) peanut butter or other nut or seed butter (almond, sunflower, sesame) with the milk. Serve topped with 1 tbsp (15 mL) fruit jelly or jam.

Prep Ahead Option

Measure the quinoa and salt into the mug; cover and store at room temperature. Measure the dried fruit, cinnamon and milk into a small airtight container; cover and refrigerate until ready to use.

Chocolate Chip Cookie Dough "Baked" Oatmeal

Go ahead, pinch yourself — you're not dreaming. This mugful of oats tastes like warm chocolate chip cookie dough, but it's also a nutritious, fiber-packed breakfast.

Prep Ahead Option

Whisk the oats, flour, cinnamon, baking powder and salt in the mug; cover and store at room temperature. Break the egg into a small airtight container and add the milk, butter, brown sugar and vanilla; cover and refrigerate until ready to use.

♦ **16-oz (500 mL) mug**

1/3 cup	quick-cooking rolled oats	75 mL
2 tbsp	all-purpose or whole wheat flour	30 mL
1/4 tsp	ground cinnamon	1 mL
1/8 tsp	baking powder	0.5 mL
1/8 tsp	salt	0.5 mL
1	large egg	1
3 tbsp	milk	45 mL
2 tsp	butter	10 mL
1 1/2 tbsp	packed brown sugar	22 mL
1/4 tsp	vanilla extract	1 mL
1 tbsp	miniature semisweet chocolate chips	15 mL

Suggested Accompaniments

Milk or half-and-half (10%) cream; diced fresh or thawed frozen fruit or berries; vanilla-flavored Greek yogurt

1. In the mug, whisk oats, flour, cinnamon, baking powder and salt until blended. Using a fork, beat in egg, milk, butter, brown sugar and vanilla until blended.

2. Microwave on High for 1 1/2 to 2 1/2 minutes (checking at 1 1/2) or until just set. Sprinkle with chocolate chips and let stand for 1 minute. Serve with any of the suggested accompaniments, as desired.

Variations

- **Gluten-Free Chocolate Chip Cookie "Baked" Oatmeal:** Use certified gluten-free oats and replace the all-purpose flour with an equal amount of almond flour or an all-purpose gluten-free flour blend.

- **Raisin Oatmeal Cookie Dough Oatmeal:** Increase the brown sugar to 2 tbsp (30 mL). Omit the chocolate chips with stir in an equal amount of raisins with the oats.

Carrot Cake Oatmeal

Carrot cake for breakfast? I know what you're thinking: it's about time! While this tastes like a mugful of your favorite cake (especially if you add a dollop of cream cheese), you can feel virtuous about digging in: it's packed with a serving of vegetables, plus a hefty dose of whole-grain fiber. You're welcome.

Tip

To make this oatmeal gluten-free, be sure to use oats that are certified gluten-free.

♦ **16-oz (500 mL) mug**

1/2 cup	quick-cooking rolled oats	125 mL
1/3 cup	finely shredded carrot	75 mL
2 tbsp	raisins or dried cranberries	30 mL
2 tsp	packed brown sugar	10 mL
1/2 tsp	pumpkin pie spice or ground cinnamon	2 mL
Pinch	salt	Pinch
3/4 cup	water	175 mL

Suggested Accompaniments

Honey nut–flavored or plain cream cheese; pure maple syrup, liquid honey or brown sugar; milk; chopped toasted walnuts or pecans

1. In the mug, combine oats, carrot, raisins, brown sugar, pumpkin pie spice, salt and water.

2. Microwave on High for 90 seconds. Stir. Microwave on High for $1^1/_2$ to $2^1/_2$ minutes or until most of the liquid is absorbed. Let stand for 1 minute. Serve with any of the suggested accompaniments, as desired.

Variations

- **Zucchini Bread Oatmeal:** Replace the carrots with shredded zucchini.

- **Pumpkin Pie Oatmeal:** Replace the carrots with an equal amount of canned pumpkin purée (not pie filling).

Prep Ahead Option

Measure the oats, carrot, raisins, brown sugar, pumpkin pie spice and salt into the mug (do not add the water); cover and refrigerate until ready to use.

Honey Breakfast Couscous

A double boost of sweetness from honey and chopped dried fruit gives this morning version of couscous a flavor boost. To sneak some whole grains into your diet first thing in the morning, opt for whole wheat couscous over regular couscous.

Tips

Adding the dried fruit with the couscous allows it to plump up from the boiling water.

An equal amount of any other sweetener — liquid or granular — can be used in place of the honey.

♦ **16-oz (500 mL) mug**

$\frac{1}{2}$ cup	water	125 mL
$\frac{1}{2}$ cup	couscous (regular or whole wheat)	125 mL
2 tbsp	chopped dried fruit (cranberries, apricots, raisins)	30 mL
$\frac{1}{8}$ tsp	salt	0.5 mL
2 tsp	butter (optional)	10 mL
1 tbsp	liquid honey	15 mL
	Milk or half-and-half (10%) cream	

1. In the mug, microwave water on High for $1\frac{1}{2}$ to 3 minutes or until boiling.
2. Stir in couscous, dried fruit, salt and butter (if using). Cover with a small plate and let stand for 5 minutes. Drizzle with honey and serve with milk.

Variations

- **Coconut Couscous:** Omit the dried fruit and replace the butter with an equal amount of virgin coconut oil. Top with flaked or shredded coconut (toasted or untoasted).
- **Cinnamon Maple Couscous:** Add $\frac{1}{4}$ tsp (1 mL) ground cinnamon with the salt and use dried cherries or cranberries for the fruit. Replace the honey with pure maple syrup.

Prep Ahead Option

Measure the couscous, dried fruit and salt into a small airtight container; cover and store at room temperature until ready to use.

Brown Sugar Vanilla Breakfast Polenta

You may have enjoyed polenta at the supper table, but have you tried it for breakfast? If not, step right up to the mug. Creamy and comforting, it is the perfect foil for any number of toppings, such as fresh fruit, toasted nuts or a sprinkle of spices.

Tips

For the dried fruit, try apricots, cranberries and/or raisins.

An equal amount of granulated sugar, maple syrup, agave nectar or liquid honey can be used in place of the brown sugar.

Stone-ground (aka coarse-grind) cornmeal produces a more toothsome texture than regular cornmeal; it also has a deeper corn flavor.

♦ 16-oz (500 mL) mug

$1/4$ cup	yellow cornmeal (preferably stone-ground)	60 mL
$1^1/2$ tbsp	chopped dried fruit (optional)	22 mL
$1/8$ tsp	salt	0.5 mL
$3/4$ cup	milk, divided	175 mL
$2/3$ cup	water	150 mL
2 tsp	butter (optional)	10 mL
$1/4$ tsp	vanilla extract	1 mL
1 tbsp	packed brown sugar	15 mL

1. In the mug, combine cornmeal, dried fruit, salt, $1/2$ cup (125 mL) milk and water.

2. Place in the microwave atop a doubled paper towel. Microwave on High for 3 minutes. Stir. Microwave on High for 2 minutes. Stir. Microwave on High for $1^1/2$ to $2^1/2$ minutes (checking at $1^1/2$) or until thickened.

3. Stir in butter (if using) and vanilla until butter is melted. Sprinkle with brown sugar and drizzle with the remaining milk.

Variation

- **Honey Lemon Breakfast Polenta:** Replace the brown sugar with an equal amount of liquid honey. Omit the vanilla and add $1/2$ tsp (2 mL) finely grated lemon zest and 1 tsp (5 mL) freshly squeezed lemon juice with the vanilla.

Prep Ahead Option

Measure the cornmeal, dried fruit and salt into the mug; cover and store at room temperature. Measure the $1/2$ cup (125 mL) milk and the water into a small airtight container; cover and refrigerate. Measure the butter and vanilla into a small airtight container; cover and refrigerate until ready to use.

Apple Butter Breakfast Mug

Apple butter is a subtly spiced applesauce that gets cooked down until it becomes a luscious, caramelized, buttery (despite having no butter) spread. Here it joins fresh apples in a perfect breakfast mug of autumnal deliciousness.

Tips

Look for jars of apple butter where jams and jellies are shelved. It's not expensive (it often costs less than many jams) and can be used on toast and bread, just like jam and preserves.

It will take about half a medium apple to yield ½ cup (125 mL) chopped apple.

♦ **12- to 16-oz (375 to 500 mL) mug**

¼ cup	wheat and barley nugget cereal (such as Grape-Nuts or Kashi 7 Whole Grain Nuggets)	60 mL
½ cup	chopped peeled apple	125 mL
½ cup	milk	125 mL
1 tbsp	apple butter	15 mL
2 tbsp	chopped pecans or walnuts	30 mL

1. In the mug, combine cereal, apple and milk.
2. Microwave on High for 90 seconds. Stir. Microwave on High for 2 to 3 minutes or until cereal and apples are tender (not all of the milk will be absorbed). Swirl in apple butter. Top with pecans.

Variation

- **Pear and Berry Breakfast Mug:** Replace the apple with an equal amount of chopped peeled pear, and replace the apple butter with 1½ tbsp (22 mL) raspberry, strawberry or blackberry jam or preserves.

Prep Ahead Option

Combine the cereal, apple and milk in the mug; cover and refrigerate. Measure the apple butter and pecans into separate small airtight containers; cover and refrigerate until ready to use.

Maple Berry Compote with Yogurt

Smooth, rich, tangy Greek yogurt provides a creamy contrast to a maple-sweetened, cinnamon-scented berry compote. It's an incredibly easy way to start the day with flair.

Tips

This also makes a not-too-sweet dessert. Try topping it with crumbled cookies or toasted almonds in place of the granola.

If you prefer, you can use vanilla- or fruit-flavored Greek yogurt in place of the plain yogurt.

Try using Mug Granola (page 68) for the granola topping.

♦ **16-oz (500 mL) mug**

1 cup	frozen mixed berries	250 mL
6 tsp	pure maple syrup, divided	30 mL
1/8 tsp	ground cinnamon	0.5 mL
1/2 cup	plain Greek yogurt	125 mL
2 tbsp	granola (optional)	30 mL

1. In the mug, combine berries, 4 tsp (20 mL) maple syrup and cinnamon.

2. Microwave on High for 1 minute. Stir with a fork, then coarsely mash the berries. Microwave on High for 60 to 90 seconds or until bubbling at edges. Let cool for 1 to 2 minutes.

3. Spoon in the yogurt, sprinkle with granola (if using) and drizzle with remaining syrup.

Variation

• **Blackberry Compote with Cardamom Yogurt:** Use frozen blackberries in place of the mixed berries and replace the maple syrup with liquid honey. Omit the cinnamon and mix a pinch of ground cardamom into the yogurt.

Prep Ahead Option

Combine the berries, 4 tsp (20 mL) maple syrup and cinnamon in the mug; cover and refrigerate. Measure the yogurt into a small airtight container; cover and refrigerate until ready to use.

Peach Breakfast Clafouti

Clafouti is a cross between a flan and a fruit-filled pancake. Traditional versions embrace cherries, but any diced fruit — fresh, canned or thawed frozen — will work perfectly in this single-serving microwave version.

Tips

One single-serve cup (4 oz/125 mL) of diced peaches, drained, is just the right amount for this recipe.

To measure the egg, whisk 1 large egg in a small airtight container. Measure 2 tbsp (30 mL) into the mug as directed. Cover and refrigerate the remaining egg (about 2 tbsp/30 mL) for up to 2 days.

One small egg can be used in place of the 2 tbsp (30 mL) beaten egg.

♦ **16-oz (500 mL) mug**

1 tbsp	butter	15 mL
3 tbsp	all-purpose flour	45 mL
2 tbsp	granulated sugar	30 mL
Pinch	salt	Pinch
¼ cup	diced fresh, thawed frozen or drained canned peaches	60 mL
2 tbsp	beaten egg	30 mL
1 tbsp	milk	15 mL
⅛ tsp	vanilla extract (optional)	0.5 mL
	Confectioners' (icing) sugar (optional)	

1. In the mug, heat butter for 15 to 25 seconds or until melted. Stir in flour, granulated sugar, salt, peaches, egg, milk and vanilla (if using) until blended.

2. Microwave on High for 75 to 90 seconds (checking at 75) or until puffed and set at the center. If desired, sprinkle with confectioners' sugar.

Variations

- **Gluten-Free Peach Clafouti:** Replace the all-purpose flour with an all-purpose gluten-free flour blend. Make sure the confectioners' sugar is gluten-free or omit it.

- **Dried Fruit Clafouti:** Replace the peaches with 2 tbsp (30 mL) chopped dried fruit (cranberries, apricots, figs). Increase the milk to 2 tbsp (30 mL).

- **Berry Clafouti:** Replace the peaches with an equal amount of fresh blueberries or raspberries.

> **Prep Ahead Option**
>
> Measure the butter into the mug; cover and refrigerate. Measure the flour, granulated sugar, salt, peaches, egg, milk and vanilla (if using) into a small airtight container; cover and refrigerate until ready to use.

Raspberry Blintz Mug

A blintz (Ukrainian for "pancake") is a thin pancake folded around a creamy, white cheese filling and very often accompanied with jam or a fruit compote. My mug rendition combines the crêpe and filling into one light and cheesy puff — jam included.

Tips

You can use any flavor of jam, jelly, preserves or marmalade in place of the raspberry jam.

An equal amount of ricotta cheese can be used in place of the cottage cheese.

To measure the egg, whisk 1 large egg in a small airtight container. Measure 2 tbsp (30 mL) into the mug as directed. Cover and refrigerate the remaining egg (about 2 tbsp/30 mL) for up to 2 days.

One small egg can be used in place of the 2 tbsp (30 mL) beaten egg.

♦ **16-oz (500 mL) mug**

1 tbsp	all-purpose flour	15 mL
1 tbsp	granulated sugar	15 mL
Pinch	salt	Pinch
¼ cup	cottage cheese	60 mL
3 tbsp	plain Greek yogurt	45 mL
2 tbsp	beaten egg	30 mL
⅛ tsp	vanilla extract (optional)	0.5 mL
2 tsp	raspberry jam or preserves	10 mL
	Confectioners' (icing) sugar	

1. In the mug, combine flour, granulated sugar, salt, cottage cheese, yogurt, egg and vanilla until well blended.
2. Microwave on High for 75 to 90 seconds (checking at 75) or until puffed and center is just set. Let stand for 5 minutes. Top with jam. If desired, sprinkle with confectioners' sugar.

Variation

- **Gluten-Free Raspberry Blintz Mug:** Replace the all-purpose flour with almond flour or an all-purpose gluten-free flour blend. Make sure the confectioners' sugar is gluten-free or omit it.

Prep Ahead Option

Measure the flour, granulated sugar and salt into the mug; cover and store at room temperature. Measure the cottage cheese, yogurt, egg and vanilla into a small airtight container; cover and refrigerate until ready to use.

Poached Egg

Wouldn't it be great if you had a technique for making perfect poached eggs? Now you do. Enjoy the egg's simplicity with a piece of toast, or place atop any salad or cooked vegetables for an instant lunch or dinner.

Tips

For the best results, use recently purchased eggs.

For an egg with a firm yolk, microwave on High for 60 to 75 seconds or until yolk is just firm.

The microwave will cook the yolk faster than the white. If you prefer a runnier yolk, stop cooking when the white is not quite set (it will continue to firm up from the heat of the water).

♦ **12- to 16-oz (375 to 500 mL) mug**

1/3 cup	water	75 mL
1/8 tsp	white or cider vinegar	0.5 mL
1	large egg	1

1. In the mug, combine water and vinegar. Carefully crack the egg into the mug, being careful not to break the yolk.

2. Cover with a small plate or saucer. Microwave on Medium-High (70%) for 75 seconds. Check the egg white to see if it is just barely set. If not, microwave on High for 15 to 30 seconds (checking at 15) or until the white is just set. Remove egg with a slotted spoon.

Variation

• **Shirred Eggs:** Replace the water and vinegar with 2 tbsp (30 mL) heavy or whipping (35%) cream. Sprinkle with a pinch each of salt and ground black pepper and cook as directed. Eat directly from mug, with the cream.

> **Prep Ahead Option**
> Combine the water and vinegar in the mug; cover and store at room temperature until ready to use.

Huevos Rancheros

On mornings when you awaken famished, huevos rancheros is just the breakfast you need. It literally translates as "rancher's eggs," meaning it is intended to provide energy for a long morning on the farm. But it's perfect for powering through a tough workout or workday, too.

Tips

For an egg with a firm yolk, microwave on High for 60 to 75 seconds or until yolk is just firm.

The microwave will cook the yolk faster than the white. If you prefer a runnier yolk, stop cooking when the white is not quite set (it will continue to firm up from the heat of the tomato mixture).

If you prefer, you can use ½ cup (125 mL) thick and chunky salsa in place of the canned tomatoes with chiles.

♦ **16-oz (500 mL) mug**

½ can	(10 oz/284 mL) diced tomatoes with green chiles, with juice	½
⅓ cup	drained rinsed canned black or pinto beans	75 mL
⅛ tsp	ground cumin (optional)	0.5 mL
1	large egg	1

Suggested Accompaniments

Warm tortilla (corn or flour); chopped green onions; chopped fresh cilantro; sour cream or plain Greek yogurt; diced avocado or guacamole; hot pepper sauce; crumbled queso blanco or shredded Cheddar cheese

1. In the mug, combine tomatoes, beans and cumin (if using). Microwave on High for 1½ to 2 minutes or until heated through.
2. Make a well in the center of the mixture and carefully crack the egg into the well, being careful not to break the yolk.
3. Cover with a small plate or saucer. Microwave on Medium-High (70%) for 60 seconds. Check the egg white to see if it is just barely set. If not, microwave on High for 15 to 20 seconds or until the white is just set. Serve with any of the suggested accompaniments, as desired.

Variation

- **Huevos Rancheros Verde:** Replace the tomatoes with ½ cup (125 mL) green enchilada sauce.

> **Prep Ahead Option**
> Combine the tomatoes, beans and cumin (if using) in the mug; cover and refrigerate until ready to use.

Essential Omelet

Simple, simple, simple! That's the best way to describe this mug omelet, though you could add delicious, healthy, versatile and cheap, too. Have fun with your customizations (a bit of this, a smidge of that) and don't limit it to breakfast.

Tips

Add up to 2 tsp (10 mL) of your favorite chopped leafy herbs (basil, parsley, cilantro) or chives to the egg mixture in step 1.

This omelet is a great way to use up small amounts of cooked vegetables, meats and cheese. Add up to 2 tbsp (30 mL) of each or up to $1/3$ cup (75 mL) combination of two or more options.

♦ **12- to 16-oz (375 to 500 mL) mug, sprayed with nonstick cooking spray**

2	large eggs	2
2 tsp	milk or water	10 mL
Pinch	salt	Pinch
Pinch	ground black pepper	Pinch

1. In the mug, whisk eggs, milk, salt and pepper until well blended.
2. Microwave on High for 30 seconds. Stir. Microwave on High for 30 to 45 seconds or until eggs are puffed and just barely set at the center.

Variations

- **Reduced-Fat Omelet:** Replace one of the whole eggs with 2 egg whites.
- **Cheese Omelet:** Add 2 to 3 tbsp (30 to 45 mL) shredded cheese (Cheddar, Swiss, Monterey Jack) or 1 tbsp (15 mL) grated Parmesan cheese to the beaten eggs.
- **Denver Omelet:** Add 2 tbsp (30 mL) chopped ham, 2 tbsp (30 mL) shredded Cheddar cheese and 1 tbsp (15 mL) chopped green bell pepper (fresh or thawed frozen) to the beaten eggs.
- **Bacon Swiss Omelet:** Add 2 tbsp (30 mL) shredded Swiss cheese and $1\frac{1}{2}$ tbsp (22 mL) ready-to-eat real bacon bits to the beaten eggs.
- **Sausage, Pepper and Onion Omelet:** Before preparing the eggs, combine 1 frozen cooked breakfast sausage link and $1/4$ cup (60 mL) frozen or fresh chopped bell pepper and onion blend in the mug. Microwave on High for 60 to 90 seconds or until both sausage and vegetables are thawed and warm. Drain off excess liquid and use a fork to crumble the sausage. Add the eggs and remaining ingredients and proceed as directed.

> **Prep Ahead Option**
> Prepare through step 1; cover and refrigerate until ready to use.

Scrambled Eggs Florentine

You'll return to this breakfast mugful again and again because it is so convenient and delivers serious satisfaction. The nutty accents of Parmesan cheese and nutmeg gently permeate the eggs, while the tomatoes and spinach proclaim freshness (despite coming from a can and the freezer).

Tips

Opt for bags, as opposed to boxes, of frozen chopped spinach, as it is easier to remove small amounts at a time.

Freeze the remaining tomatoes in a small sealable freezer bag. You can freeze the entire amount in one bag, or portion out ¼ cup (60 mL) per bag so that the tomatoes are recipe-ready. Be sure to label the bag with the contents. Store for up to 3 months. Defrost in the refrigerator or microwave before using.

◆ **12- to 16-oz (375 to 500 mL) mug**

1 cup	frozen chopped spinach	250 mL
2	large eggs	2
Pinch	ground nutmeg (optional)	Pinch
Pinch	salt	Pinch
Pinch	ground black pepper	Pinch
¼ cup	drained canned Italian-seasoned diced tomatoes	60 mL
1 tbsp	grated Parmesan cheese	15 mL

1. In the mug, microwave spinach on High for 1½ to 2 minutes or until thawed and warm. Using the tines of a fork, press down firmly on the spinach and drain off excess liquid.

2. Using a fork, beat in eggs, nutmeg (if using), salt and pepper until well blended. Stir in tomatoes and Parmesan. Microwave on High for 30 seconds. Stir. Microwave on High for 30 to 45 seconds or until eggs are puffed and just barely set at the center.

Variation

- **Greek Spinach Scramble:** Omit the tomatoes. Replace the nutmeg with ¼ tsp (1 mL) dried dillweed or ⅛ tsp (0.5 mL) dried oregano. Replace the Parmesan with 1 tbsp (15 mL) crumbled feta cheese.

Prep Ahead Option

Measure the spinach into the mug; cover and refrigerate (decrease the cooking time in step 1 to 30 seconds). Using a fork, beat the eggs in a small airtight container, then add the nutmeg (if using), salt, pepper, tomatoes and Parmesan; cover and refrigerate until ready to use.

Green Eggs and Ham

Equal amounts of basil pesto and fresh parsley add vivid color and a layer of herbaceous flavor, a lively contrast to the smoky bits of ham.

Tips

Look for prepared basil pesto in the supermarket where pasta sauces are shelved.

You can use an equal amount of chopped cooked smoked sausage or 1 tbsp (15 mL) ready-to-eat real bacon bits in place of the ham.

♦ **12- to 16-oz (375 to 500 mL) mug**

2	large eggs	2
1 tbsp	basil pesto	15 mL
2 tbsp	chopped ham	30 mL
1 tbsp	chopped fresh parsley	15 mL

1. In the mug, whisk eggs and pesto until well blended. Stir in ham and parsley.
2. Microwave on High for 30 seconds. Stir. Microwave on High for 30 to 45 seconds or until eggs are puffed and just barely set at the center.

Variations

- **Reduced-Fat Green Eggs and Ham:** Replace one of the whole eggs with 2 egg whites.
- **Green Eggs and Ricotta:** Replace the ham with an equal amount of ricotta cheese, gently stirring it in so the cheese remains in large clumps.

Prep Ahead Option
Prepare through step 1; cover and refrigerate until ready to use.

Tex-Mex Migas Mug

Migas (pronounced *MEE-guz*) is one of my favorite breakfast dishes. It's essentially scrambled eggs loaded with corn tortillas, onions, tomatoes, peppers, and cheese. My simplified mug version will make you rise and shine on any day!

Tips

You can use 1/2 cup (125 mL) coarsely crumbled tortilla chips in place of the tortilla.

An equal amount of chili powder or chipotle chile powder can be used in place of, or in addition to, the cumin.

♦ **12- to 16-oz (375 to 500 mL) mug**

2	large eggs	2
1/8 tsp	ground cumin (optional)	0.5 mL
1	small (6-inch/15 cm) corn tortilla, chopped	1
1/4 cup	thick and chunky-style salsa	60 mL
2 tbsp	shredded Monterey Jack or Cheddar cheese	30 mL

Suggested Accompaniments

Chopped fresh cilantro; chopped green onions; sour cream or plain Greek yogurt; additional salsa; diced avocado or guacamole

1. In the mug, whisk eggs and cumin (if using) until well blended. Stir in tortilla and salsa.

2. Microwave on High for 30 seconds. Stir, then sprinkle with cheese. Microwave on High for 30 to 60 seconds or until eggs are puffed and just barely set at the center. Let cool for 1 minute. Serve with any of the suggested accompaniments, as desired.

Variations

• **Reduced-Fat Migas:** Replace one of the whole eggs with 2 egg whites.

• **Black Bean Migas:** Add 3 tbsp (45 mL) drained rinsed canned black beans with the tortilla.

> **Prep Ahead Option**
>
> Whisk the eggs and cumin (if using) in the mug, then stir in salsa; cover and refrigerate. Measure the tortilla and cheese into separate small airtight containers; cover and refrigerate until ready to use.

French Toast

I'm a firm believer that breakfast is the most important meal of the day, not just for the usual reasons, but also simply because the offerings — from bacon to cheesy eggs to cinnamon rolls — are so scrumptious. French toast proves my point. With the help of a mug and the microwave, it's now an any-day option, even on the busiest mornings. Don't forget the syrup!

Tip

Add up to 2 tbsp (30 mL) raisins or chopped dried fruit, or 1 tbsp (15 mL) miniature semisweet chocolate chips with the bread.

♦ **16-oz (500 mL) mug**

1 tbsp	granulated sugar	15 mL
$\frac{1}{8}$ tsp	salt	0.5 mL
$\frac{1}{8}$ tsp	ground cinnamon	0.5 mL
1	large egg	1
$\frac{1}{2}$ cup	milk	125 mL
$\frac{1}{4}$ tsp	vanilla extract (optional)	1 mL
$1\frac{1}{4}$ cups	bread cubes (preferably stale) or small plain croutons	300 mL

Suggested Accompaniments

Confectioners' (icing) sugar; pure maple syrup; butter

1. In the mug, use a fork to whisk sugar, salt, cinnamon, egg, milk and vanilla (if using) until very well blended. Add bread cubes, stirring and pressing them down into the custard to absorb the liquid. Let stand for at least 15 minutes (so the bread absorbs the liquid). Press bread down with a fork to compact.

2. Microwave on High for $1\frac{1}{2}$ to $2\frac{1}{2}$ minutes (checking at $1\frac{1}{2}$) or until firm to the touch and liquid is absorbed. Serve with any of the suggested accompaniments, as desired.

Variations

- **Orange Marmalade French Toast:** Replace the sugar with an equal amount of orange marmalade.

- **Buttermilk French Toast:** Replace the milk with buttermilk, and replace the cinnamon with a pinch of ground nutmeg.

- **Banana French Toast:** Reduce the milk to $\frac{1}{4}$ cup (60 mL) and add $\frac{1}{3}$ cup (75 mL) mashed very ripe banana. Replace the sugar with packed brown sugar.

> **Prep Ahead Option**
>
> Whisk the sugar, salt, cinnamon, egg, milk and vanilla (if using) in the mug, then add the bread cubes; cover and refrigerate until ready to use.

Tomato Herb Breakfast Strata

Traditional strata — a savory main course cousin of bread pudding — is best made with stale or toasted bread to absorb the egg custard. Croutons are the perfect (and so very convenient) stand-in for this microwave rendition, delivering toasty flavor without any prep work.

Tips

For variety, you can add up to 2 tbsp (30 mL) chopped ham, diced smoked sausage or ready-to-eat real bacon bits to the egg mixture.

Freeze the remaining tomatoes in a small sealable freezer bag. You can freeze the entire amount in one bag, or portion out ¼ cup (60 mL) per bag so that the tomatoes are recipe-ready. Be sure to label the bag with the contents. Store for up to 3 months. Defrost in the refrigerator or microwave before using.

♦ **16-oz (500 mL) mug**

1	large egg	1
½ cup	milk	125 mL
1 tbsp	grated Parmesan cheese	15 mL
1 tbsp	chopped fresh parsley	15 mL
¼ tsp	dried Italian seasoning	1 mL
¼ cup	diced fresh or drained canned tomatoes	60 mL
1 cup	small plain croutons	250 mL

1. In the mug, use a fork to whisk egg, milk, Parmesan, parsley (if using) and Italian seasoning until very well blended. Stir in tomatoes. Add croutons, stirring and gently pressing them down into the custard to absorb the liquid. Let stand for at least 15 minutes (so the croutons absorb the liquid). Press croutons down with a fork to compact.

2. Microwave on High for 1½ to 2½ minutes (checking at 1½) or until firm to the touch and liquid is absorbed.

Variations

- **Mushroom Swiss Strata:** Replace the Parmesan with 2 tbsp (30 mL) shredded Swiss cheese. Replace the tomatoes with 3 tbsp (45 mL) drained canned or jarred mushroom pieces.

- **Roasted Pepper and Goat Cheese Strata:** Replace the Parmesan with 2 tbsp (30 mL) crumbled goat cheese. Replace the tomatoes with 3 tbsp (45 mL) chopped drained jarred roasted red bell peppers.

- **Chipotle Cheddar Strata:** Replace the Parmesan with 2 tbsp (30 mL) shredded Cheddar cheese. Replace the tomatoes with an equal amount of chipotle salsa.

> **Prep Ahead Option**
>
> Prepare through step 1; cover and refrigerate. Measure the croutons into a small airtight container; cover and store at room temperature until ready to use.

Ham and Hash Brown Breakfast Casserole

I love hash browns for breakfast because of their delicious, savory simplicity. Throw in some bits of ham, Cheddar cheese and green onions, and bind everything with a creamy egg custard, and things only get better.

Tip

An equal amount of diced hash browns with peppers and onions can be used in place of the shredded hash browns.

♦ **12- to 16-oz (375 to 500 mL) mug**

³⁄₄ cup	frozen shredded hash browns	175 mL
1	large egg	1
2 tbsp	chopped ham or cooked smoked sausage	30 mL
2 tbsp	shredded Cheddar cheese (or cheese of choice)	30 mL
1 tbsp	chopped green onions	15 mL
1 tbsp	sour cream or plain Greek yogurt	15 mL
	Salt and ground black pepper	

1. In the mug, microwave hash browns on High for $1\frac{1}{2}$ to 2 minutes or until warmed through.

2. Using a fork, beat in egg. Stir in ham, cheese, green onions and sour cream until blended. Season with salt and pepper. Microwave for 45 to 75 seconds or until just set.

Variations

- **Herbed Hash Brown Casserole:** Omit the ham. Add ¼ tsp (1 mL) dried basil and 1 tbsp (15 mL) chopped fresh parsley to the egg mixture.

- **Tomato Bacon Hash Brown Casserole:** Omit the ham and green onions. Add 2 tbsp (30 mL) chopped plum (Roma) tomato, 1 tbsp (15 mL) ready-to-eat real bacon bits and ¼ tsp (1 mL) dried Italian seasoning to the egg mixture.

> **Prep Ahead Option**
> Measure the hash browns into the mug; cover and refrigerate (decrease the cooking time in step 1 by 30 seconds). Whisk the egg in a small airtight container and add the ham, cheese, green onions and sour cream; cover and refrigerate until ready to use.

Southern Sausage and Grits Casserole

Grits are iconic Southern food fare, but they are very similar to Italian dishes like risotto and polenta. Pair them up with other Italian favorites — sausage, peppers and Parmesan cheese — and they demonstrate their multi-cuisine versatility.

Tips

You can use 2 tbsp (30 mL) chopped cooked smoked sausage in place of the breakfast sausage.

Be sure to use quick-cooking grits (typically sold in containers), not regular grits, which take much longer to prepare.

♦ **12- to 16-oz (375 to 500 mL) mug**

3 tbsp	quick-cooking grits	45 mL
2 tbsp	frozen or fresh chopped bell pepper and onion blend (optional)	30 mL
½ cup	milk	125 mL
¼ cup	water	60 mL
1	large egg	1
1	frozen cooked breakfast sausage link, thawed and chopped	1
1 tbsp	grated Parmesan cheese	15 mL
	Salt and ground black pepper	

1. In the mug, combine grits, peppers and onions (if using), milk and water. Microwave on High for 1 minute. Stir. Microwave on High for 60 to 90 seconds (checking at 60) or until thickened and creamy.

2. Using a fork, beat in egg, sausage and cheese. Microwave on High for 45 to 75 seconds or until just set. Let stand for 30 seconds. Season to taste with salt and pepper.

Variations

- **Italian Grits Casserole:** Replace the sausage with 2 tbsp (30 mL) chopped ham and add ¼ tsp (1 mL) dried Italian seasoning.

- **Pepper Jack Bacon Grits Casserole:** Replace the sausage with 1 tbsp (15 mL) ready-to-eat real bacon bits, and replace the Parmesan with 2 tbsp (30 mL) shredded pepper Jack cheese.

Prep Ahead Option

Measure the grits into the mug; cover and store at room temperature. Whisk the egg in a small airtight container and add the sausage and cheese; cover and refrigerate until ready to use.

Cheese and Bacon Breakfast Puffs

Part muffin, part omelet, these tender, popover-like puffs are perfect when you cannot decide which you feel like eating.

Tips

An equal amount of ricotta cheese can be used in place of the cottage cheese.

Look for ready-to-eat real bacon bits where salad dressings and croutons are shelved in the grocery store, or near the regular bacon in the packaged meat or deli department.

♦ 12- to 16-oz (375 to 500 mL) mug

1½ tbsp	all-purpose or whole wheat flour	22 mL
¼ tsp	baking powder	1 mL
1	large egg	1
¼ cup	cottage cheese	60 mL
3 tbsp	shredded Monterey Jack, Cheddar or Swiss cheese	45 mL
1 tbsp	ready-to-eat real bacon bits	15 mL
2 tsp	vegetable oil	10 mL

1. In the mug, whisk flour, baking powder, egg, cottage cheese, Monterey Jack cheese, bacon and oil until well blended.
2. Microwave on High for 60 to 75 seconds (checking at 60) or until puffed and just set at the center.

Variations

- **Gluten-Free Breakfast Puffs:** Replace the all-purpose flour with an all-purpose gluten-free flour blend. Be sure the baking powder is gluten-free.
- **Smoked Sausage Dill Puffs:** Replace the bacon with 2 tbsp (30 mL) chopped cooked smoked sausage. Add ¼ tsp (1 mL) dried dillweed.
- **Goat Cheese and Chive Puffs:** Replace the shredded cheese with 3 tbsp (45 mL) crumbled goat cheese, and replace the bacon with an equal amount of finely chopped chives.

Prep Ahead Option

Whisk the egg in the mug and add the cottage cheese, Monterey Jack cheese and oil; cover and refrigerate. Measure the flour, baking powder and bacon into a small airtight container; cover and refrigerate until ready to use.

Cinnamon Roll in a Mug

Cinnamon is arguably one of the best scents in the world, and it permeates this delectable mug rendition of a cinnamon roll.

Tips

To measure the egg, whisk 1 large egg in a small airtight container. Measure 2 tbsp (30 mL) into the mug as directed. Cover and refrigerate the remaining egg (about 2 tbsp/30 mL) for up to 2 days.

One small egg can be used in place of the 2 tbsp (30 mL) beaten egg.

An equal amount of virgin coconut oil or vegetable oil can be used in place of the butter.

In place of the icing, consider frosting the finished roll with honey-sweetened tub-style cream cheese.

For extra flavor, add a drop of vanilla extract to the icing.

Try replacing the cinnamon with an equal amount of pumpkin pie spice.

♦ **16-oz (500 mL) mug, sprayed with nonstick cooking spray**

Cake

1 tbsp	butter	15 mL
2 tbsp	beaten egg	30 mL
1 tbsp	milk	15 mL
1/4 tsp	vanilla extract	1 mL
1/3 cup	all-purpose flour	75 mL
2 1/2 tbsp	packed brown sugar	37 mL
3/4 tsp	ground cinnamon	3 mL
1/4 tsp	baking powder	1 mL
1/8 tsp	salt	0.5 mL

Icing

3 tbsp	confectioners' (icing) sugar	45 mL
3/4 tsp	milk	3 mL

1. *Cake:* In the mug, microwave butter on High for 20 to 25 seconds or until melted. Stir in egg, milk and vanilla until blended. Using a fork, stir in flour, brown sugar, cinnamon, baking powder and salt until well blended and smooth.

2. Microwave on High for 60 to 90 seconds (checking at 60) or until puffed and center is just set.

3. *Icing:* In a small bowl or cup, combine confectioners' sugar and milk until blended and smooth.

4. Spread or drizzle icing over cinnamon roll. Eat directly from mug or gently remove to a small plate.

Variation

- **Gluten-Free Cinnamon Roll:** Replace the all-purpose flour with an all-purpose gluten-free flour blend. Make sure the baking powder and confectioners' sugar are gluten-free.

> ### Prep Ahead Option
> Prepare the cake through step 1, but omit the baking powder; cover and refrigerate. Measure the baking powder into a small airtight container; cover and store at room temperature. Whisk the baking powder into the batter when ready to cook. Prepare the icing as directed; cover and refrigerate until ready to use.

Cranberry Nut Scone

This scone is a cinch to prepare. Nevertheless, it's important to follow the instructions for working the cold butter into the flour — melted butter or oil will not suffice. Cranberry nut scones are a personal favorite, but you can vary the flavors and mix-ins in multiple ways.

Tip

Packed brown sugar can be used in place of the granulated sugar.

Prep Ahead Option

Whisk the flour mixture in the mug and work in the butter as directed, then stir in the cranberries and pecans; cover and refrigerate. Place the egg yolk, buttermilk and vanilla (if using) in a small airtight container; cover and refrigerate until ready to use.

Storage Tip

The scone can be made in advance. Remove from mug and let cool completely, then tightly wrap in plastic wrap, parchment paper or foil, or store in an airtight container. Store at room temperature for up to 1 day or in the refrigerator for up to 2 days.

♦ **12- to 16-oz (375 to 500 mL) mug, sprayed with nonstick cooking spray**

3 tbsp	all-purpose flour	45 mL
2 tbsp	wheat germ	30 mL
4 tsp	granulated sugar	20 mL
1/4 tsp	baking powder	1 mL
1/8 tsp	ground cinnamon (optional)	0.5 mL
Pinch	salt	Pinch
4 tsp	cold butter, cut into small pieces	20 mL
1 tbsp	dried cranberries	15 mL
1 tbsp	chopped pecans or walnuts	15 mL
1	large egg yolk	1
2 tbsp	buttermilk or milk	30 mL
1/8 tsp	vanilla extract (optional)	0.5 mL

1. In the mug, use a fork to whisk together flour, wheat germ, sugar, baking powder, cinnamon (if using) and salt. Using your fingers, work in butter until mixture resembles coarse crumbs. Stir in cranberries and pecans. Using a fork, stir in egg yolk, buttermilk and vanilla (if using) until blended.

2. Microwave on High for $1\frac{1}{2}$ to 2 minutes (checking at $1\frac{1}{2}$) or until center is set and top of scone appears dry. Gently remove to a small plate and let cool for at least 5 minutes before eating.

Variations

- **Gluten-Free Scone:** Replace the all-purpose flour with an all-purpose gluten-free flour blend. Replace the wheat germ with ground flax seeds (flaxseed meal). Be sure the baking powder is gluten-free.

- **Apricot Almond Scone:** Replace the cranberries with chopped dried apricots, and replace the pecans with chopped plain or roasted almonds.

- **Ginger Lemon Scone:** Omit the cranberries and pecans. Add 1/2 tsp (2 mL) ground ginger and 1/2 tsp (2 mL) finely grated lemon zest.

- **Brown Sugar Oat Scone:** Omit the cranberries and pecans. Replace the granulated sugar with packed brown sugar and add 1/4 tsp (1 mL) ground cinnamon.

Crumb Coffeecake

Crumb coffeecake is an addictive treat for lazy weekend mornings. Now, with a mug and a microwave, this wonderfully rich, cinnamon-scented cake can be part of your weekday breakfast rotation.

Tip

The crumb topping has a pronounced cinnamon flavor; for a subtler flavor, simply reduce the amount to ½ tsp (2 mL) or ¼ tsp (1 mL).

Prep Ahead Option

Prepare the topping in the mug and transfer to a small airtight container; cover and refrigerate. Whisk the egg in a small airtight container and add the yogurt and vanilla; cover and refrigerate. Measure the flour, baking powder and salt into a small airtight container; cover and store at room temperature until ready to use.

♦ **16-oz (500 mL) mug, sprayed with nonstick cooking spray**

Topping

1 tbsp	butter	15 mL
2 tbsp	all-purpose flour	30 mL
1 tbsp	packed brown sugar	15 mL
1 tsp	ground cinnamon	5 mL

Cake

1½ tbsp	butter	22 mL
2 tbsp	granulated sugar	30 mL
2 tbsp	beaten egg	30 mL
1½ tbsp	plain Greek yogurt	22 mL
⅛ tsp	vanilla extract	0.5 mL
¼ cup	all-purpose flour	60 mL
¼ tsp	baking powder	1 mL
Pinch	salt	Pinch

1. *Topping:* In the mug, microwave butter on High for 10 to 15 seconds or until softened (not melted). Using a fork, stir in flour, brown sugar and cinnamon until crumbly. Transfer to a small bowl or cup.

2. *Cake:* In the mug (no need to clean it), heat butter for 10 to 15 seconds or until softened (not melted). Using a fork, stir in sugar until fluffy. Stir in egg, yogurt and vanilla until blended. Stir in flour, baking powder and salt until blended. Sprinkle with topping.

3. Microwave on High for 60 to 75 seconds (checking at 60) or until puffed and center is just set. Eat directly from mug or gently remove to a small plate.

Variations

- **Gluten-Free Crumb Coffeecake:** Replace the all-purpose flour with an all-purpose gluten-free flour blend. Be sure the baking powder is gluten-free.

- **Cranberry Spice Coffeecake:** Replace the cinnamon with pumpkin pie spice. Add 1 tbsp (15 mL) dried cranberries to the cake batter.

- **Blueberry Coffeecake:** Add 8 to 12 blueberries (depending on size) to the cake batter.

Fruit and Fiber Breakfast Cookie

Meet your new favorite portable breakfast. Vary the fruit, nuts and seeds to your heart's content, or spice things up with a bit of ground cinnamon, ginger or allspice.

Tip

The corn syrup (or brown rice syrup) does more than sweeten this cookie; it helps bind it. Other liquid sweeteners, such as honey and maple syrup, will not hold the cookie together.

Storage Tip

The cookie can be made in advance. Place in an airtight container and store in the refrigerator for up to 1 week or in the freezer for up to 1 month.

♦ **16-oz (500 mL) mug, sprayed with nonstick cooking spray**

♦ **Square of waxed paper, parchment paper, plastic wrap or foil**

1½ tbsp	corn syrup or brown rice syrup	22 mL
1 tbsp	peanut butter	15 mL
⅓ cup	crispy rice cereal	75 mL
2 tbsp	chopped roasted or raw nuts or seeds	30 mL
2 tbsp	chopped dried fruit	30 mL
1 tbsp	ground flax seeds (flaxseed meal)	15 mL

1. In the mug, combine corn syrup and peanut butter. Microwave on High for 25 to 35 seconds or until very hot and bubbly.

2. Stir in cereal, nuts, dried fruit and flax seeds until well coated. Turn mixture out onto waxed paper. Fold paper over the mixture and gently mold into a mound. Refrigerate for at least 30 minutes or until firm.

Prep Ahead Option

Combine the corn syrup and peanut butter in the mug; cover and store at room temperature. Measure the cereal, nuts, dried fruit and flax seeds into a small airtight container; cover and store at room temperature until ready to use.

Chocolate Chip Protein Breakfast Cookie

Say goodbye to overpriced, underwhelming packaged protein bars and hello to yummy, inexpensive, customizable protein cookies. They make a great on-the-go breakfast, but you can munch on one any time of day for instant energy.

Tips

If using vegan protein powder, reduce the total amount to 1½ tbsp (22 mL). For the best flavor and nutrition, opt for an all-natural powder.

Any other creamy nut or seed butter (cashew, sunflower, sesame) can be used in place of the peanut butter.

Storage Tip

The cookie can be made in advance. Place in an airtight container and store in the refrigerator for up to 1 week or in the freezer for up to 1 month.

♦ **12- to 16-oz (375 to 500 mL) mug, sprayed with nonstick cooking spray**

♦ **Square of waxed paper, parchment paper, plastic wrap or foil**

2 tbsp	creamy peanut butter	30 mL
1 tbsp	liquid honey, pure maple syrup or agave nectar	15 mL
1 tbsp	milk	15 mL
3 tbsp	quick-cooking or large-flake (old-fashioned) rolled oats	45 mL
2 tbsp	vanilla whey protein powder (see tip, at left)	30 mL
1 tbsp	chopped nuts or seeds (almonds, chia seeds, sunflower seeds)	15 mL
1 tbsp	miniature semisweet chocolate chips	15 mL

1. In the mug, combine peanut butter, honey and milk. Microwave on High for 25 to 35 seconds or until peanut butter is melted. Stir until blended.
2. Stir in oats, protein powder, nuts and chocolate chips until well coated. Refrigerate for 30 minutes.
3. Scoop mixture into a mound on waxed paper. Fold paper over the mound, pressing down to form a round. Freeze for 10 to 15 minutes or until set.

Variations

- **Gluten-Free Breakfast Cookie:** Use certified gluten-free oats and gluten-free protein powder.
- **Dried Fruit Protein Cookie:** Replace the chocolate chips with chopped dried fruit (apricots, prunes, raisins).
- **Double Chocolate Protein Cookie:** Replace the vanilla protein powder with an equal amount of chocolate whey protein powder.

Prep Ahead Option

Combine the peanut butter, honey and milk in the mug; cover and refrigerate. Measure the oats, protein powder, nuts and chocolate chips into a small airtight container; cover and store at room temperature until ready to use.

Bread and Muffins

Irish Brown Bread

Soda bread made in a mug — in the microwave, no less — may not be traditional, but whole wheat flour, buttermilk and the molasses flavor of brown sugar bring the flavor of true Irish brown bread to the table in a quick and delicious way.

Tips

An equal amount of granulated sugar can be used in place of the brown sugar.

Try adding 1 tbsp (15 mL) chopped nuts (such as pecans or walnuts) or 2 tsp (10 mL) toasted sesame seeds with the buttermilk.

Storage Tip

The bread can be made in advance. Remove from mug and let cool completely, then tightly wrap in plastic wrap, parchment paper or foil, or store in an airtight container. Store at room temperature for up to 1 day or in the refrigerator for up to 2 days.

♦ **12- to 16-oz (375 to 500 mL) mug, sprayed with nonstick cooking spray**

1/4 cup	whole wheat flour	60 mL
4 tsp	all-purpose flour	20 mL
1/4 tsp	baking soda	1 mL
1/8 tsp	salt	0.5 mL
3 tbsp	buttermilk	45 mL
1 tbsp	packed brown sugar	15 mL
1 tbsp	vegetable oil	15 mL
1 tbsp	raisins or currants (optional)	15 mL

1. In the mug, combine whole wheat flour, all-purpose flour, baking soda and salt. Stir in buttermilk, brown sugar, oil and raisins (if using) until blended.

2. Cover mug with a small plate or saucer and microwave on Medium (50%) for 2 minutes. Microwave on Medium (50%) for 2 to 4 minutes or until center is just set. Let cool for 5 minutes in mug. Eat directly from mug or gently remove to a small plate.

Variations

- **Irish Soda Bread:** Omit the whole wheat flour and add an additional 1/4 cup (60 mL) all-purpose flour. Replace the brown sugar with an equal amount of granulated sugar.

- **Irish Caraway Bread:** Add 1/2 tsp (2 mL) crushed caraway seeds with the baking soda. Omit the raisins.

Prep Ahead Option

Combine the whole wheat flour, all-purpose flour, baking soda and salt in the mug; cover and store at room temperature. Measure the buttermilk, brown sugar, oil and raisins (if using) into a small airtight container; cover and refrigerate until ready to use.

Quinoa Chili (page 40)

Pumpkin Sage Soup (page 35)

Pesto Chicken Couscous (page 46)

Layered Southwestern Dip (page 55)

Mug Granola (page 68)

Scrambled Eggs Florentine (page 82)

French Toast (page 85)

Cranberry Nut Scone (page 91)

Green Onion Bread

The assertive flavor of fresh green onions in this bread makes them an ideal option for enlivening a simple lunch or supper.

Tips

To measure the egg, whisk 1 large egg in a small airtight container. Measure 2 tbsp (30 mL) into the mug as directed. Cover and refrigerate the remaining egg (about 2 tbsp/30 mL) for up to 2 days.

One small egg can be used in place of the 2 tbsp (30 mL) beaten egg.

You can use 2 tbsp (30 mL) minced fresh chives in place of the green onions.

Storage Tip

The bread can be made in advance. Remove from mug and let cool completely, then tightly wrap in plastic wrap, parchment paper or foil, or store in an airtight container. Store at room temperature for up to 1 day or in the refrigerator for up to 2 days.

♦ **12- to 16-oz (375 to 500 mL) mug, sprayed with nonstick cooking spray**

3 tbsp	all-purpose flour	45 mL
1½ tbsp	yellow cornmeal	22 mL
¼ tsp	baking powder	1 mL
⅛ tsp	salt	0.5 mL
2 tbsp	beaten egg	30 mL
2 tbsp	milk	30 mL
1 tbsp	vegetable oil	15 mL
1 tsp	granulated sugar	5 mL
¼ cup	chopped green onions	60 mL

1. In the mug, combine flour, cornmeal, baking powder and salt. Stir in egg, milk, oil, sugar and green onions until very well blended.

2. Microwave on High for 1 to 2 minutes (checking at 1) or until center is just set. Let cool slightly or entirely in mug. Eat directly from mug or gently remove to a small plate.

Variations

- **Roasted Pepper Bread:** Use 3 tbsp (45 mL) chopped drained jarred roasted red bell peppers in place of the green onions. If desired, add 1 tbsp (15 mL) grated Parmesan cheese with the flour.

- **Sesame Green Onion Bread:** Replace 1 tsp (5 mL) of the vegetable oil with 1 tsp (5 mL) toasted sesame oil. Add 2 tsp (10 mL) toasted sesame seeds with the flour.

Prep Ahead Option

Combine the flour, cornmeal, baking powder and salt in the mug; cover and store at room temperature. Measure the egg, milk, oil, sugar and green onions into a small airtight container; cover and refrigerate until ready to use.

Presto Pesto Bread

A couple of spoonfuls of basil pesto take this bread from good to great in one quick move.

Tips

To measure the egg, whisk 1 large egg in a small airtight container. Measure 2 tbsp (30 mL) into the mug as directed. Cover and refrigerate the remaining egg (about 2 tbsp/30 mL) for up to 2 days.

One small egg can be used in place of the 2 tbsp (30 mL) beaten egg.

If you do not have pesto on hand, use the following ingredients in its place: 1½ tbsp (22 mL) olive oil or vegetable oil, 2 tsp (10 mL) dried basil, ¼ tsp (1 mL) garlic powder and, if desired, 2 tsp (10 mL) grated Parmesan cheese.

Storage Tip

The bread can be made in advance. Remove from mug and let cool completely, then tightly wrap in plastic wrap, parchment paper or foil, or store in an airtight container. Store at room temperature for up to 1 day or in the refrigerator for up to 2 days.

♦ **12- to 16-oz (375 to 500 mL) mug, sprayed with nonstick cooking spray**

¼ cup	all-purpose flour	60 mL
¼ tsp	baking powder	1 mL
2 tbsp	beaten egg	30 mL
2 tbsp	basil pesto	30 mL
1 tbsp	milk	15 mL

1. In the mug, combine flour and baking powder. Stir in egg, pesto and milk until very well blended.
2. Microwave on High for 1 to 2 minutes (checking at 1) or until center is just set. Let cool slightly or entirely in mug. Eat directly from mug or gently remove to a small plate.

Variation

- **Tapenade Bread:** Use 1 tbsp (15 mL) olive tapenade plus 1 tbsp (15 mL) olive oil in place of the pesto.

Prep Ahead Option

Combine the flour and baking powder in the mug; cover and store at room temperature. Measure the egg, pesto and milk into a small airtight container; cover and refrigerate until ready to use.

Double Cheese Bread

Ready for an easy upgrade to your lunchtime routine? Here's a versatile version of cheese bread that will elevate your mug of soup in an instant.

Tips

An equal amount of vegetable oil or olive oil may be used in place of the butter.

To measure the egg, whisk 1 large egg in a small airtight container. Measure 2 tbsp (30 mL) into the mug as directed. Cover and refrigerate the remaining egg (about 2 tbsp/30 mL) for up to 2 days.

One small egg can be used in place of the 2 tbsp (30 mL) beaten egg.

Storage Tip

The bread can be made in advance. Remove from mug and let cool completely, then tightly wrap in plastic wrap, parchment paper or foil, or store in an airtight container. Store at room temperature for up to 1 day or in the refrigerator for up to 2 days.

♦ **16-oz (500 mL) mug, sprayed with nonstick cooking spray**

1 tbsp	butter	15 mL
2 tbsp	beaten egg	30 mL
1 tbsp	milk	15 mL
1/4 cup	all-purpose flour	60 mL
3 tbsp	shredded sharp (old) Cheddar cheese	45 mL
1 tbsp	grated Parmesan cheese	15 mL
1/4 tsp	baking powder	1 mL

1. In the mug, microwave butter on High for 15 to 30 seconds or until melted. Using a fork, whisk in egg and milk. Still using the fork, beat in flour, Cheddar, Parmesan and baking powder until smooth.

2. Microwave on High for 1 to 2 minutes (checking at 1) or until center is just set. Let cool slightly or entirely in mug. Eat directly from mug or gently remove to a small plate.

Variations

- **Cheesy Garlic Bread:** Replace the Cheddar with shredded Italian-blend cheese. Add 1/4 tsp (1 mL) garlic powder and, if desired, 1/4 tsp (1 mL) dried Italian seasoning.

- **Parmesan Pepper Bread:** Omit the Cheddar and increase the Parmesan to 2 tbsp (30 mL). Add 1/8 tsp (0.5 mL) cracked black pepper.

- **Pepper Jack Bread:** Replace the Cheddar with shredded pepper Jack cheese. Add 1/4 tsp (1 mL) chili powder.

Prep Ahead Option

Measure the butter into the mug; cover and refrigerate. Measure the egg and milk into a small airtight container; cover and refrigerate. Measure the flour, Cheddar, Parmesan and baking powder into a small airtight container; cover and refrigerate until ready to use.

Pepperoni Pizza Bread

Cottage cheese and Parmesan add savory richness to this muffin, while pepperoni adds bold, spicy flavor.

Tips

To measure the egg, whisk 1 large egg in a small airtight container. Measure 2 tbsp (30 mL) into the mug as directed. Cover and refrigerate the remaining egg (about 2 tbsp/30 mL) for up to 2 days.

One small egg can be used in place of the 2 tbsp (30 mL) beaten egg.

Either regular or turkey pepperoni can be used.

An equal amount of vegetable oil can be used in place of the olive oil.

For added flavor, try adding $\frac{1}{2}$ tsp (2 mL) dried Italian seasoning to the batter.

Storage Tip

The bread can be made in advance. Remove from mug and let cool completely, then tightly wrap in plastic wrap, parchment paper or foil, or store in an airtight container. Store at room temperature for up to 1 day or in the refrigerator for up to 2 days.

♦ **16-oz (500 mL) mug, sprayed with nonstick cooking spray**

3 tbsp	all-purpose flour	45 mL
$\frac{1}{4}$ tsp	baking powder	1 mL
2 tbsp	beaten egg	30 mL
2 tbsp	cottage cheese	30 mL
1 tbsp	grated Parmesan cheese	15 mL
1 tbsp	chopped pepperoni	15 mL
1 tbsp	olive oil	15 mL
1 tbsp	thick marinara sauce	15 mL

1. In the mug, combine flour and baking powder. Stir in egg, cottage cheese, Parmesan, pepperoni and oil until blended. Gently stir in marinara sauce until swirled through batter.

2. Microwave on High for $1\frac{1}{2}$ to $2\frac{1}{2}$ minutes (checking at $1\frac{1}{2}$) or until center is just set. Let cool slightly or entirely in mug. Eat directly from mug or gently remove to a small plate.

Variations

- **Sausage Pizza Bread:** Replace the pepperoni with 1 cooked breakfast sausage link, crumbled or chopped.
- **Gluten-Free Pizza Bread:** Use almond flour in place of the all-purpose flour. Make sure the baking powder and pepperoni are gluten-free.

Prep Ahead Option

Combine the flour and baking powder in the mug; cover and store at room temperature. Measure the egg, cottage cheese, Parmesan, pepperoni and oil into a small airtight container; cover and refrigerate. Measure the marinara sauce into a small airtight container; cover and refrigerate until ready to use.

Cornbread

This quick version of cornbread is moist and tender, and makes a great accompaniment to any of the soups, stews or chilis (pages 120–150).

Tips

Try adding 1/4 tsp (1 mL) ground cumin and/or 1/4 tsp (1 mL) chili powder with the baking powder.

To measure the egg, whisk 1 large egg in a small airtight container. Measure 2 tbsp (30 mL) into the mug as directed. Cover and refrigerate the remaining egg (about 2 tbsp/30 mL) for up to 2 days.

One small egg can be used in place of the 2 tbsp (30 mL) beaten egg.

♦ **12- to 16-oz (375 to 500 mL) mug, sprayed with nonstick cooking spray**

2 tbsp	all-purpose flour	30 mL
2 tbsp	yellow cornmeal	30 mL
1/4 tsp	baking powder	1 mL
1/8 tsp	salt	0.5 mL
2 tbsp	beaten egg	30 mL
2 tbsp	milk	30 mL
1 tbsp	vegetable oil	15 mL
1 tsp	granulated sugar	5 mL

1. In the mug, combine flour, cornmeal, baking powder and salt. Stir in egg, milk, oil and sugar until very well blended.

2. Microwave on High for 1 to 2 minutes (checking at 1) or until center is just set. Let cool slightly or entirely in mug. Eat directly from mug or gently remove to a small plate.

Variations

- **Calico Cornbread:** Add 3 tbsp (30 mL) drained canned Mexican-style corn and pepper blend.

- **Salsa Cornbread:** Omit the sugar and replace the milk with 3 tbsp (45 mL) chunky-style salsa.

- **Honey Cornbread:** Replace the sugar with 1 tbsp (15 mL) liquid honey.

Prep Ahead Option

Combine the flour, cornmeal, baking powder and salt in the mug; cover and store at room temperature. Measure the egg, milk, oil and sugar into a small airtight container; cover and refrigerate until ready to use.

Southern Corn Spoon Bread

Spoon bread is a creamy cross between cornbread and pudding that rises like a soufflé. As its name indicates, it is best eaten (devoured) with a spoon.

Tip

Try adding ¼ tsp (1 mL) ground cumin and/ or ¼ tsp (1 mL) chili powder with the baking powder.

♦ **12- to 16-oz (375 to 500 mL) mug, sprayed with nonstick cooking spray**

1 tbsp	butter	15 mL
1	large egg	1
¼ cup	canned cream-style corn	60 mL
1 tbsp	milk	15 mL
2 tbsp	yellow cornmeal	30 mL
¼ tsp	baking powder	1 mL

1. In the mug, microwave butter on High for 15 to 30 seconds or until melted. Using a fork, whisk in egg, corn and milk. Still using the fork, beat in cornmeal and baking powder until very well blended.

2. Microwave on High for 1½ to 2½ minutes (checking at 1) or until puffed and center is just set. Let cool slightly or entirely in mug. Eat directly from mug with a spoon.

Variation

- **Triple Corn Spoon Bread:** Add 3 tbsp (30 mL) drained canned corn kernels or thawed frozen corn kernels with the cream-style corn.

> **Prep Ahead Option**
> Measure the butter into the mug; cover and refrigerate. Measure the egg, corn and milk into a small airtight container; cover and refrigerate. Measure the cornmeal and baking powder into a small airtight container; cover and store at room temperature until ready to use.

Pumpkin Bread

Embrace the flavors of autumn with this moist, delicious mug bread. Pumpkin not only lends richness and color, but is also one of the healthiest ingredients — think fiber and vitamin A, in particular — you can keep on your pantry shelf.

Tips

To measure the egg, whisk 1 large egg in a small airtight container. Measure 2 tbsp (30 mL) into the mug as directed. Cover and refrigerate the remaining egg (about 2 tbsp/30 mL) for up to 2 days.

One small egg can be used in place of the 2 tbsp (30 mL) beaten egg.

You can use an equal amount of granulated sugar in place of the brown sugar.

Try adding 1 tbsp (15 mL) dried fruit, such as raisins, cranberries, cherries or blueberries, with the egg.

Storage Tip

The bread can be made in advance. Remove from mug and let cool completely, then tightly wrap in plastic wrap, parchment paper or foil, or store in an airtight container. Store at room temperature for up to 1 day or in the refrigerator for up to 2 days.

♦ **12- to 16-oz (375 to 500 mL) mug, sprayed with nonstick cooking spray**

3 tbsp	all-purpose flour	45 mL
1/4 tsp	baking powder	1 mL
1/4 tsp	pumpkin pie spice or ground cinnamon	1 mL
1/8 tsp	salt	0.5 mL
2 tbsp	beaten egg	30 mL
2 tbsp	unsweetened pumpkin purée (not pie filling)	30 mL
1 tbsp	packed brown sugar	15 mL
1 tbsp	vegetable oil	15 mL

1. In the mug, combine flour, baking powder, pumpkin pie spice and salt. Stir in egg, pumpkin, brown sugar and oil until very well blended.
2. Microwave on High for $1^1/_2$ to $2^1/_2$ minutes (checking at $1^1/_2$) or until center is just set. Let cool slightly or entirely in mug. Eat directly from mug or gently remove to a small plate.

Variations

- **Pumpkin Praline Bread:** Sprinkle the batter with 2 tbsp (30 mL) chopped pecans and an additional 1 tbsp (15 mL) brown sugar before cooking.
- **Gluten-Free Pumpkin Muffin:** Use almond flour in place of the all-purpose flour. Make sure the baking powder is gluten-free.

Prep Ahead Option

Combine the flour, baking powder, pumpkin pie spice and salt in the mug; cover and store at room temperature. Measure the egg, pumpkin, brown sugar and oil into a small airtight container; cover and refrigerate until ready to use.

Zucchini Bread

For maximum health benefits, leave the zucchini unpeeled for this bread. Zucchini provides ample amounts of folate and potassium, and the dark green peel contains beta carotene. It also adds pretty specks of emerald throughout the bread.

Tips

To measure the egg, whisk 1 large egg in a small airtight container. Measure 2 tbsp (30 mL) into the mug as directed. Cover and refrigerate the remaining egg (about 2 tbsp/30 mL) for up to 2 days.

One small egg can be used in place of the 2 tbsp (30 mL) beaten egg.

You can use an equal amount of brown sugar or liquid honey in place of the granulated sugar.

Try adding 1 tbsp (15 mL) dried fruit, such as raisins, cranberries, cherries or blueberries, with the egg.

For even more flavor, add $\frac{1}{4}$ tsp (1 mL) vanilla extract with the oil.

♦ 12- to 16-oz (375 to 500 mL) mug, sprayed with nonstick cooking spray

3 tbsp	all-purpose flour	45 mL
$\frac{1}{4}$ tsp	ground cinnamon	1 mL
$\frac{1}{4}$ tsp	baking powder	1 mL
$\frac{1}{8}$ tsp	salt	0.5 mL
$\frac{1}{4}$ cup	shredded zucchini	60 mL
2 tbsp	beaten egg	30 mL
$1\frac{1}{2}$ tbsp	granulated sugar	22 mL
1 tbsp	vegetable oil	15 mL

1. In the mug, combine flour, cinnamon, baking powder and salt. Stir in zucchini, egg, sugar and oil until very well blended.

2. Microwave on High for $1\frac{1}{2}$ to $2\frac{1}{2}$ minutes (checking at $1\frac{1}{2}$) or until center is just set. Let cool slightly or entirely in mug. Eat directly from mug or gently remove to a small plate.

Variations

• **Carrot Bread:** Use an equal amount of shredded carrot in place of the zucchini.

• **Chocolate Zucchini Bread:** Reduce the flour to 2 tbsp (30 mL) and add 2 tbsp (30 mL) unsweetened cocoa powder. Increase the sugar to 5 tsp (25 mL). If desired, stir in 2 tsp (10 mL) miniature semisweet chocolate chips.

Prep Ahead Option

Combine the flour, cinnamon, baking powder and salt in the mug; cover and store at room temperature. Measure the zucchini, egg, sugar and oil into a small airtight container; cover and refrigerate until ready to use.

Storage Tip

The bread can be made in advance. Remove from mug and let cool completely, then tightly wrap in plastic wrap, parchment paper or foil, or store in an airtight container. Store at room temperature for up to 1 day or in the refrigerator for up to 2 days.

Banana Bread

You likely already have several recipes for banana bread, but this is the one you will turn to from now on because of its ease and speed. It doesn't hurt that it's delicious, too!

Tips

To measure the egg, whisk 1 large egg in a small airtight container. Measure 2 tbsp (30 mL) into the mug as directed. Cover and refrigerate the remaining egg (about 2 tbsp/30 mL) for up to 2 days.

One small egg can be used in place of the 2 tbsp (30 mL) beaten egg.

You can use an equal amount of granulated sugar in place of the brown sugar.

Try adding 1 tbsp (15 mL) dried fruit (raisins, cranberries, cherries, blueberries) or chopped nuts (pecans, walnuts) to the batter.

Storage Tip

The bread can be made in advance. Remove from mug and let cool completely, then tightly wrap in plastic wrap, parchment paper or foil, or store in an airtight container. Store at room temperature for up to 1 day or in the refrigerator for up to 2 days.

♦ 12- to 16-oz (375 to 500 mL) mug, sprayed with nonstick cooking spray

$1/4$ cup	all-purpose flour	60 mL
$1/4$ tsp	baking powder	1 mL
$1/4$ tsp	ground cinnamon	1 mL
$1/8$ tsp	salt	0.5 mL
$1/4$ cup	mashed very ripe banana (about $1/2$ medium-large)	60 mL
2 tbsp	beaten egg	30 mL
1 tbsp	packed brown sugar	15 mL
1 tbsp	milk	15 mL
2 tsp	vegetable oil	10 mL
$1/4$ tsp	vanilla extract (optional)	1 mL

1. In the mug, combine flour, baking powder, cinnamon, and salt. Stir in banana, egg, brown sugar, milk, oil and vanilla until very well blended.
2. Microwave on High for $1^1/2$ to $2^1/2$ minutes (checking at $1^1/2$) or until center is just set. Let cool slightly or entirely in mug. Eat directly from mug or gently remove to a small plate.

Variations

- **Chocolate Banana Bread:** Omit the cinnamon. Reduce the flour to 2 tbsp (30 mL) and add 2 tbsp (30 mL) unsweetened cocoa powder. If desired, stir in 1 tbsp (15 mL) miniature semisweet chocolate chips or chopped semisweet chocolate.
- **Gluten-Free Banana Bread:** Use almond flour in place of the all-purpose flour. Make sure the baking powder is gluten-free.
- **Cinnamon Applesauce Bread:** Use an equal amount of sweetened applesauce in place of the banana. Add an extra $1/8$ tsp (0.5 mL) cinnamon.

Prep Ahead Option

Combine the flour, baking powder, cinnamon and salt in the mug; cover and store at room temperature. Measure the banana, egg, brown sugar, milk, oil and vanilla into a small airtight container; cover and refrigerate until ready to use.

Buttermilk Biscuit

A short list of pantry ingredients and a few minutes are all that stand between you and a buttery biscuit.

Tips

An equal amount of packed brown sugar can be used in place of the granulated sugar.

Try adding 1 tbsp (15 mL) dried fruit (raisins, cranberries, cherries, blueberries), 1 tbsp (15 mL) chopped nuts (pecans, walnuts) or 2 tsp (10 mL) toasted sesame seeds with the buttermilk.

Storage Tip

The biscuit can be made in advance. Remove from mug and let cool completely, then tightly wrap in plastic wrap, parchment paper or foil, or store in an airtight container. Store at room temperature for up to 1 day or in the refrigerator for up to 2 days.

♦ **12- to 16-oz (375 to 500 mL) mug, sprayed with nonstick cooking spray**

$^1/_4$ cup	all-purpose flour	60 mL
$1^1/_2$ tbsp	wheat germ	22 mL
1 tsp	granulated sugar	5 mL
$^1/_4$ tsp	baking powder	1 mL
Pinch	salt	Pinch
1 tbsp	cold butter, cut into small pieces	15 mL
1	large egg yolk	1
1 tbsp	buttermilk or milk	15 mL

1. In the mug, use a fork to whisk together flour, wheat germ, sugar, baking powder and salt. Using your fingers, work in butter until mixture resembles coarse crumbs. Using a fork, stir in egg yolk and buttermilk until blended.

2. Microwave on High for $1^1/_2$ to $2^1/_2$ minutes (checking at $1^1/_2$) or until center is just set. Let cool slightly or entirely in mug. Eat directly from mug or gently remove to a small plate.

Variations

- **Herbed Buttermilk Biscuit:** Add 2 tsp (10 mL) minced fresh herbs (parsley, basil, dill, chives) or $^3/_4$ tsp (3 mL) dried herbs with the buttermilk.

- **Honey Biscuit:** Replace the sugar with $1^1/_2$ tsp (7 mL) liquid honey.

Prep Ahead Option

Whisk the flour mixture in the mug and work in the butter as directed; cover and refrigerate. Measure the buttermilk into a small airtight container; cover and refrigerate until ready to use.

Multigrain Muffin

This muffin is delicious proof that adding whole grains to your diet is a snap (or, more precisely, a zap)!

Tips

To measure the egg, whisk 1 large egg in a small airtight container. Measure 2 tbsp (30 mL) into the mug as directed. Cover and refrigerate the remaining egg (about 2 tbsp/30 mL) for up to 2 days.

One small egg can be used in place of the 2 tbsp (30 mL) beaten egg.

Add ⅛ tsp (0.5 mL) of your favorite ground spice or spice blend (cinnamon, ginger, cardamom, pumpkin pie spice) with the salt.

Add ¼ tsp (1 mL) vanilla extract or finely grated citrus zest (lemon, orange, lime) with the milk.

Storage Tip

The muffin can be made in advance. Remove from mug, cool completely, and then tightly wrap in plastic wrap, parchment paper or foil, or store in an airtight container. Store at room temperature for up to 1 day, or in the refrigerator for up to 2 days.

◆ **12- to 16-oz (375 to 500 mL) mug, sprayed with nonstick cooking spray**

3 tbsp	whole wheat flour	45 mL
2 tbsp	quick-cooking rolled oats	30 mL
1 tbsp	ground flax seeds (flaxseed meal)	15 mL
1 tbsp	granulated sugar	15 mL
1 tsp	baking powder	5 mL
⅛ tsp	salt	0.5 mL
2 tbsp	milk	30 mL
2 tbsp	beaten egg	30 mL
1 tbsp	vegetable oil	15 mL
1½ tbsp	chopped dried fruit, chocolate chips, seeds or nuts, or a combination (optional)	22 mL

1. In the mug, combine flour, oats, flax seeds, sugar, baking powder and salt. Using a fork, stir in milk, egg and oil until blended and smooth. Stir in dried fruit (if using).

2. Microwave on High for 1 to 2 minutes (checking at 1) or until center is just set. Let cool slightly or entirely in mug. Eat directly from mug or gently remove to a small plate.

Variations

- **Sugar-Free Multigrain Muffin:** Replace the sugar with 2 packets (about ½ tsp/2 mL) of powdered stevia or stevia-blend sweetener.

- **Savory Multigrain Muffin:** Decrease the sugar to 1 tsp (5 mL) and add ½ tsp (2 mL) dried Italian seasoning and ¼ tsp (1 mL) garlic powder with the salt.

- **Gluten-Free Multigrain Muffin:** Use an all-purpose gluten-free flour blend in place of the whole wheat flour, and use certified gluten-free oats. Make sure the baking powder is gluten-free.

Prep Ahead Option

Combine the flour, oats, flax seeds, sugar, baking powder and salt in the mug; cover and store at room temperature. Measure the milk and egg into a small airtight container and refrigerate until ready to use.

Banana Bran Muffin

Dense with whole grain, not too sweet, easy to prepare and, of course, delicious, this is everything you want your bran muffin to be.

Tips

Use an equal amount of any other dried fruit (cranberries, chopped prunes, chopped apricots) in place of the raisins.

Try adding 1 tbsp (15 mL) chopped nuts, such as pecans or walnuts, with the banana.

An equal amount of pure maple syrup, agave nectar, corn syrup or brown rice syrup can be used in place of the honey.

Storage Tip

The muffin can be made in advance. Remove from mug and let cool completely, then tightly wrap in plastic wrap, parchment paper or foil, or store in an airtight container. Store at room temperature for up to 1 day or in the refrigerator for up to 2 days.

♦ **12- to 16-oz (375 to 500 mL) mug, sprayed with nonstick cooking spray**

1/3 cup	unprocessed wheat bran (miller's bran) or natural wheat bran	75 mL
1/4 tsp	baking powder	1 mL
1/8 tsp	salt	0.5 mL
1	large egg	1
3 tbsp	mashed very ripe banana	45 mL
1 tbsp	raisins (optional)	15 mL
2 tsp	vegetable oil	10 mL
2 tsp	liquid honey	10 mL

1. In the mug, combine bran, baking powder and salt. Using a fork, stir in egg, banana, raisins (if using), oil and honey until blended.
2. Microwave on High for 1 1/2 to 2 1/2 minutes (checking at 1 1/2) or until center is just set. Let cool slightly or entirely in mug. Eat directly from mug or gently remove to a small plate.

Variations

- **Cinnamon Applesauce Bran Muffin:** Use an equal amount of applesauce in place of the banana. Replace the honey with 1 tbsp (15 mL) packed brown sugar and add 1/4 tsp (1 mL) ground cinnamon or pumpkin pie spice with the baking powder.
- **Pumpkin Spice Bran Muffin:** Use an equal amount of pumpkin purée (not pie filling) in place of the banana. Replace the honey with 1 tbsp (15 mL) pure maple syrup or packed brown sugar and add 1/4 tsp (1 mL) pumpkin pie spice with the baking powder.

Prep Ahead Option

Combine the bran, baking powder and salt in the mug; cover and store at room temperature. Measure the egg, banana, raisins (if using), oil and honey into a small airtight container; cover and refrigerate until ready to use.

All-Flax Muffin

Flax is rich in nutrients that protect against heart disease and cancer. It has a very mild taste and makes a supremely moist and delicious (and filling!) microwave muffin that can be varied in myriad ways.

Tip

Try adding $\frac{1}{4}$ tsp (1 mL) vanilla extract to the batter.

♦ **12- to 16-oz (375 to 500 mL) mug, sprayed with nonstick cooking spray**

$\frac{1}{4}$ cup	ground flax seeds (flaxseed meal)	60 mL
1 tsp	baking powder	5 mL
$\frac{1}{2}$ tsp	ground cinnamon	2 mL
$\frac{1}{8}$ tsp	salt	0.5 mL
1	large egg	1
2 tbsp	milk	30 mL
$1\frac{1}{2}$ tbsp	dried fruit (such as raisins, dried cranberries or chopped dates)	22 mL
1 tbsp	granulated sugar	15 mL

1. In the mug, combine flax seeds, baking powder, cinnamon and salt. Using a fork, stir in egg, milk, dried fruit and sugar until very well blended.

2. Microwave on High for $1\frac{1}{2}$ to $2\frac{1}{2}$ minutes (checking at $1\frac{1}{2}$) or until center is just set. Let cool slightly or entirely in mug. Eat directly from mug or gently remove to a small plate.

Variation

• **Sugar-Free All-Flax Muffin:** Replace the sugar with 2 packets (about $\frac{1}{2}$ tsp/2 mL) of powdered stevia or stevia-blend sweetener.

Prep Ahead Option

Combine the flax seeds, baking powder, cinnamon and salt in the mug; cover and store at room temperature. Measure the egg, milk, dried fruit and sugar into a small airtight container; cover and refrigerate until ready to use.

Almond Flour Muffin

Think of this recipe as the basic formula for your almond muffin, then vary the sweetener (maple syrup, agave nectar), fruit purée (mashed banana, pumpkin purée), spices, flavorings and add-ins.

Tips

You can use pure maple syrup or agave nectar in place of the honey. If you want to use granulated or brown sugar instead, add an extra 1 tbsp (15 mL) applesauce.

Try adding 2 tbsp (30 mL) dried fruit (raisins, cranberries, chopped apricots) to the batter.

Add $\frac{1}{8}$ tsp (0.5 mL) of your favorite ground spice or spice blend (cinnamon, ginger, cardamom, pumpkin pie spice) with the salt.

Add $\frac{1}{4}$ tsp (1 mL) vanilla extract or finely grated citrus zest (lemon, orange, lime) with the honey.

♦ **12- to 16-oz (375 to 500 mL) mug, sprayed with nonstick cooking spray**

$\frac{1}{4}$ cup	almond flour	60 mL
$\frac{1}{2}$ tsp	baking powder	2 mL
$\frac{1}{8}$ tsp	salt	0.5 mL
1	large egg	1
2 tbsp	applesauce	30 mL
1 tbsp	liquid honey	15 mL

1. In the mug, combine almond flour, baking powder and salt. Stir in egg, applesauce and honey until very well blended.
2. Microwave on High for $1\frac{1}{2}$ to $2\frac{1}{2}$ minutes (checking at $1\frac{1}{2}$) or until center is just set. Let cool slightly or entirely in mug. Eat directly from mug or gently remove to a small plate.

Variations

• **Banana Almond Muffin:** Use an equal amount of mashed very ripe banana in place of the applesauce.
• **Sugar-Free Almond Muffin:** Replace the sugar with 2 packets (about $\frac{1}{2}$ tsp/2 mL) of powdered stevia or stevia-blend sweetener and add an extra 1 tbsp (15 mL) applesauce.

Prep Ahead Option

Combine the almond flour, baking powder and salt in the mug; cover and store at room temperature. Whisk the egg in a small airtight container and add the applesauce and honey; cover and refrigerate until ready to use.

Low-Carb Coconut Flour Muffin

Coconut flour is a soft, naturally gluten-free flour made from dried coconut meat. It is rich in protein, fiber and fat, and is therefore very filling. It also happens to perform exceptionally well in this microwave muffin, yielding a light, tender treat that can be varied in countless ways.

Tips

A tablespoon (15 mL) of coconut flour may not sound like much, but it is extremely absorbent and expands greatly when cooked.

Try adding 1/4 tsp (1 mL) vanilla extract or finely grated citrus zest (lemon, lime or orange).

For even more flavor, add 1/8 tsp (0.5 mL) of your favorite ground spice (cinnamon, ginger, pumpkin pie spice).

♦ **12- to 16-oz (375 to 500 mL) mug, sprayed with nonstick cooking spray**

1 tbsp	coconut flour	15 mL
1/2 tsp	baking powder	2 mL
Pinch	salt	Pinch
1	large egg	1
1 tbsp	milk	15 mL
2 tsp	liquid honey	10 mL
1 1/2 tsp	vegetable oil or butter, melted	7 mL

1. In the mug, combine coconut flour, baking powder and salt. Stir in egg, milk, honey and oil until very well blended.

2. Microwave on High for 45 to 75 seconds (checking at 45) or until center is just set. Let cool slightly or entirely in mug. Eat directly from mug or gently remove to a small plate.

Variations

- **Chocolate Chip Coconut Muffin:** Add 1/4 tsp (1 mL) vanilla extract with the oil. Microwave on High for 30 seconds, then sprinkle with 2 tsp (10 mL) miniature semisweet chocolate chips and microwave for 25 to 35 seconds longer.

- **Savory Coconut Flour Muffin:** Reduce the honey to 1 tsp (5 mL). Add 1/4 tsp dried herb(s) or a savory ground spice (dill, basil, Italian seasoning, cumin) or 1 tbsp (15 mL) chopped fresh herbs (parsley, cilantro, basil). If desired, add 1 tbsp (15 mL) chopped toasted nuts or seeds (almonds, pepitas, walnuts) with the coconut flour.

Prep Ahead Option

Combine the coconut flour, baking powder and salt in the mug; cover and store at room temperature. Whisk the egg in a small airtight container and add the milk, honey and oil; cover and refrigerate until ready to use.

Cinnamon Sugar Muffin

What better way to rise and shine than with a freshly made cinnamon sugar muffin? Though it is easy to make, it is perfection in its simplicity.

Tips

Tips

To measure the egg, whisk 1 large egg in a small airtight container. Measure 2 tbsp (30 mL) into the mug as directed. Cover and refrigerate the remaining egg (about 2 tbsp/30 mL) for up to 2 days.

One small egg can be used in place of the 2 tbsp (30 mL) beaten egg.

Try replacing the cinnamon with pumpkin pie spice.

Storage Tip

The muffin can be made in advance. Remove from mug and let cool completely, then tightly wrap in plastic wrap, parchment paper or foil, or store in an airtight container. Store at room temperature for up to 1 day or in the refrigerator for up to 2 days.

♦ **12- to 16-oz (375 to 500 mL) mug, sprayed with nonstick cooking spray**

4 tsp	granulated sugar	20 mL
1/2 tsp	ground cinnamon	2 mL
1 tbsp	butter	15 mL
2 tbsp	beaten egg	30 mL
1 tbsp	milk	15 mL
1/4 tsp	vanilla extract	1 mL
1/4 cup	all-purpose flour	60 mL
1/4 tsp	baking powder	1 mL
1/8 tsp	salt	0.5 mL

1. In a small bowl or cup, combine sugar and cinnamon until blended.

2. In the mug, microwave butter on High for 15 to 30 seconds or until melted. Using a fork, whisk in egg, milk, vanilla and half the cinnamon sugar. Still using the fork, beat in flour, baking powder and salt until smooth. Sprinkle batter with remaining cinnamon sugar.

3. Microwave on High for 1 to 2 minutes (checking at 1) or until center is just set. Let cool slightly or entirely in mug. Eat directly from mug or gently remove to a small plate.

Variations

- **Blueberry Muffin:** Add 6 to 8 blueberries (depending on size) to the batter after mixing.

- **Cranberry Orange Muffin:** Add 1 1/2 tbsp (22 mL) dried cranberries and 1/2 tsp (2 mL) grated orange zest with the egg.

- **Gluten-Free Cinnamon Sugar Muffin:** Use almond flour in place of the all-purpose flour. Make sure the baking powder is gluten-free.

Prep Ahead Option

Measure the sugar and cinnamon into a small airtight container; cover and store at room temperature. Measure the butter into the mug; cover and refrigerate. Measure the flour, baking powder and salt into a small airtight container; cover and store at room temperature. Measure the egg, milk and half of the cinnamon sugar into a small airtight container; cover and refrigerate until ready to use.

Oatmeal Raisin Muffin

Oats are an excellent source of dietary fiber, plus manganese, vitamin B$_1$ and magnesium. Here, they make a delicious alternative to porridge in an easy muffin enhanced with brown sugar, cinnamon and yogurt.

Tips

Change up the dried fruit in this muffin any way you like. Try an equal amount of dried cranberries, cherries or blueberries.

You can use an equal amount of granulated sugar or liquid honey in place of the brown sugar.

Try adding $1/4$ tsp (1 mL) vanilla extract.

Storage Tip

The muffin can be made in advance. Remove from mug and let cool completely, then tightly wrap in plastic wrap, parchment paper or foil, or store in an airtight container. Store at room temperature for up to 1 day or in the refrigerator for up to 2 days.

♦ **12- to 16-oz (375 to 500 mL) mug, sprayed with nonstick cooking spray**

3 tbsp	large-flake (old-fashioned) or quick-cooking rolled oats	45 mL
$1/2$ tsp	ground cinnamon	2 mL
$1/4$ tsp	baking powder	1 mL
$1/8$ tsp	salt	0.5 mL
1	large egg	1
2 tbsp	raisins	30 mL
2 tbsp	plain yogurt	30 mL
1 tbsp	packed brown sugar	15 mL

1. In the mug, combine oats, cinnamon, baking powder and salt. Using a fork, beat in egg, raisins, yogurt and brown sugar until very well blended.

2. Microwave on High for $1^1/2$ to $2^1/2$ minutes (checking at $1^1/2$) or until center is just set. Let cool slightly or entirely in mug. Eat directly from mug or gently remove to a small plate.

Prep Ahead Option

Combine the oats, cinnamon, baking powder and salt in the mug; cover and store at room temperature. Whisk the egg in a small airtight container and add the raisins, yogurt and brown sugar; cover and refrigerate until ready to use.

Blueberry Wheat Germ Muffin

Moist and tender, with just the right balance of sweetness, this 2-minute rendition of classic blueberry muffins is destined to become one of your morning staples.

◆ 12- to 16-oz (375 to 500 mL) mug, sprayed with nonstick cooking spray

3 tbsp	toasted wheat germ	45 mL
1/2 tsp	baking powder	2 mL
1/8 tsp	salt	0.5 mL
1	large egg	1
3 tbsp	mashed very ripe banana	45 mL
1 tbsp	packed light brown sugar	15 mL
8 to 12	blueberries (depending on size)	8 to 12

1. In the mug, combine wheat germ, baking powder and salt. Stir in egg, banana and brown sugar until very well blended. Sprinkle with blueberries (some of the berries will sink as the muffin cooks).

2. Microwave on High for 80 to 90 seconds (checking at 80) or until center is just set. Let cool slightly or entirely in mug. Eat directly from mug or gently remove to a small plate.

Variations

- **Gluten-Free Banana Blueberry Muffin:** Use an equal amount of ground flax seeds (flaxseed meal) in place of the wheat germ.

- **Applesauce Blueberry Muffin:** Replace the banana with an equal amount of applesauce (sweetened or unsweetened).

- **Sugar-Free Multigrain Muffin:** Replace the brown sugar with 2 packets (about 1/2 tsp/2 mL) of powdered stevia or stevia-blend sweetener.

Prep Ahead Option

Measure the wheat germ, baking powder and salt into the mug; cover and store at room temperature. Whisk the egg in a small airtight container and add the banana and brown sugar; cover and refrigerate until ready to use.

Fresh Apple Muffin

This not-too-sweet muffin is best made with a fairly sweet apple, such as Red Delicious or Braeburn.

Tips

To measure the egg, whisk 1 large egg in a small airtight container. Measure 2 tbsp (30 mL) into the mug as directed. Cover and refrigerate the remaining egg (about 2 tbsp/30 mL) for up to 2 days.

One small egg can be used in place of the 2 tbsp (30 mL) beaten egg.

You can use an equal amount of granulated sugar in place of the brown sugar.

You can omit the nutmeg or add $1/4$ tsp (1 mL) ground cinnamon in its place.

Try adding 1 tbsp (15 mL) dried fruit, such as raisins, cranberries, cherries or blueberries, with the apple.

Storage Tip

The muffin can be made in advance. Remove from mug and let cool completely, then tightly wrap in plastic wrap, parchment paper or foil, or store in an airtight container. Store at room temperature for up to 1 day or in the refrigerator for up to 2 days.

♦ 12- to 16-oz (375 to 500 mL) mug, sprayed with nonstick cooking spray

1 tbsp	butter	15 mL
2 tbsp	beaten egg	30 mL
$1^1/_2$ tbsp	packed brown sugar	22 mL
1 tbsp	milk	15 mL
$1/_4$ cup	shredded apple (unpeeled)	60 mL
3 tbsp	all-purpose flour	45 mL
$1/_4$ tsp	baking powder	1 mL
$1/_8$ tsp	ground nutmeg	0.5 mL
$1/_8$ tsp	salt	0.5 mL

1. In the mug, microwave butter on High for 15 to 25 seconds or until melted. Using a fork, whisk in egg, brown sugar and milk. Still using the fork, beat in apple, flour, baking powder, nutmeg and salt until very well blended.

2. Microwave on High for $1^1/_2$ to $2^1/_2$ minutes (checking at $1^1/_2$) or until center is just set. Let cool slightly or entirely in mug. Eat directly from mug or gently remove to a small plate.

Variations

- **Cheddar Apple Muffin:** Omit the brown sugar and nutmeg. Add 2 tbsp (30 mL) packed shredded sharp (old) Cheddar cheese with the apple. If desired, add $1/_8$ tsp (0.5 mL) dried sage.

- **Spiced Pear Muffin:** Replace the apple with shredded firm-ripe pear.

- **Gluten-Free Apple Muffin:** Use almond flour in place of the all-purpose flour. Make sure the baking powder is gluten-free.

Prep Ahead Option

Measure the butter into the mug; cover and refrigerate. Measure the flour, baking powder, nutmeg and salt into a small airtight container; cover and store at room temperature. Measure the egg, brown sugar, milk and apple into a small airtight container; cover and refrigerate until ready to use.

Whole Wheat Cottage Cheese Muffin

Tender, moist and especially good with a schmear of fruit jam, this health-packed muffin is a perfect way to welcome any morning.

Tips

You can use an equal amount of all-purpose flour in place of the whole wheat flour.

To measure the egg, whisk 1 large egg in a small airtight container. Measure 2 tbsp (30 mL) into the mug as directed. Cover and refrigerate the remaining egg (about 2 tbsp/30 mL) for up to 2 days.

One small egg can be used in place of the 2 tbsp (30 mL) beaten egg.

Try adding 1 tbsp (15 mL) dried fruit, such as raisins, cranberries, cherries or blueberries, with the cottage cheese.

For even more flavor, add $\frac{1}{4}$ tsp (1 mL) vanilla extract with the oil.

♦ **12- to 16-oz (375 to 500 mL) mug, sprayed with nonstick cooking spray**

3 tbsp	whole wheat flour	45 mL
$\frac{1}{4}$ tsp	baking powder	1 mL
$\frac{1}{8}$ tsp	salt	0.5 mL
$\frac{1}{4}$ cup	cottage cheese	60 mL
2 tbsp	beaten egg	30 mL
1 tbsp	granulated sugar	15 mL
1 tbsp	vegetable oil	15 mL

1. In the mug, combine flour, baking powder and salt. Stir in cottage cheese, egg, sugar and oil until very well blended.

2. Microwave on High for $1\frac{1}{2}$ to $2\frac{1}{2}$ minutes (checking at $1\frac{1}{2}$) or until center is just set. Let cool slightly or entirely in mug. Eat directly from mug or gently remove to a small plate.

Variations

- **Double-Cheese Dinner Muffin:** Omit the salt and sugar, and add 1 tbsp (15 mL) grated Parmesan cheese.
- **Gluten-Free Cottage Cheese Muffin:** Use almond flour in place of the whole wheat flour. Make sure the baking powder is gluten-free.

Prep Ahead Option

Combine the flour, baking powder and salt in the mug; cover and store at room temperature. Measure the cottage cheese, egg, sugar and oil into a small airtight container; cover and refrigerate until ready to use.

Storage Tip

The muffin can be made in advance. Remove from mug and let cool completely, then tightly wrap in plastic wrap, parchment paper or foil, or store in an airtight container. Store at room temperature for up to 1 day or in the refrigerator for up to 2 days.

Chocolate Chip Oat Bran Muffin

Oat bran, the outer layer of the oat grain, contains the bulk of the grain's dietary fiber, as well as many minerals. It works particularly well in microwave quick breads, giving you a moist and filling muffin.

Tips

Try replacing the chocolate chips with 1 tbsp (15 mL) dried fruit, such as raisins, cranberries, cherries or blueberries.

For more flavor, add 1/4 tsp (1 mL) vanilla extract and/or 1/8 tsp (0.5 mL) ground cinnamon with the egg.

Storage Tip

The muffin can be made in advance. Remove from mug and let cool completely, then tightly wrap in plastic wrap, parchment paper or foil, or store in an airtight container. Store at room temperature for up to 1 day or in the refrigerator for up to 2 days.

♦ 12- to 16-oz (375 to 500 mL) mug, sprayed with nonstick cooking spray

3 tbsp	oat bran	45 mL
2 tbsp	large-flake (old-fashioned) or quick-cooking rolled oats	30 mL
1/4 tsp	baking powder	1 mL
1/8 tsp	salt	0.5 mL
1	large egg	1
3 tbsp	mashed very ripe banana	45 mL
1 tbsp	miniature semisweet chocolate chips	15 mL
1 tbsp	granulated sugar	15 mL

1. In the mug, combine oat bran cereal, oats, baking powder and salt. Using a fork, beat in egg, banana, chocolate chips and sugar until very well blended.

2. Microwave on High for 1 to 2 minutes (checking at 1) or until center is just set. Let cool slightly or entirely in mug. Eat directly from mug or gently remove to a small plate.

Variations

- **Blueberry Oat Bran Muffin:** Replace the chocolate chips with 6 to 8 blueberries (depending on size).
- **Sugar-Free Raisin Oat Bran Muffin:** Replace the sugar with 2 packets (about 1/2 tsp/2 mL) of powdered stevia or stevia-blend sweetener, and replace the chocolate chips with raisins.

Prep Ahead Option

Combine the oat bran, oats, baking powder, salt and chocolate chips in the mug; cover and store at room temperature. Whisk the egg in a small airtight container and add the banana and sugar; cover and refrigerate until ready to use.

High-Protein Chocolate Mug Muffin

Store-bought protein bars are very often full of junk ingredients, such as low-quality proteins, artificial flavors and colors, and preservatives. This quick muffin offers an easy (and delicious) alternative.

Tip

If you have a choice, opt for an all-natural protein powder (stevia-sweetened, no artificial colors or flavors). They are increasingly available in the health food sections of grocery stores.

You can use 2 tbsp (30 mL) beaten egg in place of the egg white.

♦ **16-oz (500 mL) mug, sprayed with nonstick cooking spray**

¼ cup	chocolate whey protein powder	60 mL
1½ tsp	unsweetened cocoa powder	7 mL
¼ tsp	baking powder	1 mL
Pinch	salt	Pinch
1	large egg white	1
½ cup	mashed very ripe banana	125 mL
1 tbsp	milk	15 mL

1. In the mug, combine protein powder, cocoa powder, baking powder and salt. Using a fork, beat in egg white, banana and milk until very well blended.

2. Microwave on High for 1 to 2 minutes (checking at 1) or until center is just set. Let cool slightly or entirely in mug. Eat directly from mug or gently remove to a small plate.

Variations

- **Banana Vanilla Protein Muffin:** Use vanilla whey protein powder in place of the chocolate, and omit the cocoa powder.

- **Pumpkin Spice Protein Muffin:** Use vanilla whey protein powder in place of the chocolate, and omit the cocoa powder. Replace the banana with ¼ cup (60 mL) unsweetened pumpkin purée (not pie filling) and increase the milk to ¼ cup (60 mL). Add ¼ tsp (1 mL) pumpkin pie spice or ground cinnamon and 1 packet (about ¼ tsp/1 mL) of powdered stevia or stevia-blend sweetener with the baking powder.

Prep Ahead Option

Combine the protein powder, cocoa powder, baking powder and salt in the mug; cover and store at room temperature. Whisk the egg white, banana and milk in a small airtight container; cover and refrigerate until ready to use.

Soups, Stews and Chilis

Moroccan Carrot Soup with Yogurt

I love carrots. So to me this soup, with its earthy flavor punctuated by Moroccan spices, yogurt and hints of lemon, is close to perfect.

Tips

Choose a baby food purée that contains nothing but carrots and water.

Regular yogurt works better than Greek yogurt here. If you only have Greek yogurt, whisk 2 tsp (10 mL) of it with $1\frac{1}{2}$ tsp (7 mL) milk to make drizzling consistency.

♦ **16-oz (500 mL) mug**

2	jars (each $4\frac{1}{2}$ oz/128 mL) carrot baby food purée	2
$\frac{1}{4}$ cup	ready-to-use chicken or vegetable broth	60 mL
$\frac{1}{2}$ tsp	liquid honey	2 mL
$\frac{1}{8}$ tsp	ground cumin	0.5 mL
$\frac{1}{8}$ tsp	pumpkin pie spice	0.5 mL
$\frac{1}{8}$ tsp	hot pepper sauce	0.5 mL
1 tsp	lemon juice	5 mL
1 tsp	butter or olive oil	5 mL
	Salt and ground black pepper	
1 tbsp	plain yogurt, stirred to loosen	15 mL

Suggested Accompaniments

Thinly sliced green onions; chopped fresh cilantro or parsley

1. In the mug, use a fork to whisk the carrot purée, broth, honey, cumin, pumpkin pie spice and hot pepper sauce. Microwave on High for $1\frac{1}{2}$ to $2\frac{1}{2}$ minutes (checking at $1\frac{1}{2}$) or until heated through.

2. Stir in lemon juice and butter until butter melts. Season to taste with salt and pepper, and drizzle with yogurt. Serve with any of the suggested accompaniments, as desired.

Variation

- **Carrot Soup with Ginger and Lemon:** Omit the cumin, pumpkin pie spice and hot pepper sauce, and add $\frac{1}{2}$ tsp (2 mL) finely grated lemon zest and $\frac{1}{4}$ tsp (1 mL) ground ginger with the honey.

Prep Ahead Option

Whisk the carrot purée, broth, honey, cumin, pumpkin pie spice and hot pepper sauce in the mug; cover and refrigerate. Measure the lemon juice and butter into a small airtight container; cover and refrigerate. Measure the yogurt into a small airtight container; cover and refrigerate until ready to use.

Kale and Barley Soup

Hearty fare without being heavy, this lovely green, red and white soup looks and tastes like a bowlful of Italy.

Tips

Look for quick-cooking barley near the rice or near the soups at the supermarket. If you can't find it, you can use 1/3 cup (75 mL) cooked pearl barley. Omit the cooking time in step 2.

You can use an equal amount of instant brown rice in place of the quick-cooking barley.

You can use canned chickpeas in place of the white beans if you prefer.

An equal amount of frozen chopped spinach or mustard greens can be used in place of the kale.

Freeze the remaining beans in a small sealable freezer bag. You can freeze the entire amount in one bag, or portion out 1/3 cup (75 mL) per bag so that the beans are recipe-ready. Be sure to label the bag with the contents. Store for up to 3 months. Defrost in the refrigerator or microwave before using.

♦ **16-oz (500 mL) mug**

1 cup	ready-to-use vegetable or chicken broth	250 mL
3 tbsp	quick-cooking barley	45 mL
1/3 cup	drained rinsed canned white beans (such as cannellini or great Northern)	75 mL
3/4 cup	frozen chopped kale	175 mL
1/3 cup	marinara sauce	75 mL
	Salt and ground black pepper	

1. In the mug, microwave broth on High for 60 to 90 seconds or until boiling.

2. Stir in barley. Microwave on High for 4 to 6 minutes or until barley is tender.

3. In a small bowl or cup, use a fork to coarsely mash half the beans. Stir mashed and whole beans, kale and marinara sauce into the mug. Microwave on High for 1 to 2 minutes (checking at 1) or until heated through. Season to taste with salt and pepper.

Prep Ahead Option

Measure the broth into the mug; cover and refrigerate. Measure the barley into a small airtight container; cover and store at room temperature. Mash half the beans in a small airtight container, then stir in remaining beans, kale and marinara sauce; cover and refrigerate until ready to use.

Petite Pea Soup

Regardless of your feelings about frozen peas, you'll love this soup. Its small list of humble ingredients belies its satisfaction factor and depth of flavor. The peas are more than pretty green pearls: they are rich in immune-supportive vitamin C, bone-building vitamin K and manganese, heart-healthy dietary fiber and folate, and energy-producing thiamin (vitamin B_1).

Tip

You can use a food processor instead of a blender, but purée half the peas, basil and broth at a time, to prevent leaking. The texture of the soup will not be as smooth as with a blender.

♦ **Blender**

♦ **16-oz (500 mL) mug**

³/₄ cup	frozen petite green peas, thawed	175 mL
¹/₄ cup	packed fresh basil, mint or parsley leaves	60 mL
¹/₂ cup	ready-to-use chicken or vegetable broth	125 mL
¹/₂ tsp	lemon juice	2 mL
	Salt and ground black pepper	

1. In blender, combine peas, basil and broth; purée until smooth.

2. Transfer purée to mug. Microwave on High for 1 to 2 minutes (checking at 1) or until heated through. Stir in lemon juice and season to taste with salt and pepper.

> **Prep Ahead Option**
>
> Combine the peas, basil and broth in a small airtight container; cover and refrigerate. Measure the lemon juice into a small airtight container; cover and refrigerate until ready to use.

Bistro Onion Soup

This soup takes a few more minutes to cook than others, but I promise it's worth the wait.

Tips

For onions that are meltingly tender, be sure to peel off the papery outer layer, the leathery second layer and any paper-thin membranes before cutting into thin slices.

Vegetable broth can be used in place of the beef broth.

♦ **16-oz (500 mL) mug**

1 tbsp	butter	15 mL
1	onion, halved crosswise and thinly sliced	1
1¼ cups	ready-to-use beef broth	300 mL
¼ tsp	granulated sugar	1 mL
⅛ tsp	dried thyme	0.5 mL
3 to 4	large garlic-seasoned croutons	3 to 4
1 tbsp	grated Parmesan cheese	15 mL

1. In the mug, microwave butter on High for 25 to 35 seconds or until melted.

2. Stir in onion. Microwave on High for 3 minutes. Stir. Microwave on High for 2 to 3 minutes or until onion is very soft.

3. Stir in broth, sugar and thyme. Microwave on High for 1 to 2 minutes (checking at 1) or until heated through. Top with croutons and sprinkle with Parmesan.

> **Prep Ahead Option**
> Measure the butter into the mug; cover and refrigerate. Place the onion in a small airtight container; cover and refrigerate. Measure the broth, sugar and thyme into a small airtight container; cover and refrigerate until ready to use.

Loaded Potato Soup

No need to boil potatoes for an hour, nor haul out the blender — this soup relies on instant potato flakes (simply dehydrated potatoes) to produce a perfectly creamy texture. The "loading," of shredded cheese, bacon and green onions, is where the fun comes in.

Tip

Look for ready-to-eat real bacon bits where salad dressings and croutons are shelved in the grocery store, or near the regular bacon in the packaged meat or deli department.

♦ **16-oz (500 mL) mug**

½ cup	ready-to-use chicken broth	125 mL
⅓ cup	instant potato flakes	75 mL
⅛ tsp	garlic powder	0.5 mL
½ cup	milk or half-and-half (10%) cream	125 mL
	Salt and ground black pepper	
2 tbsp	shredded sharp (old) Cheddar cheese	30 mL
1½ tbsp	ready-to-eat real bacon bits	22 mL
1 tbsp	chopped green onions	15 mL

1. In the mug, microwave broth on High for $1\frac{1}{2}$ to 2 minutes or until boiling.

2. Using a fork, whisk in potato flakes, garlic powder and milk until smooth. Microwave on High for 30 to 60 seconds (checking at 30) or until hot but not boiling. Let stand for 1 minute. Season to taste with salt and pepper. Top with cheese, bacon and green onions.

Variations

- **Pesto-Swirled Potato Soup:** Omit the Cheddar cheese, bacon and green onions. Swirl in 2 tsp (10 mL) basil pesto at the end of step 2. Sprinkle with 2 tsp (10 mL) grated Parmesan cheese.

- **Blue Cheese and Bacon Potato Soup:** Replace the Cheddar cheese with an equal amount of crumbled blue cheese. Stir half the cheese into the finished soup and sprinkle the remaining cheese on top. Add a pinch of ground nutmeg to the soup, if desired.

Prep Ahead Option

Measure the broth into the mug; cover and refrigerate. Measure the potato flakes and garlic powder into a small airtight container; cover and store at room temperature. Measure the milk into a small airtight container; cover and refrigerate. Measure the cheese, bacon bits and green onions into a small airtight container; cover and refrigerate until ready to use.

Thai Curry Pumpkin Soup

You'll love the layers of flavor that come through in this super-fast and easy Thai soup. Canned coconut milk and pumpkin purée, as well as red curry paste, keep it pantry-friendly.

Tips

A 4½-oz (128 mL) jar of winter squash baby food purée can be used in place of the pumpkin.

You can use an equal amount of mild, medium or hot curry powder in place of the curry paste.

Freeze the remaining pumpkin in a small sealable freezer bag. You can freeze the entire amount in one bag, or portion out ½ cup (125 mL) per bag so that the pumpkin is recipe-ready. Be sure to label the bag with the contents. Store for up to 3 months. Defrost in the refrigerator or microwave before using.

You can freeze extra coconut milk by placing 3 tbsp (45 mL) in each cavity of an ice cube tray. Once frozen, remove cubes from tray and store in an airtight container or freezer bag for up to 6 months. Defrost in the refrigerator or microwave.

♦ **16-oz (500 mL) mug**

½ cup	pumpkin purée (not pie filling)	125 mL
½ cup	ready-to-use chicken or vegetable broth	125 mL
1 tsp	packed brown sugar or granulated sugar	5 mL
½ tsp	Thai red curry paste	2 mL
3 tbsp	well-stirred coconut milk (not coconut water)	45 mL
1 tsp	lime juice	5 mL
	Salt and ground black pepper	

Suggested Accompaniments

Chopped fresh cilantro, basil or mint; thinly sliced green onions

1. In the mug, whisk together pumpkin, broth, brown sugar and curry paste. Microwave on High for 1 to 2 minutes (checking at 1) or until very hot but not boiling.
2. Whisk in coconut milk and lime juice. Microwave on High for 30 to 45 seconds or until heated through. Season to taste with salt and pepper. Serve with any of the suggested accompaniments, as desired.

Prep Ahead Option

Measure the pumpkin, broth, brown sugar and curry paste into the mug; cover and refrigerate. Measure the coconut milk and lime juice into a small airtight container; cover and refrigerate until ready to use.

Sweet Potato and Coconut Soup

Combining sweet potatoes and coconut in a savory dish may sound unusual, but it's quite common in a number of cuisines, including those of Southeast Asia and the Caribbean. My take leans towards the latter, but you can give it a Thai twist with my simple variation.

Tips

Choose a baby food purée that contains nothing but sweet potatoes and water.

You can use ½ cup (125 mL) canned pumpkin purée in place of the sweet potato.

You can freeze extra coconut milk by placing 2 tbsp (30 mL) in each cavity of an ice cube tray. Once frozen, remove cubes from tray and store in an airtight container or freezer bag for up to 6 months. Defrost in the refrigerator or microwave.

♦ **16-oz (500 mL) mug**

1	jar (4½ oz/128 mL) sweet potato baby food purée	1
½ cup	well-stirred coconut milk (not coconut water)	125 mL
¼ cup	ready-to-use chicken or vegetable broth	60 mL
¼ tsp	packed brown sugar	1 mL
⅛ tsp	salt	0.5 mL
⅛ tsp	ground allspice	0.5 mL
⅛ tsp	garlic powder	0.5 mL
⅛ tsp	hot pepper sauce	0.5 mL
	Salt and ground black pepper	

Suggested Accompaniments

Lime wedges; chopped fresh cilantro or thinly sliced green onions

1. In the mug, whisk sweet potato purée, coconut milk, broth, brown sugar, salt, allspice, garlic powder and hot pepper sauce until smooth.
2. Microwave on High for 75 to 90 seconds or until heated through. Season to taste with salt and pepper. Serve with any of the suggested accompaniments, as desired.

Variation

- **Thai-Spiced Sweet Potato Soup:** Omit the allspice and hot pepper sauce and add ½ tsp (2 mL) Thai red curry paste with the salt.

> **Prep Ahead Option**
> Prepare through step 1; cover and refrigerate until ready to use.

Soupe au Pistou

Soupe au pistou is a home-style vegetable soup with a good measure of pistou (the French version of pesto) stirred in right before serving. I've taken some liberties with this shortcut recipe, but I think you'll agree that the end justifies my means.

Tip

Freeze the remaining tomatoes and canned vegetables in separate small sealable freezer bags. You can freeze the entire amount in one bag, or portion out 1/4 cup (60 mL) per bag so that the tomatoes and vegetables are recipe-ready. Be sure to label the bag with the contents. Store for up to 3 months. Defrost in the refrigerator or microwave before using.

♦ **16-oz (500 mL) mug**

2 tbsp	orzo or other small pasta (such as ditalini or elbow macaroni)	30 mL
1 cup	ready-to-use chicken or vegetable broth	250 mL
1/3 cup	frozen cut green beans	75 mL
1/4 cup	canned diced tomatoes, with juice	60 mL
1/4 cup	drained canned mixed vegetables	60 mL
1 tbsp	basil pesto	15 mL
	Salt and ground black pepper	
	Grated Parmesan cheese (optional)	

1. In the mug, combine orzo and broth. Place in the microwave atop a doubled paper towel. Microwave on High for 2 minutes. Stir. Microwave on High for 3 to 5 minutes or until orzo is almost tender.

2. Stir in green beans. Microwave on High for 1 minute or until orzo is tender.

3. Stir in tomatoes and mixed vegetables. Microwave on High for 45 to 60 seconds or until heated through. Stir in pesto and season to taste with salt and pepper. If desired, sprinkle with Parmesan cheese.

Variation

- **Hearty Soupe au Pistou:** Add 1/4 cup (60 mL) diced cooked chicken, chopped ham or cooked smoked sausage with the tomatoes.

Prep Ahead Option

Measure the orzo into the mug; cover and store at room temperature. Measure each of the remaining ingredients into its own airtight container; cover and refrigerate.

Pasta e Fagioli

This cannellini-rich dish — part soup and part stew — is saucy and comforting. Once you try it, you'll understand why Tuscans proudly call themselves *mangiafagioli*, or bean eaters.

Tips

Look for ready-to-eat real bacon bits where salad dressings and croutons are shelved in the grocery store, or near the regular bacon in the packaged meat or deli department.

Freeze the remaining beans in a small sealable freezer bag. You can freeze the entire amount in one bag, or portion out $1/2$ cup (125 mL) per bag so that the beans are recipe-ready. Be sure to label the bag with the contents. Store for up to 3 months. Defrost in the refrigerator or microwave before using.

♦ **16-oz (500 mL) mug**

3 tbsp	elbow macaroni or other small tubular pasta	45 mL
2 tbsp	chopped carrots	30 mL
$3/4$ tsp	dried Italian seasoning	3 mL
1 cup	ready-to-use chicken or vegetable broth	250 mL
$1/2$ cup	drained rinsed canned white beans (such as cannellini or navy), divided	125 mL
$1/4$ cup	marinara sauce (preferably thick and chunky)	60 mL
1 tbsp	ready-to-eat real bacon bits	15 mL

Suggested Accompaniments

Grated Parmesan cheese; chopped fresh parsley

1. In the mug, combine macaroni, carrots, Italian seasoning and broth. Place in the microwave atop a doubled paper towel. Microwave on High for 2 minutes. Stir. Microwave on High for $4^1/2$ to 5 minutes or until macaroni is tender.

2. In a small bowl or cup, use a fork to coarsely mash half the beans. Stir mashed and whole beans, marinara sauce and bacon into the mug. Microwave on High for 1 to 2 minutes (checking at 1) or until heated through. Season to taste with salt and pepper. Serve with any of the suggested accompaniments, as desired.

> **Prep Ahead Option**
>
> Measure the macaroni into the mug; cover and store at room temperature. Measure the carrots, Italian seasoning and broth into a small airtight container; cover and refrigerate. Mash half the beans in a small airtight container, then add the remaining beans, marinara and bacon; cover and refrigerate until ready to use.

Spring Green Minestrone

This verdant soup is perfectly outfitted for spring with a cheery blend of green beans, petite peas and green onions, plus a swirl of basil pesto for zing.

Tips

An equal amount of frozen asparagus pieces can be used in place of the cut green beans.

Freeze the remaining beans in a small sealable freezer bag. You can freeze the entire amount in one bag, or portion out 1/2 cup (125 mL) per bag so that the beans are recipe-ready. Be sure to label the bag with the contents. Store for up to 3 months. Defrost in the refrigerator or microwave before using.

◆ 16-oz (500 mL) mug

1/2 cup	frozen cut green beans	125 mL
1 cup	ready-to-use chicken or vegetable broth	250 mL
1/2 cup	drained rinsed canned white beans (such as great Northern or cannellini), divided	125 mL
1/4 cup	frozen petite green peas	60 mL
1 1/2 tbsp	finely chopped green onions	22 mL
1 tbsp	basil pesto	15 mL

Suggested Accompaniment
Grated Parmesan cheese or crumbled goat cheese

1. In the mug, microwave green beans and broth on High for 1 1/2 to 2 minutes or until beans are heated through.

2. In a small bowl or cup, use a fork to coarsely mash half the white beans. Stir mashed and whole beans, peas and green onions into the mug. Microwave on High for 1 to 2 minutes or until heated through. Stir in pesto. Serve with a suggested accompaniment, if desired.

> **Prep Ahead Option**
>
> Combine the green beans and broth in the mug; cover and refrigerate (decrease the cooking time in step 1 by 30 seconds). Mash half the white beans in a small airtight container, then add the remaining beans, peas and onions; cover and refrigerate. Measure the pesto into a small airtight container; cover and refrigerate until ready to use.

Black Bean and Quinoa Soup

Lime zest and lime juice bring a touch of sunshine to this delicious soup, which can be made as spicy or as mellow as you like depending on the salsa you choose.

Tips

An equal amount of canned chickpeas, white beans, pinto beans or black-eyed peas can be used in place of the black beans.

You can use ¼ cup (60 mL) canned diced tomatoes with green chiles, with juice, in place of the salsa.

Freeze the remaining beans in a small sealable freezer bag. You can freeze the entire amount in one bag, or portion out ½ cup (125 mL) per bag so that the beans are recipe-ready. Be sure to label the bag with the contents. Store for up to 3 months. Defrost in the refrigerator or microwave before using.

♦ **16-oz (500 mL) mug**

1 cup	ready-to-use chicken or vegetable broth	250 mL
3 tbsp	quinoa, rinsed	45 mL
½ cup	rinsed drained canned black beans, divided	125 mL
¼ cup	salsa	60 mL
¼ tsp	finely grated lime zest	1 mL
2 tsp	freshly squeezed lime juice	10 mL
	Salt and ground black pepper	

1. In the mug, microwave broth on High for $1^1/_2$ to 2 minutes or until boiling.

2. Stir in quinoa. Microwave on High for 4 to 6 minutes or until quinoa is tender.

3. In a small bowl or cup, use a fork to coarsely mash half the beans. Stir mashed and whole beans and salsa into the mug. Microwave on High for 1 to 2 minutes or until heated through. Stir in lime zest and lime juice. Season to taste with salt and pepper.

Variation

- **Chicken and Quinoa Soup:** Replace the beans with half of a 5-oz (142 g) can of water-packed chunk chicken, drained and flaked.

Prep Ahead Option

Measure the broth into the mug; cover and refrigerate. Measure the quinoa into a small airtight container; cover and store at room temperature. Mash half the beans in a small airtight container, then add the remaining beans and salsa; cover and refrigerate. Measure the lime zest and lime juice into a small airtight container; cover and refrigerate until ready to use.

Bean and Bacon Soup

It may not be a new combination, but bean and bacon soup (one of my favorites from childhood) is so satisfying, you'll wonder how such modest ingredients can create something so pleasing.

Tips

Look for ready-to-eat real bacon bits where salad dressings and croutons are shelved in the grocery store, or near the regular bacon in the packaged meat or deli department.

Freeze the remaining beans in a small sealable freezer bag. You can freeze the entire amount in one bag, or portion out ³⁄₄ cup (175 mL) per bag so that the beans are recipe-ready. Be sure to label the bag with the contents. Store for up to 3 months. Defrost in the refrigerator or microwave before using.

♦ **16-oz (500 mL) mug**

³⁄₄ cup	drained rinsed canned white beans (such as great Northern, cannellini or navy), divided	175 mL
³⁄₄ cup	ready-to-use chicken broth	175 mL
1 tsp	packed dark brown sugar	5 mL
¹⁄₄ tsp	Dijon, coarse-grain or brown mustard	1 mL
1¹⁄₂ tbsp	ready-to-eat real bacon bits	22 mL
	Salt and ground black pepper	

1. In the mug, use a fork to coarsely mash ¹⁄₂ cup (125 mL) of the beans. Stir in remaining beans, broth, brown sugar, mustard and bacon.
2. Microwave on High for 1¹⁄₂ to 2¹⁄₂ minutes or until hot. Let stand for 1 minute. Season to taste with salt and pepper.

Variation

- **Black Bean and Bacon Soup:** Replace the great Northern beans with canned black beans. Omit the brown sugar and mustard, and add ¹⁄₂ tsp (2 mL) ground cumin and ¹⁄₈ tsp (0.5 mL) hot pepper sauce with the bacon.

Prep Ahead Option
Prepare through step 1; cover and refrigerate until ready to use.

Collard Greens and Black-Eyed Pea Soup

Collards are often used in long, slow cooking, but chopped frozen collard greens become tender with minimal cooking time. The result is bright, lively flavor that works in perfect sync with a bit of ham and creamy black-eyed peas.

Tips

Any other frozen chopped greens (kale, spinach, mustard greens) can be used in place of the collard greens.

An equal amount of diced cooked smoked sausage can be used in place of the ham.

Canned white beans can be used in place of the black-eyed peas.

You can use 1 tbsp (15 mL) ready-to-eat real bacon bits in place of the ham.

♦ **16-oz (500 mL) mug**

½ cup	frozen chopped collard greens	125 mL
¾ cup	ready-to-use chicken or vegetable broth	175 mL
⅓ cup	rinsed drained canned black-eyed peas	75 mL
2 tbsp	diced or chopped ham	30 mL
⅛ tsp	hot pepper sauce	0.5 mL

1. In the mug, microwave collard greens and broth on High for 1½ to 2 minutes or until greens are heated through.

2. Stir in black-eyed peas, ham and hot pepper sauce. Microwave on High for 60 to 90 seconds (checking at 60) or until heated through.

> **Prep Ahead Option**
>
> Combine the collard greens and broth in the mug; cover and refrigerate (decrease the cooking time in step 1 by 30 seconds). Measure the black-eyed peas, ham and hot pepper sauce into a small airtight container; cover and refrigerate until ready to use.

West African Peanut Soup

Tired of the same old vegetable soup? Try this spicy African soup for a delicious change of pace. The peanut butter adds addictive substance and depth to the broth.

Tips

Any other creamy nut or seed butter (almond, cashew, sunflower seed) can be used in place of the peanut butter.

Freeze the remaining tomatoes in a small sealable freezer bag for future use. Be sure to label the bag with the contents. Store for up to 3 months. Defrost in the refrigerator or microwave before using.

Freeze the remaining black-eyed peas in a small sealable freezer bag. You can freeze the entire amount in one bag, or portion out $1/2$ cup (125 mL) per bag so that the peas are recipe-ready. Be sure to label the bag with the contents. Store for up to 3 months. Defrost in the refrigerator or microwave before using.

♦ 16-oz (500 mL) mug

$1/2$	can (10 oz/284 mL) diced tomatoes with green chiles, with juice	$1/2$
$3/4$ cup	ready-to-use chicken or vegetable broth	175 mL
1 tbsp	creamy peanut butter	15 mL
$3/4$ tsp	curry powder	3 mL
$1/2$ cup	rinsed drained canned black-eyed peas	125 mL
	Salt and ground black pepper	
1 tbsp	chopped fresh cilantro or parsley	15 mL

1. In the mug, combine tomatoes, broth, peanut butter and curry powder. Microwave on High for 60 to 90 seconds or until heated through.

2. Stir in peas. Microwave on High for 1 to 2 minutes or until heated through. Season to taste with salt and pepper. Stir in cilantro.

Variation

- **West African Chicken and Peanut Soup:** Replace the peas with a 5-oz (142 g) can of water-packed chunk chicken, drained and flaked.

Prep Ahead Option

Combine the tomatoes, broth, peanut butter and curry powder in the mug; cover and refrigerate. Measure the black-eyed peas and cilantro into separate small airtight containers; cover and refrigerate until ready to use.

Tomato, Couscous and Chickpea Soup

If ever there was an easy dinner to brighten winter's gloom, this is it. The fresh cilantro is a must, providing bright contrast to the nutty chickpeas and spicy broth.

Tips

Either regular or whole wheat couscous can be used in the recipe.

Freeze the remaining tomatoes in a small sealable freezer bag for future use. Be sure to label the bag with the contents. Store for up to 3 months. Defrost in the refrigerator or microwave before using.

Freeze the remaining chickpeas in a small sealable freezer bag. You can freeze the entire amount in one bag, or portion out $1/2$ cup (125 mL) per bag so that the chickpeas are recipe-ready. Be sure to label the bag with the contents. Store for up to 3 months. Defrost in the refrigerator or microwave before using.

♦ **16-oz (500 mL) mug**

$1/2$	can (10 oz/284 mL) diced tomatoes with green chiles, with juice	$1/2$
$3/4$ cup	ready-to-use chicken or vegetable broth	175 mL
$1/2$ cup	rinsed drained canned chickpeas	125 mL
$1/2$ tsp	ground cumin	2 mL
$1/8$ tsp	hot pepper sauce	0.5 mL
2 tbsp	couscous	30 mL
	Salt and ground black pepper	

Suggested Accompaniments

Lemon or lime juice; chopped fresh parsley or cilantro

1. In the mug, combine tomatoes, broth, chickpeas, cumin and hot pepper sauce. Microwave on High for $1^1/2$ to 2 minutes or until boiling.

2. Stir in couscous, cover with a small plate or saucer and let stand for 3 minutes. Microwave on High for 30 seconds. Season to taste with salt and pepper. Serve with any of the suggested accompaniments, as desired.

Prep Ahead Option

Combine the tomatoes, broth, chickpeas, cumin and hot pepper sauce in the mug; cover and refrigerate. Measure the couscous into a small airtight container; cover and store at room temperature until ready to use.

Edamame Succotash Soup

This is a perfect midwinter soup, just right when you're craving something hearty but also fresh-tasting. The edamame cozies up to the corn in a way that manages to be both new and familiar.

Tips

Cream-style corn contains no cream, so if the soup is made with vegetable broth, it is vegan.

Try stirring 2 tsp (10 mL) basil pesto into the soup in place of the dried basil.

Frozen baby lima beans can be used in place of the edamame.

♦ **16-oz (500 mL) mug**

1/3 cup	frozen shelled edamame	75 mL
2/3 cup	ready-to-use chicken or vegetable broth	150 mL
1/2 cup	canned cream-style corn	125 mL
1/4 cup	frozen corn kernels	60 mL
1/4 tsp	dried basil (optional)	1 mL
	Salt and ground black pepper	

1. In the mug, microwave edamame and broth on High for 2 minutes or until edamame are tender.

2. Stir in cream-style corn, corn kernels and basil (if using). Microwave on High for 60 to 75 seconds or until heated through. Season to taste with salt and pepper.

Variation

- **Hearty Edamame Succotash Soup:** Add 3 tbsp (45 mL) cooked diced chicken, chopped ham or cooked smoked sausage with the corn.

- **Bacon Edamame Succotash Soup:** Add 1 tbsp (15 mL) ready-to-eat real bacon bits.

Prep Ahead Option

Combine the edamame and broth in the mug; cover and refrigerate (decrease the cooking time in step 1 by 30 seconds). Measure the cream-style corn, corn kernels and basil (if using) into a small airtight container; cover and refrigerate until ready to use.

Miso, Brown Rice and Tofu Soup

Be sure to use firm or extra-firm tofu for this soup, as it will hold up better. The miso is added at the very end of cooking to preserve both its flavor and its healthful qualities.

Tips

You can use $1/2$ cup (125 mL) cooked brown rice in place of the instant brown rice. Omit the cooking time in step 2.

Miso paste can be stored in an airtight container in the refrigerator for up to 6 months.

Cut the tofu into very small cubes so that they will fit onto a soup spoon.

Try adding up to 2 tbsp (30 mL) grated carrot with the rice.

♦ **16-oz (500 mL) mug**

$1^1/_4$ cups	ready-to-use vegetable or chicken broth	300 mL
$1/_2$ tsp	ground ginger	2 mL
$1/_4$ cup	instant brown rice	60 mL
1 tbsp	miso paste (any variety)	15 mL
$1/_4$ cup	diced firm or extra-firm tofu	60 mL
1 tbsp	thinly sliced green onions	15 mL

1. In the mug, combine broth and ginger. Microwave on High for $1^1/_2$ to 2 minutes or until boiling.

2. Stir in rice. Microwave on High for 5 minutes or until rice is tender.

3. Stir in miso paste until dissolved. Stir in tofu and green onions. Microwave on High for 30 seconds.

Variation

• **Miso Quinoa Soup:** Omit the tofu and replace the rice with $1/_4$ cup (60 mL) quinoa, rinsed. Increase the cooking time in step 2 to 7 minutes.

> **Prep Ahead Option**
> Measure the broth and ginger into the mug; cover and refrigerate. Measure the rice into a small airtight container; cover and store at room temperature. Measure the miso paste, tofu and green onions into a small airtight container; cover and refrigerate until ready to use.

Greek Lemon and Rice Soup

Avgolemono is Greek for egg-lemon and can refer to a range of sauces as well as soup. It is made with eggs and lemon juice mixed with hot broth. I've added a bit of brown rice to make the soup substantial enough for a light meal.

Tip

You can use ⅓ cup (75 mL) cooked brown rice in place of the instant brown rice. Reduce the cooking time in step 1 to 2 minutes.

♦ **16-oz (500 mL) mug**

3 tbsp	instant brown rice	45 mL
1⅓ cups	chicken or vegetable broth	325 mL
1	large egg	1
1 tbsp	lemon juice	15 mL
1 tbsp	chopped green onions	15 mL

1. In the mug, combine rice and broth. Microwave on High for 5 minutes or until rice is tender.

2. In a small bowl or measuring cup, use a fork to beat egg and lemon juice until foamy. Whisk about one-third of the broth into the egg. Stir egg mixture into mug.

3. Microwave on High for 30 seconds or until soup is thickened. Sprinkle with green onions.

Variation

- **Lemon Chicken and Rice Soup:** Add half of a 5-oz (142 g) can of water-packed chunk chicken, drained and flaked, at the end of step 1.

Prep Ahead Option

Measure the rice into the mug; cover and store at room temperature. Measure the broth into a small airtight container; cover and refrigerate. Beat the egg and lemon juice in a small airtight container; cover and refrigerate. Measure the green onions into a small airtight container; cover and refrigerate until ready to use.

Beef and Barley Soup

Barley is one of the oldest grains on the planet. It has a mild sweetness and a chewy, tender texture. Quick-cooking barley is ready in a matter of minutes, meaning this is sure to be your new go-to dinner when you need something hearty in a hurry.

Tips

Look for quick-cooking barley near the rice or near the soups at the supermarket. If you can't find it, you can use 1/3 cup (75 mL) cooked pearl barley. Omit the cooking time in step 2.

You can use an equal amount of instant brown rice in place of the quick-cooking barley.

Freeze the remaining mixed vegetables in a small sealable freezer bag. You can freeze the entire amount in one bag, or portion out 1/4 cup (60 mL) per bag so that the vegetables are recipe-ready. Be sure to label the bag with the contents. Store for up to 3 months. Defrost in the refrigerator or microwave before using.

◆ **16-oz (500 mL) mug**

2	frozen cooked beef meatballs	2
1/4 cup	drained canned mixed vegetables	60 mL
3 tbsp	quick-cooking barley	45 mL
1/8 tsp	dried thyme (optional)	0.5 mL
1 cup	ready-to-use beef or vegetable broth	250 mL
1/8 tsp	cider vinegar or wine vinegar	0.5 mL

1. In the mug, microwave meatballs on High for 1 to 2 minutes or until completely warmed through. Transfer to a small bowl and break apart with a fork. Wipe out mug with a paper towel.

2. In the mug, use a fork to coarsely mash the mixed vegetables. Stir in barley, thyme (if using) and broth. Microwave on High for 5 minutes or until barley is tender.

3. Stir in crumbled meatballs and vinegar. Let stand for 1 minute before serving.

Variation

- **Sausage and Barley Soup:** Use 2 frozen cooked breakfast sausage links in place of the meatballs.

> **Prep Ahead Option**
>
> Measure the meatballs into the mug; cover and refrigerate (decrease the cooking time in step 1 to 30 to 45 seconds). Mash the mixed vegetables in a small airtight container, then stir in the barley, thyme (if using) and broth; cover and refrigerate until ready to use.

Vietnamese Pho

In Vietnam, people are fiercely loyal to their favorite version of pho. After a taste of this quick, light version, you'll start to feel the same sense of devotion. Serve it with Asian chili sauce (such as Sriracha) for diners who want to add some heat.

Tips

If using broken spaghetti, break into 1- to 1½- inch (2.5 to 4 cm) pieces for best results.

For best results, select a deli roast beef that has no additional flavorings (such as Italian herbs or barbecue seasoning).

◆ 16-oz (500 mL) mug

1 cup	ready-to-use beef broth	250 mL
1 tsp	granulated sugar	5 mL
½ tsp	ground ginger	2 mL
1½ tsp	soy sauce	7 mL
¼ cup	cut or broken spaghetti	60 mL
1 oz	sliced deli roast beef, halved crosswise and cut lengthwise into 1-inch (2.5 cm) strips	30 g
2 tsp	lime juice	10 mL

Suggested Accompaniments

Mung bean sprouts; sliced fresh basil; fresh cilantro leaves; chopped green onions

1. In the mug, combine broth, sugar, ginger and soy sauce. Stir in spaghetti. Place in the microwave atop a doubled paper towel. Microwave on High for 2 minutes. Stir. Microwave on High for 4½ minutes or until spaghetti is tender.

2. Stir in beef and lime juice. Let stand for 1 minute. Serve with any of the suggested accompaniments, as desired.

Variation

- **Vegetarian Pho:** Use vegetable broth in place of the beef broth, and diced firm tofu in place of the roast beef.

Prep Ahead Option

Combine the broth, sugar, ginger and soy sauce in the mug; cover and refrigerate. Measure the spaghetti into a small airtight container; cover and store at room temperature. Measure the beef and lime juice into separate small airtight containers; cover and refrigerate until ready to use.

Smoked Sausage and Potato Chowder

Smoky sausage, hearty potatoes and corn make this a substantial, satisfying soup.

Tip

An equal amount of diced ham can be used in place of the smoked sausage.

♦ **16-oz (500 mL) mug**

1/3 cup	frozen diced hash brown potatoes with peppers and onions	75 mL
1/4 cup	ready-to-use chicken or vegetable broth	60 mL
1/3 cup	cream-style corn	75 mL
1/3 cup	diced cooked smoked sausage	75 mL
1/4 cup	half-and-half (10%) cream or milk	60 mL
	Salt and ground black pepper	
2 tsp	chopped fresh parsley (optional)	10 mL

1. In the mug, microwave hash browns and broth on High for $1^1/_2$ to 2 minutes or until hot but not boiling.

2. Stir in corn and sausage. Microwave on High for $1^1/_2$ to 2 minutes or until potatoes are very soft.

3. Stir in cream. Microwave on High for 30 to 45 seconds or until heated through. Season to taste with salt and pepper. Sprinkle with parsley, if desired.

> **Prep Ahead Option**
>
> Combine the hash browns and broth in the mug; cover and refrigerate (decrease the cooking time in step 1 by 30 seconds). Measure the corn and sausage into a small airtight container; cover and refrigerate. Measure the cream and parsley into separate small airtight containers; cover and refrigerate until ready to use.

Chicken Pot Pie Soup

Chicken, a mix of vegetables and sage-scented cream sauce make a satisfying main course in minutes. Don't forget your biscuit accompaniment!

Tips

An equal amount of poultry seasoning or dried thyme can be used in place of the sage.

Freeze the remaining mixed vegetables in a small sealable freezer bag. You can freeze the entire amount in one bag, or portion out ⅓ cup (75 mL) per bag so that the vegetables are recipe-ready. Be sure to label the bag with the contents. Store for up to 3 months. Defrost in the refrigerator or microwave before using.

♦ **16-oz (500 mL) mug**

1	can (5 oz/142 g) water-packed chunk chicken, drained and flaked	1
⅓ cup	drained canned mixed vegetables	75 mL
⅛ tsp	dried rubbed sage	0.5 mL
¾ cup	ready-to-use chicken broth	175 mL
⅓ cup	light Alfredo sauce	75 mL
	Salt and ground black pepper	
1	prepared biscuit (such as the Buttermilk Biscuit, page 106)	1

1. In the mug, combine chicken, vegetables, sage and broth. Microwave on High for 75 to 90 seconds or until heated through.
2. Stir in Alfredo sauce. Microwave on High for 30 to 45 minutes or until heated through. Season to taste with salt and pepper. Serve with biscuit.

> **Prep Ahead Option**
>
> Combine the chicken, vegetables, sage and broth in the mug; cover and refrigerate. Measure the Alfredo sauce into a small airtight container; cover and refrigerate until ready to use. Wrap the biscuit separately and store at room temperature until ready to use.

Green Chile and Chicken Posole

This revamped version of posole — a traditional Latin American soup that has been served since pre-Columbian time — showcases the citrusy flavor of tomatillos.

Tips

Look for salsa verde (green salsa made with green chiles and tomatillos) where other salsas are shelved.

Canned hominy is inexpensive and readily available. You can find it where canned corn is shelved, or in the Mexican or Latin foods section.

♦ **16-oz (500 mL) mug**

¹⁄₂ cup	drained canned yellow hominy, divided	125 mL
1	can (5 oz/142 g) water-packed chunk chicken, drained and flaked	1
³⁄₄ cup	ready-to-use chicken or vegetable broth	175 mL
¹⁄₄ cup	salsa verde	60 mL
¹⁄₄ tsp	ground cumin	1 mL
1¹⁄₂ tbsp	minced fresh cilantro	22 mL

Suggested Accompaniments

Crumbled queso blanco or shredded Jack cheese; plain Greek yogurt or sour cream; tortilla chips

1. In the mug, use a fork to mash 2 tbsp (30 mL) of the hominy. Stir in remaining hominy, chicken, broth, salsa and cumin.

2. Microwave on High for 1¹⁄₂ to 2 minutes (checking at 1¹⁄₂) or until very hot but not boiling. Stir in cilantro. Serve with any of the suggested accompaniments, as desired.

Variations

- **White Chicken Chili:** Use an equal amount of rinsed drained canned white beans (such as cannellini or great Northern) in place of the hominy.

- **Vegetarian Green Chile Posole:** Omit the chicken and increase the hominy by ¹⁄₄ cup (60 mL). Use vegetable broth.

Prep Ahead Option

Mash the 2 tbsp (30 mL) hominy in the mug, then add the remaining hominy, chicken, broth, salsa and cumin; cover and refrigerate. Measure the cilantro into a small airtight container; cover and refrigerate until ready to use.

Salmon Chowder

Making salmon chowder is usually impractical for the home cook, especially on a weeknight. But my microwave version makes it a cinch, thanks to canned salmon, ready-to-eat bacon bits and some cream.

Tip

Look for ready-to-eat real bacon bits where salad dressings and croutons are shelved in the grocery store, or near the regular bacon in the packaged meat or deli department.

♦ **16-oz (500 mL) mug**

1	can (4 oz/114 g) salmon, with liquid, flaked	1
1/2 cup	bottled clam juice or ready-to-use chicken broth	125 mL
1 tbsp	ready-to-eat real bacon bits	15 mL
1/2 tsp	dried dillweed	2 mL
2/3 cup	half-and-half (10%) cream or evaporated milk	150 mL
2 tsp	finely chopped green onions	10 mL
	Salt and ground black pepper	

1. In the mug, combine salmon, clam juice, bacon and dill. Microwave on High for 1 1/2 to 2 minutes or until hot but not boiling.

2. Stir in cream and green onions. Microwave on High for 30 to 45 seconds (checking at 30) or until heated through. Season to taste with salt and pepper.

Prep Ahead Option

Combine the salmon, clam juice, bacon and dill in the mug; cover and refrigerate. Measure the cream and green onions into a small airtight container; cover and refrigerate until ready to use.

Manhattan Clam Chowder

Unlike New England clam chowder, Manhattan clam chowder (also known as Fulton Fish Market clam chowder) has clear broth, plus tomato for color and flavor. Canned clams make it a snap to prepare in the microwave.

Tips

A 4- to 5-oz (114 to 142 g) can of lump crabmeat, flaked, or tiny shrimp (undrained) can be used in place of the clams.

Look for ready-to-eat real bacon bits where salad dressings and croutons are shelved in the grocery store, or near the regular bacon in the packaged meat or deli department.

♦ **16-oz (500 mL) mug**

¼ cup	frozen diced hash brown potatoes with peppers and onions	60 mL
¾ cup	ready-to-use chicken or vegetable broth	175 mL
¼ cup	marinara sauce	60 mL
1 tbsp	ready-to-eat real bacon bits	15 mL
⅛ tsp	dried thyme	0.5 mL
1	can (6 oz/170 mL) chopped clams, with liquid	1
	Salt and ground black pepper	
2 tsp	chopped fresh parsley (optional)	10 mL

1. In the mug, microwave hash browns and broth on High for 1½ to 2 minutes or until hot but not boiling.

2. Stir in marinara sauce, bacon and thyme. Microwave on High for 1½ to 2 minutes or until potatoes are very soft.

3. Stir in clams. Microwave on High for 30 seconds or until heated through. Season to taste with salt and pepper. Sprinkle with parsley, if desired.

> **Prep Ahead Option**
> Combine the hash browns and broth in the mug; cover and refrigerate (decrease the cooking time in step 1 by 30 seconds). Measure the marinara sauce, bacon and thyme into a small airtight container; cover and refrigerate. Measure the clams and parsley into separate small airtight containers; cover and refrigerate until ready to use.

Southern Corn Spoon Bread (page 102)

Cinnamon Sugar Muffin (page 112)

Loaded Potato Soup (page 124)

Italian Meatball Stew (page 146)

Spiced Lentils with Yogurt, Almonds and Mint (page 164)

Tomato and Zucchini Crumble (page 157)

Barbecued Chinese Chicken Lettuce Wraps (page 208)

Tuna Niçoise Mug (page 212)

Caldillo

Caldillo is a Mexican version of beef stew, rich with potatoes, tomatoes, chiles and spices. A few handy ingredients from the freezer and pantry make this rendition ready in minutes.

Tip

Freeze the remaining tomatoes in a small sealable freezer bag for future use. Be sure to label the bag with the contents. Store for up to 3 months. Defrost in the refrigerator or microwave before using.

♦ **16-oz (500 mL) mug**

1/2 cup	frozen diced hash brown potatoes with peppers and onions	125 mL
1/4 cup	ready-to-use beef or vegetable broth	60 mL
4	frozen cooked beef meatballs	4
1/2	can (10 oz/284 mL) tomatoes with green chiles, with juice	1/2
1/4 tsp	ground cumin	1 mL
	Salt and ground black pepper	

Suggested Accompaniments

Chopped fresh cilantro; lime wedges; tortilla chips; plain Greek yogurt or sour cream

1. In the mug, combine hash browns and broth. Place meatballs on top. Microwave on High for 2 to 3 minutes or until meatballs are heated through and potatoes are almost tender. Break meatballs apart with a fork.

2. Stir in tomatoes and cumin. Microwave on High for 1 1/2 to 2 minutes or until heated through. Season to taste with salt and pepper. Serve with any of the suggested accompaniments, as desired.

Variation

- **Caldo de Pollo:** Omit the meatballs. Add a 5-oz (142 g) can of water-packed chunk chicken, drained and flaked, with the tomatoes. Use chicken broth instead of beef broth.

Prep Ahead Option

Combine the hash browns and broth in the mug, then place the meatballs on top; cover and refrigerate (decrease the cooking time in step 1 to 30 to 45 seconds). Measure the tomatoes and cumin into a small airtight container; cover and refrigerate until ready to use.

Italian Meatball Stew

Ready-made meatballs add quick and delicious heft, while mixed vegetables, marinara and mushrooms enrich store-bought broth for a quick and truly delicious Italian meal in a mug.

Tips

Chicken or vegetable broth can be used in place of the beef broth.

Freeze the remaining mixed vegetables in a small sealable freezer bag. You can freeze the entire amount in one bag, or portion out $1/3$ cup (75 mL) per bag so that the vegetables are recipe-ready. Be sure to label the bag with the contents. Store for up to 3 months. Defrost in the refrigerator or microwave before using.

♦ **16-oz (500 mL) mug**

4	frozen beef meatballs	4
$1/2$ cup	marinara sauce	125 mL
$1/3$ cup	ready-to-use beef broth	75 mL
$1/3$ cup	drained canned mixed vegetables	75 mL
2 tbsp	drained canned or jarred mushroom pieces	30 mL
	Salt and ground black pepper	

Suggested Accompaniments

Grated Parmesan cheese or shredded Italian-blend cheese; chopped fresh parsley

1. In the mug, microwave meatballs on High for 1 to 2 minutes or until completely warmed through. Using a fork, cut meatballs in half.

2. Stir in marinara sauce, broth, mixed vegetables and mushrooms. Microwave on High for $1^1/2$ to 2 minutes or until heated through. Season to taste with salt and pepper. Serve with any of the suggested accompaniments, as desired.

Variation

- **Vegetarian Meatball Stew:** Replace the beef meatballs with ready-to-use vegetarian or vegan meatballs, and use vegetable broth in place of the beef broth.

Prep Ahead Option

Place the meatballs in the mug; cover and refrigerate (decrease the cooking time in step 1 to 30 to 45 seconds). Measure the marinara sauce, broth, mixed vegetables and mushrooms into a small airtight container; cover and refrigerate until ready to use.

Chicken and Vegetable Stew

Don't dial for pizza delivery the next time you're mad hungry. Whip up a batch of this comforting — and easy — chicken stew instead.

Tips

If your can of tomatoes is larger, measure $2/3$ cup (150 mL) diced tomatoes with juice.

For a spicier stew, use $2/3$ cup (150 mL) canned diced tomatoes with green chiles in place of the tomatoes with Italian seasoning.

Freeze the remaining tomatoes in a small sealable freezer bag for future use. Be sure to label the bag with the contents. Store for up to 3 months. Defrost in the refrigerator or microwave before using.

Freeze the remaining mixed vegetables in a small sealable freezer bag. You can freeze the entire amount in one bag, or portion out $1/2$ cup (125 mL) per bag so that the vegetables are recipe-ready. Be sure to label the bag with the contents. Store for up to 3 months. Defrost in the refrigerator or microwave before using.

♦ **16-oz (500 mL) mug**

1	can (5 oz/142 g) water-packed chunk chicken, drained and flaked	1
$1/2$	can (14 to 15 oz/398 to 425 mL) diced tomatoes with Italian seasoning, with juice	$1/2$
$1/2$ cup	drained canned mixed vegetables	125 mL
	Ground black pepper	
1 tbsp	grated Parmesan cheese	15 mL

1. In the mug, combine chicken, tomatoes and vegetables.
2. Microwave on High for $1^1/2$ to $2^1/2$ minutes or until heated through. Season to taste with pepper. Sprinkle with Parmesan.

> **Prep Ahead Option**
> Combine the chicken, tomatoes and vegetables in the mug; cover and refrigerate. Measure the Parmesan into a small airtight container; cover and refrigerate until ready to use.

Smoky Bacon Chili

Chili from a can pales beside this 3-minute, bacon-enriched version. Thick, rich and smoky, it's a seriously satisfying meal any day of the week.

Tips

Look for ready-to-eat real bacon bits where salad dressings and croutons are shelved in the grocery store, or near the regular bacon in the packaged meat or deli department.

Freeze the remaining tomatoes in a small sealable freezer bag for future use. Be sure to label the bag with the contents. Store for up to 3 months. Defrost in the refrigerator or microwave before using.

♦ **16-oz (500 mL) mug**

2	frozen cooked beef meatballs	2
³⁄₄ cup	chili-seasoned pinto beans, with liquid, divided	175 mL
¹⁄₂	can (10 oz/284 mL) diced tomatoes with green chiles, with juice	¹⁄₂
2 tbsp	ready-to-eat real bacon bits	30 mL
¹⁄₄ tsp	ground cumin	1 mL
	Salt and ground black pepper	

Suggested Accompaniments

Shredded Cheddar or Monterey Jack cheese; thinly sliced green onions; tortilla chips

1. In the mug, microwave meatballs on High for 60 to 90 seconds or until heated through. Break apart with a fork. Add ¹⁄₄ cup (60 mL) of the beans to the mug and coarsely mash with the fork.

2. Stir in remaining beans, tomatoes, bacon and cumin. Microwave on High for 1¹⁄₂ to 2 minutes or until heated through. Season to taste with salt and pepper. Serve with any of the suggested accompaniments, as desired.

> **Prep Ahead Option**
>
> Place the meatballs in the mug; cover and refrigerate (decrease the cooking time in step 1 to 30 to 45 seconds). Mash ¹⁄₄ cup (60 mL) of the beans in a small airtight container, then add the remaining beans, tomatoes, bacon and cumin; cover and refrigerate until ready to use.

Winter Squash, Sausage and White Bean Chili

This light-colored chili gets its rich, autumnal flavor from a stealth ingredient: winter squash baby food purée. Most vegetable baby food purées on the market (especially organic varieties) contain nothing more than the vegetable (in this case, butternut squash) and a bit of water. Pretty nifty! And so delicious in this easy sausage chili.

Tips

Choose a baby food purée that contains nothing but squash and water.

Freeze the remaining beans in a small sealable freezer bag. You can freeze the entire amount in one bag, or portion out ¾ cup (175 mL) per bag so that the beans are recipe-ready. Be sure to label the bag with the contents. Store for up to 3 months. Defrost in the refrigerator or microwave before using.

♦ **16-oz (500 mL) mug**

3	frozen cooked breakfast sausage links	3
¾ cup	drained rinsed canned white beans (such as great Northern or cannellini), divided	175 mL
1	jar (4½ oz/128 mL) winter squash baby food purée	1
⅓ cup	thick and chunky salsa	75 mL
¼ tsp	dried rubbed sage	1 mL
	Salt and ground black pepper	

Suggested Accompaniments

Crumbled goat cheese or shredded Cheddar or Monterey Jack cheese; chopped fresh parsley; tortilla chips

1. In the mug, microwave sausages on High for 60 to 75 seconds or until heated through. Break apart with a fork. Add ¼ cup (60 mL) of the beans to the mug and coarsely mash with the fork.

2. Stir in remaining beans, squash purée, salsa and sage. Microwave on High for 1½ to 2 minutes or until heated through. Season to taste with salt and pepper. Serve with any of the suggested accompaniments, as desired.

Variation

- **Vegetarian Squash and White Bean Chili:** Omit the sausages and increase the beans to 1¼ cups (300 mL) total.

> **Prep Ahead Option**
>
> Place the sausages in the mug; cover and refrigerate (decrease the cooking time in step 1 to 30 seconds). Mash ¼ cup (60 mL) of the beans in a small airtight container, then add the remaining beans, squash purée, salsa and sage; cover and refrigerate until ready to use.

Black-Eyed Pea Chili with Ham

I like beans — a lot — but I love black-eyed peas. They're also known as cow peas and are used in a number of cuisines, including India, West Africa, the Caribbean and the American South. Here, they star in a quick, Louisiana-influenced chili that is eminently satisfying.

Tips

Canned white beans (such as cannellini or great Northern) can be used in place of the black-eyed peas.

Freeze the remaining black-eyed peas in a small sealable freezer bag. You can freeze the entire amount in one bag, or portion out ³⁄₄ cup (175 mL) per bag so that the peas are recipe-ready. Be sure to label the bag with the contents. Store for up to 3 months. Defrost in the refrigerator or microwave before using.

Freeze the remaining tomatoes in a small sealable freezer bag. Be sure to label the bag with the contents. Store for up to 3 months. Defrost in the refrigerator or microwave before using.

♦ 16-oz (500 mL) mug

³⁄₄ cup	rinsed drained canned black-eyed peas, divided	175 mL
¹⁄₂	can (10 oz/284 mL) diced tomatoes with green chiles, with juice	¹⁄₂
¹⁄₃ cup	diced or chopped ham	75 mL
¹⁄₄ cup	ready-to-use chicken or vegetable broth	60 mL
¹⁄₄ tsp	ground cumin	1 mL
¹⁄₈ tsp	dried thyme	0.5 mL
	Salt and hot pepper sauce	

Suggested Accompaniments

Shredded Monterey Jack cheese; chopped fresh parsley or thinly sliced green onions; tortilla chips

1. In the mug, use a fork to coarsely mash ¹⁄₄ cup (60 mL) of the peas. Stir in remaining peas, tomatoes, ham, broth, cumin and thyme.

2. Microwave on High for 1¹⁄₂ to 2¹⁄₂ minutes or until heated through. Season to taste with salt and hot pepper sauce. Serve with any of the suggested accompaniments, as desired.

Prep Ahead Option

Mash ¹⁄₄ cup (60 mL) of the peas in the mug, then add the remaining peas, tomatoes, ham, broth, cumin and thyme; cover and refrigerate until ready to use.

Meatless Main Dishes

Cauliflower and Goat Cheese Casserole

Zesty goat cheese and a toasty crumb topping bring out cauliflower's best, turning this otherwise humble vegetable into delectable dinner fare.

Tips

Try adding a pinch of ground nutmeg or $\frac{1}{8}$ tsp (0.5 mL) dried Italian seasoning with the Alfredo sauce.

Freeze the remaining beans in a small sealable freezer bag. You can freeze the entire amount in one bag, or portion out $\frac{1}{2}$ cup (125 mL) per bag so that the beans are recipe-ready. Be sure to label the bag with the contents. Store for up to 3 months. Defrost in the refrigerator or microwave before using.

♦ **16-oz (500 mL) mug**

1 cup	coarsely chopped fresh or thawed frozen cauliflower florets	250 mL
$\frac{1}{2}$ cup	rinsed drained canned white beans (such as cannellini or great Northern)	125 mL
3 tbsp	light Alfredo sauce	45 mL
2 tbsp	chopped drained jarred roasted red bell peppers	30 mL
	Salt and ground black pepper	
2 tbsp	crumbled goat cheese	30 mL
2 tbsp	crushed garlic croutons	30 mL

1. In the mug, microwave cauliflower on High for $1\frac{1}{2}$ to 2 minutes or until warmed through and almost tender. Drain off excess liquid.

2. Stir in beans, Alfredo sauce and roasted peppers. Season to taste with salt and pepper, and sprinkle with goat cheese. Microwave on High for 60 to 90 seconds (checking at 60) or until heated through. Sprinkle with croutons.

Variation

- **Asparagus and Goat Cheese Casserole:** Use an equal amount of frozen cut asparagus in place of the cauliflower.

Prep Ahead Option

Place the cauliflower in the mug; cover and refrigerate. Measure the beans, Alfredo sauce, peppers and goat cheese into a small airtight container; cover and refrigerate. Measure the croutons into a small airtight container; cover and store at room temperature until ready to use.

Curried Cauliflower and Peas

Vegetable curries are all about contrasting textures and flavors, but their real success hinges on great spices — in this case, a single spice blend, curry powder. Make sure the one you use is aromatic and fresh, for optimal flavor.

Tip

Frozen hash browns with onions and peppers are often labeled "O'Brien" potatoes.

♦ 16-oz (500 mL) mug

³/₄ cup	frozen cauliflower pieces	175 mL
¹/₂ cup	frozen diced hash brown potatoes with onions and peppers	125 mL
¹/₄ cup	frozen petite green peas	60 mL
3 tbsp	tomato sauce or marinara sauce	45 mL
1 tsp	curry powder	5 mL
	Salt and ground black pepper	

Suggested Accompaniments

Chopped fresh cilantro; plain yogurt; chutney; raisins; chopped cashews

1. In the mug, microwave cauliflower and hash browns on High for 2 to 3 minutes or until vegetables are tender. Drain off excess liquid.

2. Stir in peas, tomato sauce and curry powder. Microwave on High for 45 to 75 seconds or until heated through. Let stand for 1 minute. Season to taste with salt and pepper. Serve with any of the suggested accompaniments, as desired.

Variation

- **Tempeh and Cauliflower Curry:** Omit the hash browns. Add ²/₃ cup (150 mL) diced or crumbled tempeh with the peas.

> **Prep Ahead Option**
> Measure the cauliflower and hash browns into the mug; cover and refrigerate (decrease the cooking time in step 1 by 30 to 60 seconds). Measure the peas, tomato sauce and curry powder into a small airtight container; cover and refrigerate until ready to use.

Eggplant Parmesan Mug

In a matter of minutes, the microwave renders eggplant tender and slightly sweet. It then finds great flavor contrast with classic eggplant Parmesan flavors: marinara sauce, mozzarella and a toasty crumb topping.

Tips

Try using an equal amount of diced zucchini (peeled or unpeeled) in place of the eggplant.

If you eat meat, try adding 1 or 2 cooked frozen beef meatballs (heated on High for 60 to 90 seconds, then crumbled with a fork) to the marinara sauce, to make the meal more substantial.

♦ **16-oz (500 mL) mug**

1½ cups	diced peeled eggplant	375 mL
2 tsp	olive oil	10 mL
⅛ tsp	salt	0.5 mL
⅓ cup	marinara sauce	75 mL
¼ cup	shredded mozzarella or Italian-blend cheese, divided	60 mL
1 tbsp	grated Parmesan cheese	15 mL
2 tbsp	crushed garlic-seasoned croutons	30 mL
2 tsp	chopped fresh parsley	10 mL

1. In the mug, combine eggplant, oil and salt, tossing to coat. Microwave on High for 1½ to 2½ minutes or until tender. Let stand for 1 minute. Drain off excess liquid.

2. Stir in marinara sauce, half the mozzarella, and Parmesan. Sprinkle with remaining mozzarella. Microwave on High for 60 to 90 seconds or until heated through and cheese is melted. Sprinkle with croutons and parsley.

> **Prep Ahead Option**
> Combine the eggplant, oil and salt in the mug; cover and refrigerate. Measure the marinara sauce, half the mozzarella, and Parmesan into a small airtight container; cover and refrigerate. Measure the remaining mozzarella into a small airtight container; cover and refrigerate. Measure the croutons and parsley into a small airtight container; cover and refrigerate until ready to use.

Portobello and Potato Casserole

Robust mushrooms, creamy Alfredo sauce and the heartiness of hash browns come together in this substantial mug casserole. A small salad (sure, you can put it in a mug to continue the theme) is perfect alongside.

Tip

The portobello mushroom can be replaced by $2/3$ cup (150 mL) sliced fresh white or other mushrooms or $1/2$ cup (125 mL) drained canned or jarred mushroom pieces.

♦ **16-oz (500 mL) mug**

1	large portobello mushroom, trimmed and coarsely chopped	1
1 cup	frozen diced hash brown potatoes	250 mL
$1/4$ cup	chopped drained jarred roasted red bell peppers	60 mL
1 tbsp	chopped green onions	15 mL
1 tbsp	grated Parmesan cheese	15 mL
3 tbsp	light Alfredo sauce	45 mL

1. In the mug, microwave mushroom and hash browns on High for $1^1/2$ to $2^1/2$ minutes or until vegetables are tender.

2. Stir in roasted peppers, green onions, Parmesan and Alfredo sauce. Microwave on High for 60 to 90 seconds (checking at 60) or until heated through. Stir.

Variation

• **Portobello and White Bean Casserole:** Omit the hash browns and decrease the cooking time in step 1 to 45 seconds. Add $3/4$ cup (175 mL) rinsed drained canned white beans (such as cannellini or great Northern) with the Alfredo sauce and increase the cooking time in step 2 to 60 to 75 seconds.

> **Prep Ahead Option**
>
> Measure the mushroom and hash browns into the mug; cover and refrigerate (decrease the cooking time in step 1 by 30 seconds). Measure the roasted peppers, green onions, Parmesan and Alfredo sauce into a small airtight container; cover and refrigerate until ready to use.

Spinach Saag Paneer

Paneer is a fresh, firm, white Indian cheese that is often cubed or crumbled into vegetarian dishes for a quick protein boost. It can be hard to find outside of Indian grocery stores, so I've included the option to use Mexican white cheese (queso blanco) or mild feta cheese.

Tips

Opt for bags, as opposed to boxes, of frozen chopped spinach, as it is easier to remove small amounts at a time.

If a frozen pepper and onion stir-fry blend isn't available, use $1/3$ cup (75 mL) mixed sliced fresh bell peppers and onions and, in step 1, cook for about 2 minutes or until vegetables are tender-crisp.

◆ **16-oz (500 mL) mug**

$1^1/_2$ cups	frozen chopped spinach	375 mL
$1/3$ cup	frozen sliced bell pepper and onion stir-fry blend	75 mL
1 tbsp	butter	15 mL
$1/_4$ tsp	ground cumin	1 mL
$1/_4$ tsp	ground ginger	1 mL
$1/_8$ tsp	salt	0.5 mL
$1/_8$ tsp	hot pepper sauce	0.5 mL
2 oz	paneer, queso blanco or mild feta cheese, cut into small cubes	60 g
1 tbsp	plain yogurt (regular or Greek)	15 mL

1. In the mug, microwave spinach and stir-fry blend on High for $1^1/_2$ to $2^1/_2$ minutes or until thawed and warm. Using the tines of a fork, press down firmly on the vegetables and drain off excess liquid.

2. Add butter to the mug and let stand for 1 minute to melt. Using a fork, stir in cumin, ginger, salt and hot pepper sauce, breaking up the spinach. Gently mix in cheese. Microwave on High for 30 to 40 seconds or until heated through. Serve dolloped with yogurt.

> **Prep Ahead Option**
> Measure the spinach and stir-fry blend into the mug; cover and refrigerate (decrease the cooking time in step 1 by 30 seconds). Measure the butter, cumin, ginger, salt and hot pepper sauce into a small airtight container; cover and refrigerate. Measure the cheese and yogurt into separate small airtight containers; cover and refrigerate until ready to use.

Tomato and Zucchini Crumble

This meaty yet meat-free mug — a filling mix of tomatoes, squash and white beans — gets a boost from a buttery toasted garlic topping.

Tips

An equal amount of frozen Italian-blend vegetables can be used in place of the zucchini. Microwave the vegetable blend for $1\frac{1}{2}$ to $2\frac{1}{2}$ minutes or until tender before adding the tomatoes and beans; drain off excess liquid. Add the tomatoes and beans and microwave for 45 to 60 seconds or until hot, then add the crouton topping.

Try replacing 2 tbsp (30 mL) of the crushed croutons with 2 tbsp (30 mL) toasted or roasted chopped almonds, walnuts or pecans.

Freeze the remaining tomatoes in a small sealable freezer bag. You can freeze the entire amount in one bag, or portion out $\frac{3}{4}$ cup (175 mL) per bag so that the tomatoes are recipe-ready. Be sure to label the bag with the contents. Store for up to 3 months. Defrost in the refrigerator or microwave before using.

♦ **16-oz (500 mL) mug**

1 tbsp	butter	15 mL
$\frac{1}{4}$ cup	crushed garlic-seasoned croutons	60 mL
1 tbsp	grated Parmesan cheese	15 mL
$\frac{3}{4}$ cup	canned diced tomatoes with Italian seasoning, with juice	175 mL
$\frac{3}{4}$ cup	diced zucchini or yellow summer squash	175 mL
$\frac{1}{3}$ cup	rinsed drained canned white beans (such as cannellini or great Northern)	75 mL

1. In the mug, microwave butter on High for 15 to 25 seconds or until melted. Using a fork, stir in croutons and Parmesan. Transfer to a small bowl or cup.

2. In the mug (no need to clean it), combine tomatoes, zucchini and beans. Microwave on High for $1\frac{1}{2}$ to 2 minutes (checking at $1\frac{1}{2}$) or until bubbling and zucchini is tender.

3. Sprinkle with crouton mixture. Microwave on High for 20 seconds. Let stand for 1 minute before eating.

> **Prep Ahead Option**
> Prepare through step 1 and transfer topping to a small airtight container; cover and store at room temperature. Measure the tomatoes, zucchini and beans into the mug; cover and refrigerate until ready to use.

Zucchini Lasagna

Lasagna is a classic Italian dish, but watch what happens when the noodles are replaced with tender slices of zucchini and amped up with plenty of ricotta and mozzarella. *Fantastico.*

Tip

Try adding $\frac{1}{4}$ tsp (1 mL) garlic powder and/ or $\frac{1}{4}$ tsp (1 mL) dried Italian seasoning to the ricotta cheese.

◆ **16-oz (500 mL) mug**

$\frac{1}{2}$	small zucchini, thinly sliced crosswise	$\frac{1}{2}$
6 tbsp	marinara sauce, divided	90 mL
$\frac{2}{3}$ cup	ricotta cheese, divided	150 mL
4 tbsp	drained canned or jarred mushroom pieces, divided	60 mL
6 tbsp	shredded mozzarella or Italian-blend cheese, divided	90 mL

1. Lay zucchini slices on a small plate. Microwave on High for 45 to 60 seconds or until slightly softened. Let stand for 2 to 3 minutes to cool. Drain off any liquid.

2. Spread 2 tbsp (30 mL) marinara sauce in the mug. Layer one-third of the zucchini slices on top. Using the back of a spoon, spread half the ricotta over the zucchini. Sprinkle with half the mushrooms and 2 tbsp (30 mL) mozzarella. Repeat layers. Layer remaining zucchini on top, followed by the remaining marinara sauce and mozzarella.

3. Cover with a small plate or saucer. Microwave on High for $1\frac{1}{2}$ to 2 minutes or until sauce is bubbling at the edges. Uncover and let stand for 2 minutes.

Variation

- **Sausage Zucchini Lasagna:** Before assembling lasagna, microwave 2 to 3 frozen cooked breakfast sausage links in the mug for 60 to 90 seconds or until warmed through. Remove to a plate and break apart with a fork. Replace the mushrooms with the sausage, adding half the sausage in each layer.

Prep Ahead Option
Prepare through step 1; cover and refrigerate until ready to use.

Lemon Gnocchi with Peas and Parmesan

Soft pillows of potato gnocchi are offset by the sweetness of green peas and the zing of lemon in this quick, creamy meal.

Tips

Look for shelf-stable gnocchi near other pastas in the Italian section of supermarkets.

Refrigerate or freeze the remaining gnocchi in a small sealable freezer bag. You can put the entire amount in one bag, or portion out 4 oz (113 g) per bag so that the gnocchi are recipe-ready. Be sure to label the bag with the contents. Refrigerate for up to 3 weeks or freeze for up to 3 months. Thaw frozen gnocchi in the refrigerator or microwave before using.

♦ **16-oz (500 mL) mug**

1 cup	water	250 mL
¼	package (16 oz/454 g) shelf-stable gnocchi	¼
¼ cup	frozen petite green peas	60 mL
2 tbsp	light Alfredo sauce	30 mL
¼ tsp	finely grated lemon zest	1 mL
1 tsp	freshly squeezed lemon juice	5 mL
2 tsp	grated Parmesan cheese	10 mL

1. In the mug, microwave water on High for 2 to 3 minutes or until boiling.

2. Carefully add gnocchi. Place in the microwave atop a doubled paper towel. Microwave on High for 2 to 3 minutes or until gnocchi float to the top.

3. Add peas and let stand for 30 seconds. Carefully pour water out of mug.

4. Stir in Alfredo sauce, lemon zest and lemon juice. Microwave on High for 30 to 60 seconds or until heated through. Sprinkle with Parmesan.

> **Prep Ahead Option**
> Measure the gnocchi into a small airtight container; cover and refrigerate. Measure the peas into a small airtight container; cover and refrigerate. Measure the Alfredo sauce, lemon zest and lemon juice into a small airtight container; cover and refrigerate. Measure the Parmesan into a small airtight container; cover and refrigerate until ready to use.

Gnocchi with Marinara, Olives and Basil

Briny olives, nutty cheese and herbaceous basil elevate store-bought gnocchi from good to grand (use your grandest mug).

Tips

Look for shelf-stable gnocchi near other pastas in the Italian section of supermarkets.

Refrigerate or freeze the remaining gnocchi in a small sealable freezer bag. You can put the entire amount in one bag, or portion out 4 oz (113 g) per bag so that the gnocchi are recipe-ready. Be sure to label the bag with the contents. Refrigerate for up to 3 weeks or freeze for up to 3 months. Thaw frozen gnocchi in the refrigerator or microwave before using.

♦ 16-oz (500 mL) mug

1 cup	water	250 mL
¼	package (16 oz/454 g) shelf-stable gnocchi	¼
1 tbsp	thinly sliced fresh basil	15 mL
2 tbsp	marinara sauce	30 mL
1 tbsp	coarsely chopped drained brine-cured or green olives	15 mL
1 tsp	olive oil	5 mL
1 tbsp	grated Parmesan cheese	15 mL

1. In the mug, microwave water on High for 2 to 3 minutes or until boiling.

2. Carefully add gnocchi. Place in the microwave atop a doubled paper towel. Microwave on High for 2 to 3 minutes or until gnocchi float to the top. Carefully pour water out of mug.

3. Stir in basil, marinara sauce, olives and oil. Microwave on High for 30 to 60 seconds or until heated through. Sprinkle with Parmesan.

> **Prep Ahead Option**
>
> Measure the gnocchi into a small airtight container; cover and refrigerate. Measure the basil, marinara sauce, olives and oil into a small airtight container; cover and refrigerate. Measure the Parmesan into a small airtight container; cover and refrigerate until ready to use.

Gnocchi with Mushrooms and Sage

Mushrooms, cloaked in sage-scented Alfredo sauce, add both complexity and comfort to the tender gnocchi in this mug.

Tips

Look for shelf-stable gnocchi near other pastas in the Italian section of supermarkets.

Refrigerate or freeze the remaining gnocchi in a small sealable freezer bag. You can put the entire amount in one bag, or portion out 4 oz (113 g) per bag so that the gnocchi are recipe-ready. Be sure to label the bag with the contents. Refrigerate for up to 3 weeks or freeze for up to 3 months. Thaw frozen gnocchi in the refrigerator or microwave before using.

♦ **16-oz (500 mL) mug**

1 cup	water	250 mL
1/4	package (16 oz/454 g) shelf-stable gnocchi	1/4
3 tbsp	drained canned or jarred mushroom pieces	45 mL
3 tbsp	light Alfredo sauce	45 mL
1/8 tsp	dried rubbed sage	0.5 mL
1 tbsp	grated Parmesan cheese	15 mL

1. In the mug, microwave water on High for 2 to 3 minutes or until boiling.

2. Carefully add gnocchi. Place in the microwave atop a doubled paper towel. Microwave on High for 2 to 3 minutes or until gnocchi float to the top. Carefully pour water out of mug.

3. Stir in mushrooms, Alfredo sauce and sage. Microwave on High for 30 to 60 seconds or until heated through. Sprinkle with Parmesan.

> **Prep Ahead Option**
> Measure the gnocchi into a small airtight container; cover and refrigerate. Measure the mushrooms, Alfredo sauce and sage into a small airtight container; cover and refrigerate. Measure the Parmesan into a small airtight container; cover and refrigerate until ready to use.

Gnocchi with Creamy Pumpkin Sauce

The combination of pumpkin, thyme and Parmesan cheese makes an ideal foil for pillowy, ready-to-use gnocchi.

Tips

Look for shelf-stable gnocchi near other pastas in the Italian section of supermarkets.

Refrigerate or freeze the remaining gnocchi in a small sealable freezer bag. You can put the entire amount in one bag, or portion out 4 oz (113 g) per bag so that the gnocchi are recipe-ready. Be sure to label the bag with the contents. Refrigerate for up to 3 weeks or freeze for up to 3 months. Thaw frozen gnocchi in the refrigerator or microwave before using.

♦ **16-oz (500 mL) mug**

1 cup	water	250 mL
$\frac{1}{4}$	package (16 oz/454 g) shelf-stable gnocchi	$\frac{1}{4}$
$1\frac{1}{2}$ tbsp	light Alfredo sauce	22 mL
2 tsp	pumpkin purée (not pie filling)	10 mL
$\frac{1}{8}$ tsp	dried thyme	0.5 mL
1 tbsp	grated Parmesan cheese	15 mL

1. In the mug, microwave water on High for 2 to 3 minutes or until boiling.
2. Carefully add gnocchi. Place in the microwave atop a doubled paper towel. Microwave on High for 2 to 3 minutes or until gnocchi float to the top. Carefully pour water out of mug.
3. Stir in Alfredo sauce, pumpkin and thyme. Microwave on High for 30 to 60 seconds or until heated through. Sprinkle with Parmesan.

> **Prep Ahead Option**
>
> Measure the gnocchi into a small airtight container; cover and refrigerate. Measure the Alfredo sauce, pumpkin and thyme into a small airtight container; cover and refrigerate. Measure the Parmesan into a small airtight container; cover and refrigerate until ready to use.

Warm Lentils Vinaigrette

My husband lived in Paris for a year while he was a graduate student and swears that the majority of his diet was lentils (supplemented with coffee and pastries). This lentil dish is right up his alley — *très simple* and *très français*.

Tips

If available, you can use vacuum-packed lentils in place of canned ones. They are typically found in the produce section, near the tofu products.

You can use ⅓ cup (75 mL) canned diced tomatoes, with juice, in place of the plum tomato.

Canned white beans or chickpeas can be used in place of the lentils.

♦ **16-oz (500 mL) mug**

⅓ cup	frozen pearl onions, or fresh or frozen chopped onions	75 mL
1 cup	rinsed drained canned lentils	250 mL
⅛ tsp	dried thyme or Italian seasoning	0.5 mL
1 tbsp	olive oil	15 mL
1 tsp	balsamic or red wine vinegar	5 mL
⅛ tsp	prepared mustard (preferably Dijon or coarse-grain)	0.5 mL
1	small plum (Roma) tomato, chopped	1
1 tbsp	chopped fresh parsley	15 mL

1. In the mug, microwave onions on High for 60 to 90 seconds or until heated through.

2. Stir in lentils, thyme, oil, vinegar and mustard. Microwave on High for $1\frac{1}{2}$ to 2 minutes or until heated through. Stir in tomato and parsley.

> **Prep Ahead Option**
> Measure the onions into the mug; cover and refrigerate. Measure the lentils, thyme, oil, vinegar and mustard into a small airtight container; cover and refrigerate. Measure the tomato and parsley into a small airtight container; cover and refrigerate until ready to use.

Spiced Lentils with Yogurt, Almonds and Mint

Zesty tomatoes and chiles, warm spices and earthy lentils are the stars of this lively vegetarian mug. A trio of toppings — yogurt, almonds and fresh mint — heightens the wow factor.

Tips

If available, you can use vacuum-packed lentils in place of canned ones. They are typically found in the produce section, near the tofu products.

Canned black beans or pinto beans can be used in place of the lentils.

An equal amount of chopped fresh parsley or cilantro, or minced fresh chives, can be used in place of the mint.

Freeze the remaining tomatoes in a small sealable freezer bag for future use. Be sure to label the bag with the contents. Store for up to 3 months. Defrost in the refrigerator or microwave before using.

◆ 16-oz (500 mL) mug

1 cup	rinsed drained canned lentils	250 mL
1/2	can (10 oz/285 mL) diced tomatoes with green chiles, with juice	1/2
1/2 tsp	ground cumin	2 mL
1/4 tsp	ground ginger	1 mL
1/8 tsp	hot pepper sauce	0.5 mL
1 tbsp	plain Greek yogurt	15 mL
1 tbsp	chopped roasted salted almonds	15 mL
2 tsp	chopped fresh mint	10 mL

Suggested Accompaniment
Warm naan, pita or flour tortilla

1. In the mug, combine lentils, tomatoes, cumin, ginger and hot pepper sauce.
2. Microwave on High for $1\frac{1}{2}$ to $2\frac{1}{2}$ minutes or until hot. Top with yogurt and sprinkle with almonds and mint. Serve with a suggested accompaniment, if desired.

> **Prep Ahead Option**
> Combine the lentils, tomatoes, cumin, ginger and hot pepper sauce in the mug; cover and refrigerate. Measure the yogurt, almonds and mint into a small airtight container; cover and refrigerate until ready to use.

Koshari

Koshari is to Egyptians what chili is to Americans. Made of lentils, rice, pasta, tomato sauce and a kick of spice, it is a fast-food staple offered by street vendors in cities such as Cairo. To streamline the dish for a microwave mug meal, I've combined the rice and pasta into one ingredient by using orzo (small rice-shaped pasta).

Tips

If available, you can use vacuum-packed lentils in place of canned ones. They are typically found in the produce section, near the tofu products.

Feta cheese is similar to the Egyptian cheese *gibna beida*, a traditional topping for koshari.

♦ **16-oz (500 mL) mug**

⅓ cup	orzo	75 mL
⅔ cup	water	150 mL
½ cup	rinsed drained canned lentils	125 mL
¼ tsp	ground cumin	1 mL
½ cup	chunky marinara sauce	125 mL
⅛ tsp	hot pepper sauce	0.5 mL

Suggested Accompaniments

Chopped fresh mint or parsley; crumbled feta cheese

1. In the mug, combine orzo and water. Place in the microwave atop a doubled paper towel. Microwave on High for 2 minutes. Stir. Microwave on High for 3 minutes. If the mixture appears dry, add 1 tbsp (15 mL) water to the mug. Microwave on High for 1 to 2 minutes or until orzo is tender.

2. Stir in lentils, cumin, marinara sauce and hot pepper sauce. Microwave on High for 60 to 75 seconds or until heated through. Serve with any of the suggested accompaniments, as desired.

Prep Ahead Option

Measure the orzo into the mug; cover and store at room temperature. Measure the lentils, cumin, marinara sauce and hot pepper sauce into a small airtight container; cover and refrigerate until ready to use.

Butternut Squash and Black Bean Mug

A bit of tangy yogurt and fresh green onions stealthily round out the interplay of sweet and umami in this simple (and simply delicious) combination of butternut squash and black beans.

Tips

Look for bags of ready-to-use diced butternut squash in the produce section. Leftover squash can be frozen in airtight containers or plastic bags for up to 3 months.

An equal amount of finely diced sweet potatoes can be used in place of the squash.

Freeze the remaining beans in a small sealable freezer bag. You can freeze the entire amount in one bag, or portion out 1/2 cup (125 mL) per bag so that the beans are recipe-ready. Be sure to label the bag with the contents. Store for up to 3 months. Defrost in the refrigerator or microwave before using.

♦ 16-oz (500 mL) mug

3/4 cup	ready-to-use fresh or frozen diced butternut squash	175 mL
1/4 cup	ready-to-use vegetable broth or water	60 mL
1/2 cup	rinsed drained canned black beans	125 mL
3 tbsp	salsa	45 mL
1/4 tsp	ground cumin or chili powder	1 mL
1 tbsp	plain Greek yogurt	15 mL
1 tbsp	chopped green onions or chopped fresh cilantro	15 mL

1. In the mug, combine squash and broth. Cover with a small plate or saucer. Microwave on High for 4 to 8 minutes or until squash is tender.

2. Stir in beans, salsa and cumin. Microwave, uncovered, on High for 45 to 75 seconds or until heated through. Top with yogurt and sprinkle with green onions.

Prep Ahead Option

Combine the squash and broth in the mug; cover and refrigerate. Measure the beans, salsa and cumin into a small airtight container; cover and refrigerate. Measure the yogurt and green onions into a small airtight container; cover and refrigerate until ready to use.

Unstuffed Pepper Mug

Stuffing normally appears inside bell peppers, but here the two are mixed together in one easy mugful. A savory mixture of rice and black beans lends textural contrast to the rustic roasted peppers, and seasoned tomatoes jazz up the flavor.

Tips

You can use $2/3$ cup (150 mL) cooked brown rice (or any other cooked grain, such as quinoa, barley or bulgur) in place of the instant brown rice. Omit the water and all of step 1. Add the cooked rice with the roasted peppers.

Canned lentils, white beans or chickpeas can be used in place of the black beans.

Freeze the remaining beans and tomatoes in separate small sealable freezer bags. You can freeze the entire amount in one bag, or portion out $1/2$ cup (125 mL) per bag so that the beans and tomatoes are recipe-ready. Be sure to label the bags with the contents. Store for up to 3 months. Defrost in the refrigerator or microwave before using.

♦ **16-oz (500 mL) mug**

$1/3$ cup	instant brown rice	75 mL
$2/3$ cup	water	150 mL
$1/2$ cup	coarsely chopped drained jarred roasted red bell peppers	125 mL
$1/2$ cup	rinsed drained canned black beans	125 mL
$1/2$ cup	canned diced tomatoes with Italian seasoning, with juice	125 mL
1 tbsp	chopped fresh parsley (optional)	15 mL
	Salt and ground black pepper	
$1/3$ cup	shredded Italian-blend or Cheddar cheese	75 mL

1. In the mug, combine rice and water. Cover with a small plate or saucer and microwave on High for 5 to 6 minutes or until rice is tender. Remove from oven and let stand, covered, for 1 minute to absorb water.

2. Stir in roasted peppers, beans, tomatoes and parsley (if using). Season to taste with salt and pepper. Microwave, uncovered, on High for 30 seconds or until heated through.

3. Sprinkle with cheese. Microwave on High for 25 to 30 seconds or until cheese is melted. Let stand for 30 seconds before eating.

Prep Ahead Option

Measure the rice into the mug; cover and store at room temperature. Measure the roasted peppers, beans, tomatoes and parsley (if using) into a small airtight container; cover and refrigerate. Measure the cheese into a small airtight container; cover and refrigerate until ready to use.

Egyptian Beans with Zucchini (*Ful Medames*)

Ful medames is a traditional Egyptian stew (arguably the national stew) made with fava beans, vegetables, garlic, lemon juice and olive oil. It is typically served for breakfast, but you can choose to eat it at any time of day.

Tips

Canned cannellini (white kidney) beans can be used in place of the fava beans.

Freeze the remaining beans and tomatoes in separate small sealable freezer bags. You can freeze the entire amount in one bag, or portion out $3/4$ cup (175 mL) per bag (for the beans) or $1/3$ cup (75 mL) per bag (for the tomatoes) so that they are recipe-ready. Be sure to label the bags with the contents. Store for up to 3 months. Defrost in the refrigerator or microwave before using.

◆ 16-oz (500 mL) mug

$1/2$ cup	diced zucchini	125 mL
2 tsp	olive oil	10 mL
Pinch	salt	Pinch
$3/4$ cup	rinsed drained canned fava beans, lightly mashed with a fork	175 mL
$1/3$ cup	canned diced tomatoes with green chiles, with juice	75 mL
$1/4$ tsp	ground cumin	1 mL
$1/8$ tsp	garlic powder	0.5 mL
1 tsp	lemon juice	5 mL
$1/4$ tsp	hot pepper sauce	1 mL
	Salt and ground black pepper	
2 tsp	chopped fresh mint or cilantro	10 mL

Suggested Accompaniments

Chopped or sliced hard-cooked egg; plain regular or Greek yogurt

1. In the mug, combine zucchini, oil and salt. Microwave on High for $1^1/2$ to $2^1/2$ minutes or until zucchini is tender.

2. Stir in beans, tomatoes, cumin, garlic powder, lemon juice and hot pepper sauce. Microwave on High for 1 to 2 minutes or until heated through. Season to taste with salt and pepper, and sprinkle with mint. Serve with any of the suggested accompaniments, as desired.

> **Prep Ahead Option**
>
> Combine the zucchini, oil and salt in the mug; cover and refrigerate. Measure the beans, tomatoes, cumin, garlic powder, lemon juice and hot pepper sauce into a small airtight container; cover and refrigerate. Measure the mint into a small airtight container; cover and refrigerate until ready to use.

Moroccan Date and Chickpea Tagine

You might think a dish with a name like this is far too fussy and time-consuming for a weeknight meal. Think again. In less than 5 minutes, you can capture the juicy flavors of Morocco in your mug.

Tips

Canned white beans (such as cannellini or great Northern) can be used in place of the chickpeas.

Freeze the remaining chickpeas and tomatoes in separate small sealable freezer bags. You can freeze the entire amount in one bag, or portion out 1 cup (250 mL) per bag (for the chickpeas) or ½ cup (125 mL) per bag (for the tomatoes) so that they are recipe-ready. Be sure to label the bags with the contents. Store for up to 3 months. Defrost in the refrigerator or microwave before using.

♦ **16-oz (500 mL) mug**

2 tsp	olive oil	10 mL
⅛ tsp	ground cumin	0.5 mL
⅛ tsp	pumpkin pie spice	0.5 mL
2	whole pitted dates, chopped	2
1 cup	rinsed drained canned chickpeas	250 mL
½ cup	diced canned tomatoes with Italian seasoning, with juice	125 mL
1 tbsp	chopped fresh mint or cilantro	15 mL
2 tsp	lemon juice	10 mL
	Salt and ground black pepper	

Suggested Accompaniments

Plain Greek yogurt; warm naan, pita or flour tortilla; hot cooked couscous

1. In the mug, combine oil, cumin and pumpkin pie spice. Microwave on High for 15 to 30 seconds or until fragrant.

2. Stir in dates, chickpeas and tomatoes. Microwave on High for 1½ to 2½ minutes or until heated through. Stir in mint and lemon juice. Season to taste with salt and pepper. Serve with any of the suggested accompaniments, as desired.

> **Prep Ahead Option**
>
> Combine the oil, cumin and pumpkin pie spice in the mug; cover and refrigerate. Measure the dates, chickpeas and tomatoes into a small airtight container; cover and refrigerate. Measure the mint and lemon juice into separate small airtight containers; cover and refrigerate until ready to use.

Chickpea Potato Masala

A bit of butter adds silky richness to this South Indian–style mug meal.

Tips

Frozen hash browns with onions and peppers are often labeled "O'Brien" potatoes.

Use any heat level of curry powder — mild, medium or hot — according to your taste.

An equal amount of virgin coconut oil can be used in place of the butter.

Freeze the remaining chickpeas in a small sealable freezer bag. You can freeze the entire amount in one bag, or portion out ⅔ cup (150 mL) per bag so that the chickpeas are recipe-ready. Be sure to label the bag with the contents. Store for up to 3 months. Defrost in the refrigerator or microwave before using.

♦ **16-oz (500 mL) mug**

⅔ cup	frozen diced hash brown potatoes with onions and peppers	150 mL
⅔ cup	rinsed drained canned chickpeas	150 mL
3 tbsp	thick and chunky salsa	45 mL
1 tbsp	butter	15 mL
¾ tsp	curry powder	3 mL
1 tsp	lime juice	5 mL
	Salt and ground black pepper	

Suggested Accompaniments

Plain Greek or regular yogurt; chopped fresh cilantro; golden or dark raisins; warm naan, pita or flour tortilla

1. In the mug, microwave hash browns on High for 1½ to 2 minutes or until warmed through.

2. Stir in chickpeas, salsa, butter and curry powder. Microwave on High for 1½ to 2 minutes or until hot. Stir in lime juice. Season to taste with salt and pepper. Serve with any of the suggested accompaniments, as desired.

Prep Ahead Option

Measure the hash browns into the mug; cover and refrigerate (decrease the cooking time in step 1 by 30 seconds). Measure the chickpeas, salsa, butter and curry powder into a small airtight container; cover and refrigerate. Measure the lime juice into a small airtight container; cover and refrigerate until ready to use.

Marinara Chickpeas with Poached Egg and Feta

A poached egg centerpiece gives some extra protein to this hearty, no-fuss, high-flavor meal.

Tips

For an egg with a firm yolk, microwave on High for 1 minute.

The microwave will cook the yolk faster than the white. If you prefer a runnier yolk, stop cooking when the white is not quite set (it will continue to firm up from the heat of the chickpea mixture).

Canned white beans or lentils can be used in place of the chickpeas.

An equal amount of grated Parmesan cheese can be used in place of the feta.

Freeze the remaining chickpeas in a small sealable freezer bag. You can freeze the entire amount in one bag, or portion out ½ cup (125 mL) per bag so that the chickpeas are recipe-ready. Be sure to label the bag with the contents. Store for up to 3 months. Defrost in the refrigerator or microwave before using.

◆ **16-oz (500 mL) mug**

½ cup	rinsed drained canned chickpeas	125 mL
½ cup	thick and chunky marinara sauce	125 mL
1	large egg	1
	Salt and ground black pepper	
2 tbsp	crumbled feta cheese	30 mL
2 tsp	chopped fresh parsley	10 mL

Suggested Accompaniment
Crusty bread

1. In the mug, combine chickpeas and marinara sauce. Microwave on High for 60 to 75 seconds or until just heated through.

2. Make a well in the center of the mixture and carefully crack the egg into the well, being careful not to break the yolk. Cover with a small plate or saucer. Microwave on Medium-High (70%) for 60 seconds. Check the egg white to see if it is just barely set. If not, microwave on High for 15 to 30 seconds or until the white is just set. Season egg to taste with salt and pepper. Sprinkle with feta and parsley. Serve with crusty bread, if desired.

> **Prep Ahead Option**
> Combine the chickpeas and marinara sauce in the mug; cover and refrigerate. Measure the feta and parsley into separate small airtight containers; cover and refrigerate until ready to use.

Quiche in a Mug

Seasoned croutons, stirred right into the egg custard, make the "crust" for this easy quiche, while cream cheese adds instant decadence.

Tips

Either brick-style or soft tub-style cream cheese may be used.

Cottage cheese, ricotta cheese or garlic-and-herb-flavored spreadable cheese may be used in place of the cream cheese.

Any variety of small croutons can be used. If the croutons are unseasoned, add a pinch of salt to the egg mixture.

Crusty bread or a bagel can be torn or cut into small pieces and used in place of the croutons.

♦ **12- to 16-oz (375 to 500 mL) mug**

1	large egg	1
2 tbsp	milk	30 mL
⅛ tsp	Dijon or coarse-grain mustard	0.5 mL
Pinch	ground black pepper	Pinch
2 tbsp	small garlic-seasoned croutons	30 mL
2 tbsp	plain cream cheese, cut into small bits	30 mL
2 tsp	finely chopped fresh chives or green onions (optional)	10 mL
Pinch	dried thyme (optional)	Pinch

1. In the mug, use a fork to whisk egg, milk, mustard and pepper until blended. Stir in croutons, cream cheese, chives (if using) and thyme (if using). Let stand for 1 minute.

2. Microwave on High for 60 to 90 seconds (checking at 60) or until just set.

Variations

- **Tomato Basil Quiche:** Omit the chives and thyme. Add 3 tbsp (45 mL) diced cherry tomatoes or plum (Roma) tomato and 2 tsp (10 mL) sliced fresh basil or ⅛ tsp (0.5 mL) dried basil.

- **Mushroom Quiche:** Add 1 tbsp (15 mL) drained canned or jarred mushroom pieces with the croutons.

Prep Ahead Option

Whisk the egg, milk, mustard and pepper in the mug, then stir in cream cheese, chives (if using) and thyme (if using); cover and refrigerate. Measure the croutons into a small airtight container; cover and store at room temperature until ready to use.

Chile Rellenos Mug Casserole

This riff on chile rellenos uses diced green chiles (as opposed to whole), delivering the great flavor of the classic dish with mug-and-spoon simplicity.

Tip

Freeze the remaining green chiles in a small sealable freezer bag for future use. Be sure to label the bag with the contents. Store for up to 3 months. Defrost in the refrigerator or microwave before using.

♦ **16-oz (500 mL) mug**

2	large eggs	2
1 tbsp	all-purpose flour	15 mL
1/4 tsp	baking powder	1 mL
1/4 tsp	ground cumin	1 mL
1/4 cup	cottage cheese	60 mL
1/8 tsp	hot pepper sauce	0.5 mL
1/2	can (4 1/2 oz/127 mL) diced green chiles	1/2
1/3 cup	shredded Cheddar or Monterey Jack cheese	75 mL

Suggested Accompaniments

Salsa; sour cream or plain Greek yogurt; chopped fresh cilantro or green onions

1. In the mug, use a fork to beat eggs until blended. Beat in flour, baking powder, cumin, cottage cheese and hot pepper sauce until blended. Stir in chiles and Cheddar.

2. Microwave on High for 1 1/2 to 2 minutes (checking at 1 1/2) or until puffed and just set at the center. Serve with any of the suggested accompaniments, as desired.

Variation

• **Roasted Pepper Goat Cheese Casserole:** Replace the cumin with an equal amount of dried Italian seasoning, replace the green chiles with 1/3 cup (75) drained chopped jarred roasted red bell peppers, and replace the Cheddar cheese with 3 tbsp (45 mL) crumbled goat cheese or feta cheese.

Prep Ahead Option

Beat the eggs in the mug, then beat in cottage cheese, hot pepper sauce, chiles and Cheddar; cover and refrigerate. Measure the flour, baking powder and cumin into a small airtight container; cover and store at room temperature until ready to use.

Spanish Tortilla

Tortilla Española, a thick omelet made with fried potatoes, onions and eggs, is the most commonly served dish in Spain. Here, kettle-cooked potato chips stand in for the fried potatoes, with *muy delicioso* results.

Tips

Although this is best with kettle-cooked potato chips, regular potato chips can be used in their place.

Add instant flavor and variety by choosing flavored potato chips, such as jalapeño, Parmesan or chipotle.

♦ **12- to 16-oz (375 to 500 mL) mug**

2	large eggs	2
1 cup	kettle-cooked potato chips, coarsely crushed	250 mL
1 tbsp	chopped green onions (optional)	15 mL
	Hot pepper sauce or ground black pepper	

1. In the mug, use a fork to whisk eggs until blended. Stir in potato chips and green onions (if using). Season with hot pepper sauce. Let stand for 1 minute.
2. Microwave on High for 45 to 90 seconds (checking at 45) or until eggs are just set.

Variation

• **Sweet Potato Spanish Tortilla:** Use sweet potato chips in place of the potato chips.

> **Prep Ahead Option**
>
> Whisk the eggs in the mug; cover and refrigerate. Measure the potato chips and green onions (if using) into a small airtight container; cover and store at room temperature until ready to use.

Korean Vegetable Puff (*Pa Jeon*)

Literally translating as "green onion pancakes," *pa jeon* are a beloved Korean dish that can be eaten as a snack or a full meal.

Tip

Consider the vegetables in this dish (other than the green onions) entirely variable; the beauty of *pa jeon* is that it is perfect for using up bits and pieces of whatever vegetables you have on hand.

♦ **16-oz (500 mL) mug**

1	large egg	1
1½ tbsp	water	22 mL
½ tsp	toasted sesame oil or vegetable oil	2 mL
⅛ tsp	hot pepper sauce	0.5 mL
2 tbsp	all-purpose flour	30 mL
⅛ tsp	salt	0.5 mL
2 tbsp	chopped green onions	30 mL
2 tbsp	shredded carrots	30 mL
2 tbsp	drained canned or jarred mushroom pieces	30 mL

Suggested Accompaniment
Teriyaki sauce or soy sauce

1. In the mug, use a fork to beat egg, water, oil and hot pepper sauce until blended. Beat in flour and salt until blended and smooth. Stir in green onions, carrots and mushrooms.

2. Microwave on High for 75 to 90 seconds (checking at 75) or until puffed and just set at the center. Serve with a suggested accompaniment, if desired.

> **Prep Ahead Option**
> Beat the egg, water, oil and hot pepper sauce in the mug; cover and refrigerate. Measure the flour and salt into a small airtight container; cover and store at room temperature. Measure the green onions, carrots and mushrooms into a small airtight container; cover and refrigerate until ready to use.

Mu Shu Mug

Mu shu dishes appear on almost every Chinese takeout menu, but it's extremely satisfying to be able to make a faster, healthier version in the microwave.

Tips

Look for bags of precut coleslaw mix in the produce section, with the bagged salads.

Look for jars of hoisin sauce in the Asian foods section, near the soy sauce.

For a higher-protein meal, add up to $1/3$ cup (75 mL) diced tempeh or drained firm tofu with the mushrooms.

♦ 16-oz (500 mL) mug

$1\frac{1}{2}$ cups	cut coleslaw mix (shredded cabbage and carrots)	375 mL
1 tsp	water	5 mL
$\frac{1}{4}$ cup	drained canned or jarred mushroom pieces	60 mL
2 tbsp	thinly sliced green onions	30 mL
2 tsp	hoisin sauce	10 mL
$\frac{1}{2}$ tsp	toasted sesame oil (optional)	2 mL
1	large egg, lightly beaten	1

Suggested Accompaniments

Warm flour tortilla; additional hoisin sauce

1. In the mug, combine coleslaw mix and water. Cover with a small plate or saucer. Microwave on High for 60 to 90 seconds or until cabbage is wilted. Drain off excess water.

2. Stir in mushrooms, green onions, hoisin sauce and oil (if using).

3. Push cabbage mixture to one side of the mug and pour egg into the other side. Microwave, uncovered, on High for 20 to 40 seconds (checking at 20) or until egg is just set. Break up egg with fork, mixing it in with the cabbage mixture. Let stand for 30 seconds. Serve with any of the suggested accompaniments, as desired.

> **Prep Ahead Option**
>
> Measure the coleslaw mix into the mug; cover and refrigerate. Measure the mushrooms, green onions, hoisin sauce and oil (if using) into a small airtight container; cover and refrigerate until ready to use.

Black Pepper Tofu

Spiced with black pepper and ginger and coated in a gently sweet sauce, this satisfying tofu dish deserves its billing as a main course (especially if you make some instant brown rice on the side).

Tip

An equal amount of cubed tempeh can be used in place of the tofu.

♦ **16-oz (500 mL) mug**

2 tsp	packed dark brown sugar	10 mL
1/4 tsp	freshly cracked black pepper	1 mL
1/8 tsp	ground ginger	0.5 mL
1/8 tsp	garlic powder	0.5 mL
1 tbsp	soy sauce	15 mL
1/2 tsp	vegetable oil	2 mL
1 cup	diced drained firm or extra-firm tofu	250 mL
2 tbsp	chopped green onions	30 mL

1. In the mug, use a fork to whisk brown sugar, pepper, ginger, garlic powder, soy sauce and oil until blended. Microwave on High for 30 to 60 seconds (checking at 30) or until sugar is dissolved and mixture is hot.

2. Add tofu and green onions, gently tossing to coat. Microwave on High for 1 to $1\frac{1}{2}$ minutes (checking at 1) or until tofu is heated through.

Prep Ahead Option

Measure the brown sugar, pepper, ginger, garlic powder, soy sauce and oil into the mug; cover and refrigerate. Measure the tofu and green onions into a small airtight container; cover and refrigerate until ready to use.

Cashew Tofu with Cucumber

This quick-to-the-table tofu dish couldn't be simpler or more satisfying. Consider making a mug of brown rice to accompany it.

Tip

Chopped roasted almonds or peanuts can be used in place of the cashews.

♦ **12- to 16-oz (375 to 500 mL) mug**

1 tbsp	hoisin sauce	15 mL
1/2 tsp	toasted sesame oil or vegetable oil	2 mL
1 cup	diced drained firm or extra-firm tofu, pressed dry between paper towels	250 mL
1 1/2 tbsp	chopped roasted cashews	22 mL
1/3 cup	diced or shredded seeded peeled cucumber	75 mL

1. In the mug, use a fork to whisk hoisin sauce and oil until blended. Add tofu, gently tossing to coat.
2. Microwave on High for 1 to 1 1/2 minutes (checking at 1) or until tofu is heated through. Sprinkle with cashews and top with cucumber.

Variations

- **Cashew Tempeh with Cucumber:** Replace the tofu with an equal amount of diced tempeh.
- **Peanut Tofu with Pineapple:** Replace the cashews with chopped roasted peanuts, and replace the cucumber with 1/3 cup (75 mL) diced fresh, canned or thawed frozen pineapple tossed with 2 tsp (10 mL) minced fresh cilantro.

> **Prep Ahead Option**
> Prepare through step 1; cover and refrigerate. Measure the cashews into a small airtight container; cover and store at room temperature. Measure the cucumber into a small airtight container; cover and refrigerate until ready to use.

Tofu and Green Beans with Coconut Sauce

If you like coconut in savory dishes, you'll love this recipe. The sauce is rich with coconut flavor and packs just the right amount of heat and sweet.

Tips

Frozen snow peas or sugar snap peas can be used in place of the green beans.

An equal amount of cubed or crumbled tempeh can be used in place of the tofu.

Any other creamy nut or seed butter can be used in place of the peanut butter.

You can freeze extra coconut milk by placing 3 tbsp (45 mL) in each cavity of an ice cube tray. Once frozen, remove cubes from tray and store in an airtight container or freezer bag for up to 6 months. Defrost in the refrigerator or microwave.

♦ **16-oz (500 mL) mug**

¹⁄₂ cup	frozen cut green beans	125 mL
¹⁄₂ tsp	granulated sugar	2 mL
3 tbsp	well-stirred coconut milk (not coconut water)	45 mL
2 tsp	soy sauce	10 mL
1 tsp	creamy peanut butter	5 mL
1 tsp	lime juice	5 mL
¹⁄₈ tsp	hot pepper sauce	0.5 mL
1 cup	diced drained firm or extra-firm tofu	250 mL
2 tbsp	chopped drained jarred roasted red bell peppers	30 mL

Suggested Accompaniments

Chopped roasted peanuts; chopped fresh mint, basil or cilantro; warm flour tortilla

1. In the mug, microwave green beans on High for 1¹⁄₂ to 2 minutes or until heated through. Drain off excess liquid.

2. Stir in sugar, coconut milk, soy sauce, peanut butter, lime juice and hot pepper sauce. Let stand for 30 seconds to melt the peanut butter, then stir until blended.

3. Add tofu and roasted peppers, gently tossing to coat. Microwave on High for 1 to 1¹⁄₂ minutes (checking at 1) or until tofu is heated through. Serve with any of the suggested accompaniments, as desired.

> **Prep Ahead Option**
>
> Measure the green beans into the mug; cover and refrigerate (decrease the cooking time in step 1 to 60 seconds). Measure the sugar, coconut milk, soy sauce, peanut butter, lime juice, hot pepper sauce, tofu and peppers into a small airtight container; cover and refrigerate until ready to use.

Snow Peas and Tofu with Spicy Sauce

Favorite stir-fry ingredients — snow peas, tofu, sesame oil and ginger — join forces in this mug main dish, whose flavors belie its ease of preparation (and cleanup).

Tips

Frozen cut green beans or sugar snap peas can be used in place of the snow peas.

An equal amount of cubed or crumbled tempeh can be used in place of the tofu.

♦ **16-oz (500 mL) mug**

1/2 cup	frozen snow peas	125 mL
1/2 tsp	granulated sugar	2 mL
1/4 tsp	ground ginger	1 mL
2 tsp	soy sauce	10 mL
1/2 tsp	toasted sesame oil	2 mL
1/8 tsp	hot pepper sauce	0.5 mL
1 cup	diced drained firm or extra-firm tofu	250 mL

Suggested Accompaniments

Toasted sesame seeds; chopped fresh cilantro or green onions; warm flour tortilla; hot cooked instant brown rice

1. In the mug, microwave snow peas on High for $1^1/_2$ to 2 minutes or until heated through. Drain off excess liquid.

2. Stir in sugar, ginger, soy sauce, oil and hot pepper sauce. Add tofu, gently tossing to coat. Microwave on High for 1 to $1^1/_2$ minutes (checking at 1) or until tofu is heated through. Serve with any of the suggested accompaniments, as desired.

Prep Ahead Option

Measure the snow peas into the mug; cover and refrigerate (decrease the cooking time in step 1 to 60 seconds). Measure the sugar, ginger, soy sauce, oil, hot pepper sauce and tofu into a small airtight container; cover and refrigerate until ready to use.

Barbecued Tempeh and Peppers

Meaty tempeh stands up deliciously to spicy barbecue sauce, peppers and onions. Eat it straight from the mug or pile the finished dish on a bun or into a wrap for a satisfying sandwich.

Tips

If a frozen pepper and onion stir-fry blend isn't available, use $2/3$ cup (150 mL) mixed sliced fresh bell peppers and onions and, in step 1, cook for about 2 minutes or until vegetables are tender-crisp.

You can use $3/4$ cup (175 mL) diced drained firm or extra-firm tofu in place of the tempeh.

♦ **16-oz (500 mL) mug**

$2/3$ cup	frozen sliced bell pepper and onion stir-fry blend	150 mL
$1/2$	package (8 oz/227 g) tempeh, cut into strips	$1/2$ $1/2$
1 tbsp	thinly sliced green onions	15 mL
$1^{1}/2$ tbsp	barbecue sauce	22 mL

1. In the mug, microwave stir-fry blend on High for $1^{1}/2$ to 2 minutes or until heated through. Drain off excess liquid.
2. Stir in tempeh, green onions and barbecue sauce, gently tossing to coat. Microwave on High for 1 to $1^{1}/2$ minutes (checking at 1) or until tempeh is heated through. Stir.

Prep Ahead Option

Measure the stir-fry blend into the mug; cover and refrigerate (decrease the cooking time in step 1 by 30 seconds). Measure the tempeh, green onions (if using) and barbecue sauce into a small airtight container; cover and refrigerate until ready to use.

Tempeh Provençal

Fresh orange zest and piquant olives give sprightliness to the robust Mediterranean flavors of the tempeh, tomatoes and peppers.

Tip

You can use ¾ cup (175 mL) diced drained firm or extra-firm tofu in place of the tempeh.

♦ **16-oz (500 mL) mug**

½	package (8 oz/227 g) tempeh, diced or crumbled	½
2 tsp	olive oil	10 mL
	Salt and ground black pepper	
⅔ cup	chopped diced tomatoes with Italian seasoning, with juice	150 mL
¼ cup	coarsely chopped drained jarred roasted red bell peppers	60 mL
1 tbsp	sliced or chopped drained brine-cured olives	15 mL
⅛ tsp	finely grated orange or lemon zest	0.5 mL
	Sliced fresh basil or chopped fresh parsley (optional)	

Suggested Accompaniments

Crumbled goat cheese; crusty bread

1. In the mug, combine tempeh and oil. Season to taste with salt and pepper. Microwave on High for 45 to 60 seconds or until heated through.

2. Stir in tomatoes, roasted peppers, olives and orange zest. Microwave on High for 1 to 1½ minutes or until heated through. Sprinkle with basil, if desired. Serve with any of the suggested accompaniments, as desired.

Prep Ahead Option

Combine the tempeh and oil in the mug; cover and refrigerate. Measure the tomatoes, roasted peppers, olives and orange zest into a small airtight container; cover and refrigerate. Place the basil in a small airtight container; cover and refrigerate until ready to use.

Tempeh Bolognese

In this meatless take on bolognese, crumbled tempeh replaces the beef or veal to delicious effect.

Tips

You can use ¾ cup (175 mL) diced drained firm or extra-firm tofu in place of the tempeh.

Milk can be used in place of the cream, but the sauce will not be as rich.

♦ **16-oz (500 mL) mug**

3 tbsp	finely chopped carrot	45 mL
3 tbsp	finely chopped celery	45 mL
2 tsp	olive oil	10 mL
	Salt and ground black pepper	
½	package (8 oz/227 g) tempeh, crumbled	½
⅓ cup	thick and chunky marinara sauce	75 mL
1 tbsp	half-and-half (10%) cream	15 mL
	Chopped fresh parsley (optional)	

Suggested Accompaniments

Grated Parmesan cheese; crusty bread; hot cooked cut or broken spaghetti or macaroni

1. In the mug, combine carrot, celery and oil. Season to taste with salt and pepper. Microwave on High for $1\frac{1}{2}$ to $2\frac{1}{2}$ minutes or vegetables are very soft.

2. Stir in tempeh and marinara sauce. Microwave on High for 75 to 90 seconds or until tempeh is heated through. Stir in cream. Sprinkle with parsley, if desired. Serve with any of the suggested accompaniments, as desired.

> **Prep Ahead Option**
>
> Combine the carrot, celery and oil in the mug; cover and refrigerate. Measure the tempeh and marinara sauce into a small airtight container; cover and refrigerate. Place the cream and parsley (if using) in a small airtight container; cover and refrigerate until ready to use.

Spicy Tempeh and Vegetable "Stir-Fry"

A hearty mingling of sweet and spicy flavors, this Szechuan-inspired meal is reason enough to keep a package of tempeh in the refrigerator or freezer.

Tips

An equal amount of diced drained firm or extra-firm tofu can be used in place of the tempeh.

You can use any mix of frozen vegetables you prefer. If you have a small amount of several different types of frozen vegetables, this is a good recipe for using them up.

♦ **16-oz (500 mL) mug**

1 cup	frozen vegetable stir-fry blend	250 mL
1/4 tsp	packed brown sugar or granulated sugar	1 mL
1/8 tsp	garlic powder	0.5 mL
1/8 tsp	ground ginger	0.5 mL
2 tsp	soy sauce	10 mL
1/4 tsp	toasted sesame oil (optional)	1 mL
1/8 tsp	hot pepper sauce	0.5 mL
3/4 cup	diced tempeh	175 mL

1. In the mug, microwave stir-fry blend on High for $1\frac{1}{2}$ to 2 minutes or until vegetables are tender. Drain off excess liquid.

2. Stir in brown sugar, garlic powder, ginger, soy sauce, oil (if using) and hot pepper sauce. Stir in tempeh. Microwave on High for 45 seconds or until tempeh is heated through. Stir gently. Let stand for 1 minute before eating.

Prep Ahead Option

Measure the stir-fry blend into the mug; cover and refrigerate (decrease the cooking time in step 1 by 30 seconds). Measure the brown sugar, garlic powder, ginger, soy sauce, oil (if using) and hot pepper sauce into a small airtight container; cover and refrigerate. Measure the tempeh into a small airtight container; cover and refrigerate until ready to use.

Meat, Poultry and Seafood Main Dishes

Philly Cheesesteak Mug

Frozen peppers and onions, together with humble mushrooms and shredded cheese, turn deli roast beef into a mugful of deliciousness.

Tips

If a frozen pepper and onion stir-fry blend isn't available, use ³/₄ cup (175 mL) mixed sliced fresh bell peppers and onions and, in step 1, cook for about 2 minutes or until vegetables are tender-crisp.

If you prefer, scoop the mug mixture directly onto a roll or biscuit and eat as a sandwich.

◆ 16-oz (500 mL) mug

³/₄ cup	frozen sliced bell pepper and onion stir-fry blend	175 mL
2 oz	deli roast beef, thinly sliced into short strips	60 g
¹/₄ cup	drained canned or jarred sliced mushrooms	60 mL
2 tbsp	light Alfredo sauce	30 mL
¹/₄ tsp	dried Italian seasoning (optional)	1 mL
¹/₃ cup	shredded Italian-blend cheese	75 mL

Suggested Accompaniment
Breadsticks, crusty roll or biscuit

1. In the mug, microwave stir-fry blend on High for 1¹/₂ to 2 minutes or until heated through. Drain off excess liquid.

2. Stir in roast beef, mushrooms, Alfredo sauce and Italian seasoning (if using). Sprinkle with cheese. Microwave on High for 45 to 60 seconds or until cheese is melted and mixture is heated through. Serve with a suggested accompaniment, if desired.

Variations

- **Chicken Cheesesteak Mug:** Replace the roast beef with half a 5-oz (142 g) can of water-packed chunk chicken, drained and flaked.

- **Tempeh Cheesesteak Mug:** Replace the roast beef with 2 oz (60 g) tempeh, thinly sliced into short strips.

Prep Ahead Option

Measure the stir-fry blend into the mug; cover and refrigerate (decrease the cooking time in step 1 by 30 seconds). Measure the roast beef, mushrooms, Alfredo sauce and Italian seasoning (if using) into a small airtight container; cover and refrigerate. Measure the cheese into a small airtight container; cover and refrigerate until ready to use.

Picadillo

Picadillo is a savory Latin American dish of beef, onions and tomato, punctuated by olives and raisins. Here, it becomes a homey one-mug meal.

Tips

Another dried fruit (cranberries, chopped prunes, chopped apricots) can be used in place of the raisins.

Chopped ripe (black) olives can be used in place of the green olives.

♦ **16-oz (500 mL) mug**

4	frozen cooked beef meatballs	4
3 tbsp	salsa	45 mL
1 tbsp	sliced green olives with pimentos	15 mL
1 tbsp	raisins	15 mL
$\frac{1}{8}$ tsp	ground cinnamon	0.5 mL
$\frac{1}{8}$ tsp	ground cumin	0.5 mL

Suggested Accompaniments

Chopped fresh cilantro; chopped green onions; tortillas (corn or flour); tortilla chips

1. In the mug, microwave meatballs on High for 1 to 2 minutes or until completely warmed through. Break apart with a fork.
2. Stir in salsa, olives, raisins, cinnamon and cumin. Microwave on High for 30 to 45 seconds (checking at 30) or until heated through. Serve with any of the suggested accompaniments, as desired.

Variation

- **Vegetarian Picadillo:** Replace the meatballs with $\frac{2}{3}$ cup (150 mL) coarsely chopped tempeh or coarsely mashed rinsed drained canned black beans.

Prep Ahead Option

Place the meatballs in the mug; cover and refrigerate (decrease the cooking time in step 1 to 30 to 45 seconds). Measure the salsa, olives, raisins, cinnamon and cumin into a small airtight container; cover and refrigerate until ready to use.

Thai-Style Beef and Peppers Mug

Don't be intimidated by peanut butter in a main-dish mug. It mingles with the soy sauce, lime and curry paste to create an instant and eminently delicious sauce.

Tips

For a more authentic flavor, use an equal amount of Asian fish sauce (nam pla) in place of the soy sauce.

Any other nut or seed butter can be used in place of the peanut butter.

♦ 16-oz (500 mL) mug

4	frozen cooked beef meatballs	4
³⁄₄ cup	frozen stir-fry vegetable blend	175 mL
1 tbsp	creamy peanut butter	15 mL
2 tsp	soy sauce	10 mL
2 tsp	lime juice	10 mL
1 tsp	packed brown sugar	5 mL
1 tsp	Thai red curry paste or curry powder	5 mL

Suggested Accompaniments

Lettuce leaves; chopped fresh cilantro, mint or basil; chopped green onions; chopped roasted peanuts; flaked or shredded coconut

1. In the mug, microwave meatballs on High for 1 to 2 minutes or until completely warmed through. Transfer to a small bowl and break apart with a fork.

2. In the mug, microwave vegetable blend on High for 1¹⁄₂ to 2 minutes or until heated through. Drain off excess liquid.

3. Stir in peanut butter, soy sauce, lime juice, brown sugar and curry paste until blended. Stir in crumbled meatballs. Microwave on High for 45 to 60 seconds or until warmed through. Serve with any of the suggested accompaniments, as desired.

Variation

• **Thai-Style Chicken and Peppers Mug:** Replace the meatballs with a 5-oz (142 g) can of water-packed chunk chicken, drained and flaked.

Prep Ahead Option

Place the meatballs in the mug; cover and refrigerate (decrease the cooking time in step 1 to 30 to 45 seconds). Measure the vegetable blend into a small airtight container; cover and refrigerate (decrease the cooking time in step 2 by 30 seconds). Measure the peanut butter, soy sauce, lime juice, brown sugar and curry paste into a small airtight container; cover and refrigerate until ready to use.

Joe's Special

Joe's Special originates from New Joe's Italian restaurant on Broadway Street in San Francisco. Folklore has it that, back in the 1930s, a customer ordered a spinach omelet. It was late at night and he was especially hungry, so he asked the chef to add something extra to the dish. The chef added some hamburger and turned the dish into a scramble, and Joe's Special was born (and soon after, added to the menu). You'll undoubtedly add it to your list of favorites too.

Tips

Opt for bags, as opposed to boxes, of frozen chopped spinach, as it is easier to remove small amounts at a time.

Swap in another chopped frozen green (kale, mustard greens) for the spinach.

Three frozen cooked breakfast sausage links can be used in place of the meatballs.

♦ **16-oz (500 mL) mug**

3	frozen cooked beef meatballs	3
1 cup	frozen chopped spinach	250 mL
1	large egg	1
2 tbsp	chopped green onions	30 mL
1 tbsp	grated Parmesan cheese	15 mL
1/8 tsp	salt	0.5 mL
1/8 tsp	ground black pepper	0.5 mL
Pinch	ground nutmeg (optional)	Pinch

1. In the mug, microwave meatballs on High for 1 to 2 minutes or until completely warmed through. Transfer to a small bowl and break apart with a fork.

2. In the mug, microwave spinach on High for 1 to 2 minutes or until thawed and warm. Using the tines of a fork, press down firmly on the spinach and drain off excess liquid.

3. Stir in crumbled meatballs, egg, green onions, Parmesan, salt, pepper and nutmeg (if using). Microwave on High for 30 to 45 seconds (checking at 30) or until egg is just set.

Variations

- **Tomato Joe's Special:** Add 1/4 cup (60 mL) drained canned diced tomatoes with Italian seasoning with the egg.

- **Roasted Pepper Joe's Special:** Add 3 tbsp (45 mL) drained jarred roasted red bell peppers with the egg.

> **Prep Ahead Option**
> Place the meatballs in the mug; cover and refrigerate (decrease the cooking time in step 1 to 30 to 45 seconds). Measure the spinach into a small airtight container; cover and refrigerate (decrease the cooking time in step 2 to 30 to 45 seconds). Whisk the egg in a small airtight container, then add green onions, Parmesan, salt, pepper and nutmeg (if using); cover and refrigerate until ready to use.

Mug Meatloaf

Meatloaf is tried-and-true comfort food for families and crowds, but for something new, try this streamlined "loaf" for one. You can customize it any way you choose!

Tips

Ground pork, bison, turkey or chicken can be used in place of the beef.

Divide a 16-oz (454 g) package of ground beef into four equal portions. Wrap each portion in waxed paper, plastic wrap or parchment paper, then place in an airtight container or sealable food storage bag. Freeze for up to 3 months. Defrost each portion in the refrigerator or microwave as needed.

Finely crushed corn flakes, croutons or bread crumbs can be used in place of the oats.

♦ **12- to 16-oz (375 to 500 mL) mug**

4 oz	extra-lean ground beef	125 g
2 tbsp	quick-cooking rolled oats	30 mL
2 tbsp	chopped green onions	30 mL
2 tbsp	ketchup, divided	30 mL
1/8 tsp	salt	0.5 mL
1/8 tsp	ground black pepper	0.5 mL

1. In a small bowl, gently combine beef, oats, green onions, 1 tbsp (15 mL) ketchup, salt and pepper until just blended. Gently shape into a ball, without compacting the meat. Place in mug.

2. Place mug in the microwave atop a doubled paper towel. Microwave on Medium-High (70%) for 9 minutes. Cut into center of meatloaf; if still pink inside, microwave on Medium-High (70%) for 1 to 3 minutes or until no longer pink. Spread remaining ketchup over meatloaf and let stand for 2 minutes.

Variations

- **BBQ Meatloaf:** Replace the ketchup with barbecue sauce.
- **Salsa Meatloaf:** Replace the ketchup with salsa. Add 1/2 tsp (2 mL) chili powder and/or 1/4 tsp (1 mL) ground cumin with the salt.

> **Prep Ahead Option**
> Prepare through step 1; cover and refrigerate until ready to use.

Upside-Down Shepherd's Pie

Welcome the first chill of autumn with this easy, but still hearty, spin on shepherd's pie.

Tip

Freeze the remaining mixed vegetables and tomatoes in separate small sealable freezer bags. You can freeze the entire amount in one bag, or portion out 1/3 cup (75 mL) per bag so that the vegetables and tomatoes are recipe-ready. Be sure to label the bags with the contents. Store for up to 3 months. Defrost in the refrigerator or microwave before using.

Prep Ahead Option

Place the meatballs in the mug; cover and refrigerate (decrease the cooking time in step 1 to 30 to 45 seconds). Measure the vegetables and tomatoes into a small airtight container; cover and refrigerate. Measure the potato flakes, salt and pepper into a small airtight container; cover and store at room temperature. Measure the water and milk into a small airtight container; cover and refrigerate until ready to use.

♦ **16-oz (500 mL) mug**

4	frozen cooked beef meatballs	4
1/3 cup	drained canned mixed vegetables	75 mL
1/3 cup	canned diced tomatoes with Italian seasoning, with juice	75 mL
1/2 cup	instant potato flakes	125 mL
1/8 tsp	salt	0.5 mL
Pinch	ground black pepper	Pinch
1/2 cup	water	125 mL
1/4 cup	milk	60 mL
2 tsp	butter	10 mL
2 tbsp	shredded Cheddar cheese (optional)	30 mL

1. In the mug, microwave meatballs on High for 1 to 2 minutes or until completely warmed through. Transfer to a small bowl and break apart with a fork. Stir in vegetables and tomatoes.

2. Wipe out mug with paper towel. In the mug, use a fork to whisk potato flakes, salt, pepper, water and milk until blended. Add butter. Microwave on High for 60 to 90 seconds or until hot and just starting to bubble at edges. Stir. Microwave on High for 60 to 90 seconds (checking at 60) or until thickened but not dry.

3. Stir in cheese, if using. Spoon in meatball mixture. Microwave on High for 30 to 60 seconds or until warmed through.

Variations

- **Italian Shepherd's Pie:** Use 4 frozen cooked breakfast sausage links in place of the meatballs. Replace the Cheddar cheese with 1 tbsp (15 mL) grated Parmesan cheese.

- **Alfredo Shepherd's Pie:** Replace the tomatoes with 1/4 cup (60 mL) light Alfredo sauce.

Tamale Mug Pie

Here I've recreated one of my favorite comfort foods of childhood – tamale pie – into an ultra-easy mug meal.

♦ 16-oz (500 mL) mug

4	frozen cooked beef meatballs	4
1/4 cup	frozen corn kernels	60 mL
1/4 cup	salsa	60 mL
1/2 tsp	ground cumin or chili powder (optional)	2 mL
1/4 cup	dry buttermilk pancake mix	60 mL
2 tbsp	yellow cornmeal	30 mL
1	large egg	1
1 tbsp	milk	15 mL
2 tbsp	shredded Cheddar cheese (optional)	30 mL

Suggested Accompaniments

Sliced ripe olives; sour cream or plain Greek yogurt; additional salsa; shredded lettuce

1. In the mug, microwave meatballs on High for 1 to 2 minutes or until completely warmed through. Break apart with a fork.

2. Add corn, salsa and cumin (if using). Microwave on High for 30 to 60 seconds or until heated through. Stir.

3. In a small bowl, use a fork to whisk pancake mix, cornmeal, egg and milk until well blended. Stir in cheese (if using). Pour over meatball mixture in mug. Microwave on High for 75 to 90 seconds (checking at 75) or until puffed and just set at the center. Serve with any of the suggested accompaniments, as desired.

Variation

• **Vegetarian Tamale Mug Pie:** Replace the meatballs with 2/3 cup (150 mL) coarsely chopped tempeh or coarsely mashed rinsed drained canned black beans.

Shrimp, Sausage and Brown Rice Jambalaya (page 216)

Spinach, Chickpea and Feta Pasta (page 224)

Brown Rice with Edamame and Pineapple (page 238)

Chocolate Trail Mix Bark (page 255)

Spicy Thai Peanut Dip (page 264)

Double Lemon Cake (page 277)

Rice Pudding (page 296)

Brownie Batter Dip (page 300)

Beef Burrito Mug

Instead of drive-through tacos or mini-mart burritos, try this fantastic Tex-Mex mug instead. It's a perfect balancing act of all your favorite *taqueria* ingredients: beef, beans, rice, salsa, corn, cheese and any or all of the fixings you crave.

Tip

Freeze the remaining beans in a small sealable freezer bag. You can freeze the entire amount in one bag, or portion out ½ cup (125 mL) per bag so that the beans are recipe-ready. Be sure to label the bag with the contents. Store for up to 3 months. Defrost in the refrigerator or microwave before using.

Prep Ahead Option

Place the meatballs in the mug; cover and refrigerate (decrease the cooking time in step 1 to 30 to 45 seconds). Measure the rice into an airtight container; cover and store at room temperature. Measure the corn, beans, salsa and cumin (if using) into a small airtight container; cover and refrigerate (note that the corn will be added with the beans instead of being cooked with the rice). Measure cheese into an airtight container; cover and refrigerate until ready to use.

♦ **16-oz (500 mL) mug**

3	frozen cooked beef meatballs	3
¼ cup	instant brown rice	60 mL
½ cup	water	125 mL
¼ cup	frozen corn kernels	60 mL
½ cup	rinsed drained canned black beans or pinto beans	125 mL
¼ cup	salsa	60 mL
¼ tsp	ground cumin or chili powder (optional)	1 mL
3 tbsp	shredded Cheddar or Monterey Jack cheese	45 mL

Suggested Accompaniments

Chopped green onions; tortilla chips; light sour cream or plain Greek yogurt; chopped fresh cilantro

1. In the mug, microwave meatballs on High for 1 to 2 minutes or until completely warmed through. Transfer to a small bowl and break apart with a fork.

2. In the mug, combine rice and water. Top with corn. Cover with a small plate or saucer. Microwave on High for 5 to 6 minutes or until almost all the water has been absorbed. Remove from oven and let stand, covered, for 1 minute to absorb the remaining water.

3. Stir in crumbled meatballs, beans, salsa and cumin (if using). Microwave, uncovered, on High for 45 to 75 seconds or until heated through. Sprinkle with cheese. Cover with plate and let stand for 1 minute. Serve with any of the suggested accompaniments, as desired.

Variation

- **Chicken Burrito Mug:** Replace the meatballs with half a 5-oz (142 g) can of water-packed chunk chicken, drained and flaked.

Not-So-Sloppy Joe Mug

So long, sloppy; this version keeps the mess under control while maintaining the carefree ease of the original. The result is hearty, healthy (with red beans standing in for some of the meat) and delicious — perfect for a weeknight dinner.

Tips

If you prefer, you can use 2 additional frozen meatballs in place of the beans.

Freeze the remaining beans in a small sealable freezer bag. You can freeze the entire amount in one bag, or portion out ½ cup (125 mL) per bag so that the beans are recipe-ready. Be sure to label the bag with the contents. Store for up to 3 months. Defrost in the refrigerator or microwave before using.

Freeze the remaining tomatoes in a small sealable freezer bag. Be sure to label the bag with the contents. Store for up to 3 months. Defrost in the refrigerator or microwave before using.

♦ **16-oz (500 mL) mug**

3	frozen cooked beef meatballs	3
½ cup	rinsed drained canned red beans or kidney beans	125 mL
½	can (10 oz/284 mL) diced tomatoes with green chiles, with juice	½
1 tbsp	ketchup	15 mL
½ tsp	Worcestershire sauce	2 mL
¼ tsp	packed brown sugar	1 mL
¼ tsp	prepared mustard (yellow, Dijon or coarse-grain)	1 mL
	Shredded Cheddar or pepper Jack cheese (optional)	

1. In the mug, microwave meatballs on High for 1 to 2 minutes or until completely warmed through. Break apart with a fork.

2. Add beans, coarsely mashing them with the fork. Stir in tomatoes, ketchup, Worcestershire sauce, brown sugar and mustard until blended. Microwave on High for 60 to 75 seconds or until heated through. Top with cheese, if desired.

Variations

- **Sausage Joe:** Replace the meatballs with 4 frozen cooked breakfast sausage links.

- **Sloppy Joe Sandwich:** Spoon the prepared sloppy Joe mixture onto a bun, a roll, bread or a biscuit.

> **Prep Ahead Option**
> Place the meatballs in the mug; cover and refrigerate (decrease the cooking time in step 1 to 30 to 45 seconds). Measure the beans into a small airtight container; cover and refrigerate. Measure the tomatoes, ketchup, Worcestershire sauce, brown sugar and mustard into a small airtight container; cover and refrigerate until ready to use.

Sausage, White Bean and Rosemary Mug

This mugful of comfort food is so versatile. You can use crumbled breakfast sausage or diced ham in place of the smoked sausage, stir in some goat cheese and pesto in place of the Parmesan and parsley, or swap chickpeas or butter (lima) beans for the white beans.

Tips

To brighten the flavor, stir in $1/4$ tsp (1 mL) lemon juice before sprinkling with Parmesan.

Freeze the remaining beans in a small sealable freezer bag. You can freeze the entire amount in one bag, or portion out 1 cup (250 mL) per bag so that the beans are recipe-ready. Be sure to label the bag with the contents. Store for up to 3 months. Defrost in the refrigerator or microwave before using.

♦ **16-oz (500 mL) mug**

1 cup	rinsed drained canned white beans (such as great Northern or cannellini)	250 mL
$1/2$ cup	diced cooked smoked sausage	125 mL
$1/2$ cup	ready-to-use chicken or vegetable broth	125 mL
2 tsp	chopped fresh parsley	10 mL
$1/4$ tsp	dried rosemary, crumbled	1 mL
	Salt and ground black pepper	
1 tbsp	grated Parmesan cheese	15 mL

1. In the mug, use a fork to coarsely mash half the beans. Stir in the remaining beans, sausage, broth, parsley and rosemary.

2. Microwave on High for 75 to 90 seconds (checking at 75) or until heated through. Season to taste with salt and pepper. Sprinkle with Parmesan.

Variation

- **Thyme, Chickpea and Sausage Mug:** Replace the white beans with chickpeas and replace the rosemary with dried thyme.

> **Prep Ahead Option**
> Prepare through step 1; cover and refrigerate until ready to use.

Irish Champ with Smoked Sausage

Champ is a beloved Irish potato dish that's as simple as can be: hot mashed or smashed potatoes prepared with hot milk, butter and lots of green onions or chives. I've stepped it up to main dish status by adding smoked sausage. For a crispy-crunchy finish, top with ready-made fried onions.

Tip

An equal amount of diced ham, or 2 tbsp (30 mL) ready-to-eat real bacon bits, can be used in place of the smoked sausage.

◆ **16-oz (500 mL) mug**

¹⁄₂ cup	instant potato flakes	125 mL
³⁄₄ cup	milk	175 mL
2 tsp	butter	10 mL
²⁄₃ cup	diced cooked smoked sausage	150 mL
2 tbsp	chopped green onions	30 mL
Pinch	ground nutmeg (optional)	Pinch
	Salt and ground black pepper	

Suggested Accompaniment

Crispy french-fried onions (from a can)

1. In the mug, use a fork to whisk potato flakes and milk until blended. Add butter. Microwave on High for 60 to 90 seconds or until hot and just starting to bubble at edges.
2. Stir in sausage, green onions and nutmeg (if using). Microwave on High for 60 to 90 seconds (checking at 60) or until thickened but not dry. Top with french-fried onions, if desired.

> **Prep Ahead Option**
> Measure the potato flakes into the mug; cover and store at room temperature. Measure the milk and butter into a small airtight container; cover and refrigerate. Measure the sausage, green onions and nutmeg (if using) into a small airtight container; cover and refrigerate until ready to use.

Oktoberfest Mug

Prost! You will love how the smokiness of the sausage tempers the sharpness of the sauerkraut, which in turn is smoothed out by mellow hash browns. This makes a great autumn dinner, perfect with a green salad alongside.

Tips

Frozen hash browns with onions and peppers are often labeled "O'Brien" potatoes.

Shredded hash browns can be used in place of the diced hash browns with onions and peppers.

Diced ham can be used in place of the smoked sausage.

Do not rinse the sauerkraut; some recipes advise that you should, but not here. Rinsing the kraut will erase its flavorful acidity.

♦ **16-oz (500 mL) mug**

⅔ cup	frozen diced hash brown potatoes with onions and peppers	150 mL
⅔ cup	diced cooked smoked sausage	150 mL
⅓ cup	drained sauerkraut	75 mL
1 tsp	coarse-grain, yellow or Dijon mustard	5 mL
½ tsp	packed brown sugar	2 mL
	Ground black pepper	

1. In the mug, microwave hash browns on High for $1\frac{1}{2}$ to 2 minutes or until warmed through.
2. Stir in sausage, sauerkraut, mustard and brown sugar. Season to taste with pepper. Microwave on High for 30 to 40 seconds or until heated through.

> **Prep Ahead Option**
>
> Measure the hash browns into the mug; cover and refrigerate (decrease the cooking time in step 1 by 30 seconds). Measure the sausage, sauerkraut, mustard and brown sugar into a small airtight container; cover and refrigerate until ready to use.

Cowboy Hash

Combining sausage, potatoes and peppers guarantees supper success on a busy weeknight. Adding a fried egg on top makes the hash enormously satisfying.

Tips

Two frozen cooked beef meatballs can be used in place of the sausages.

Frozen hash browns with onions and peppers are often labeled "O'Brien" potatoes.

Shredded hash browns can be used in place of the diced hash browns with onions and peppers.

If a frozen pepper and onion stir-fry blend isn't available, use $1/2$ cup (125 mL) mixed sliced fresh bell peppers and onions and, in step 2, cook for about 2 minutes, until vegetables are tender-crisp.

♦ **16-oz (500 mL) mug**

3	frozen cooked breakfast sausage links	3
$3/4$ cup	frozen diced hash brown potatoes with onions and peppers	175 mL
$1/2$ cup	frozen sliced bell pepper and onion stir-fry blend	125 mL
$1/2$ tsp	chili powder	2 mL
	Salt and ground black pepper	
1	large egg	1

1. In the mug, microwave sausages on High for 60 to 75 seconds or until heated through. Transfer to a small bowl and break apart with a fork.

2. In the mug, microwave hash browns and stir-fry blend on High for $1^1/_2$ to $2^1/_2$ minutes or until warmed through. Stir in sausage and chili powder.

3. Make a well in the center of the mixture and carefully crack the egg into the well, being careful not to break the yolk. Cover with a small plate or saucer. Microwave on Medium-High (70%) for 60 seconds. Check the egg white to see if it is just barely set. If not, microwave on High for 15 to 30 seconds or until the white is just set.

Prep Ahead Option

Place the sausages in the mug; cover and refrigerate (decrease the cooking time in step 1 to 30 seconds). Measure the hash browns and stir-fry blend into a small airtight container (decrease the cooking time in step 2 by 30 seconds); cover and refrigerate. Measure the chili powder into a small airtight container; cover and store at room temperature until ready to use.

Artichoke, Ham and Swiss Supper

Ham and Swiss cheese is a combination that flatters artichokes, and somehow, with a backdrop of potatoes and peppers, the effect is doubled here.

Tips

Frozen hash browns with onions and peppers are often labeled "O'Brien" potatoes.

Look for jarred marinated artichoke hearts where canned vegetables are shelved.

♦ **16-oz (500 mL) mug**

1¼ cups	frozen diced hash brown potatoes with onions and peppers	300 mL
¼ cup	ready-to-use chicken or vegetable broth	60 mL
¼ cup	chopped drained jarred marinated artichoke hearts	60 mL
¼ cup	diced ham or cooked smoked sausage	60 mL
1 tbsp	chopped green onions	15 mL
¼ cup	shredded Swiss cheese	60 mL
	Salt and ground black pepper	

1. In the mug, microwave hash browns and broth on High for 1 minute. Stir. Microwave on High for 1½ to 2 minutes or until warmed through.

2. Stir in artichoke hearts, ham and green onions. Microwave on High for 30 to 60 seconds or until heated through.

3. Sprinkle with cheese. Microwave on High for 15 to 20 seconds or until cheese is hot and bubbly. Let stand for 30 seconds. Season to taste with salt and pepper.

Variations

- **Ham, Swiss and Mushroom Supper:** Replace the artichokes with drained canned or jarred mushroom pieces.

- **Tomato, Bacon and Swiss Supper:** Replace the artichokes with ⅓ cup (75 mL) drained canned diced tomatoes with Italian seasoning. Replace the ham with 2 tbsp (30 mL) ready-to-eat real bacon bits.

Prep Ahead Option

Measure the hash browns and broth into the mug; cover and refrigerate (decrease the cooking time in step 1 by 30 seconds). Measure the artichoke hearts, ham and green onions into a small airtight container; cover and refrigerate. Measure the cheese into a small airtight container; cover and refrigerate until ready to use.

Cauliflower and Ham Gratin

Cauliflower and ham make a very fine couple. The addition of nutty Parmesan cheese and a crisp crumble of croutons gives the impression of a baked gratin — in seconds.

Tips

If the cauliflower florets are large, thaw them slightly and coarsely chop before using.

To crush croutons, place them in a small sealable plastic bag. Seal, then pound the croutons with a heavy object (such as a can, mallet or book) until crushed.

You can use crushed potato chips or tortilla chips in place of the croutons.

♦ **16-oz (500 mL) mug**

1¼ cups	frozen cauliflower florets	300 mL
⅔ cup	diced ham or cooked smoked sausage	150 mL
2 tbsp	chopped green onions	30 mL
Pinch	ground nutmeg	Pinch
3 tbsp	light Alfredo sauce	45 mL
2 tsp	grated Parmesan cheese	10 mL
2	garlic-seasoned croutons, crushed	2

1. In the mug, microwave cauliflower on High for 1½ to 2½ minutes or until heated through and tender. Drain off excess liquid.

2. Stir in ham, green onions, nutmeg and Alfredo sauce. Sprinkle with Parmesan. Microwave on High for 45 to 60 seconds or until heated through. Sprinkle with croutons.

Variation

- **Broccoli and Ham Gratin:** Use broccoli florets in place of the cauliflower. Replace the nutmeg with ¼ tsp (1 mL) dried basil or Italian seasoning.

Prep Ahead Option

Measure the cauliflower into the mug; cover and refrigerate (decrease the cooking time in step 1 by 30 seconds). Measure the ham, green onions, nutmeg, Alfredo sauce and Parmesan into a small airtight container; cover and refrigerate until ready to use. Crush the croutons (see tip, at left) and store them in the bag at room temperature until ready to use.

Chicken Cordon Bleu Mug

Chicken gets gussied up with an indulgent mix of ham, Swiss cheese and cream sauce in this quick contemporary take on chicken Cordon Bleu.

Tip

An equal amount of crushed potato chips can be used in place of the croutons.

♦ **16-oz (500 mL) mug**

1	can (5 oz/142 g) water-packed chunk chicken, drained and flaked	1
1/3 cup	shredded Swiss cheese or Italian-blend cheese	75 mL
1/4 cup	chopped ham	60 mL
2 tbsp	light Alfredo sauce	30 mL
1/2 tsp	Dijon mustard	2 mL
1/8 tsp	ground black pepper	0.5 mL
1/3 cup	garlic-and-herb-seasoned croutons, coarsely crushed	75 mL

1. In the mug, combine chicken, cheese, ham, Alfredo sauce, mustard and pepper.

2. Microwave on High for 75 to 90 seconds or until heated through. Sprinkle with croutons.

Variations

- **Spinach Chicken Cordon Bleu Mug:** In the mug, microwave 3/4 cup (175 mL) frozen chopped spinach on High for 1 to 2 minutes or until thawed and warm. Using the tines of a fork, press down firmly on the spinach and drain off excess liquid. Add the remaining ingredients and heat as directed.

- **Chicken Cordon Bleu Cheese Mug:** Omit the mustard. Increase the Alfredo sauce to 3 tbsp (45 mL) and replace the Swiss cheese with 3 tbsp (45 mL) crumbled blue cheese.

> **Prep Ahead Option**
> Prepare through step 1; cover and refrigerate. Measure the croutons into a small airtight container; cover and store at room temperature until ready to use.

Buffalo Chicken Mug

Hot pepper sauce and butter are linchpins of so many buffalo chicken recipes, and here the combination adds its inimitable sass to everyday hash browns and canned chicken. Don't forget the accompaniments: the fresh crunch of celery and the creaminess of blue cheese or sour cream can help quell the spice.

Tips

You can use $^2/_3$ cup (150 mL) diced cooked chicken or turkey in place of the canned chicken.

If you don't have any paprika on hand, you can use $1^1/_2$ tsp (7 mL) tomato paste or 1 tbsp (15 mL) tomato or marinara sauce in its place. The flavor will not be the same, but the color will be close.

♦ **12- to 16-oz (375 to 500 mL) mug**

$^3/_4$ cup	frozen diced hash brown potatoes	175 mL
1	can (5 oz/142 g) water-packed chunk chicken, drained and flaked	1
1 tsp	paprika	5 mL
$^1/_4$ tsp	garlic powder	1 mL
1 tbsp	butter	15 mL
1 tsp	hot pepper sauce (or to taste)	5 mL

Suggested Accompaniments

Chopped celery; chopped green onions; crumbled blue cheese; sour cream or plain Greek yogurt

1. In the mug, microwave hash browns on High for $1^1/_2$ to 2 minutes or until warmed through.

2. Stir in chicken, paprika, garlic powder, butter and hot pepper sauce. Microwave on High for 60 to 75 seconds (checking at 60) or until heated through. Stir. Serve with any of the suggested accompaniments, as desired.

Variation

- **Buffalo Chicken Sandwich:** Spoon the finished mug contents into a toasted split roll or a pita pocket half. Add any of the suggested accompaniments, as desired.

Prep Ahead Option

Measure the hash browns into the mug; cover and refrigerate (decrease the cooking time in step 1 by 30 seconds). Measure the chicken, paprika, garlic powder, butter and hot pepper sauce into a small airtight container; cover and refrigerate until ready to use.

BBQ Chicken Mashed Potato Bowl

Barbecue chicken and mashed potatoes make a perfect pair. Here, the complementary duo becomes a meal-in-one for convenience (and yumminess) sake.

Tips

Try adding 1 tbsp (15 mL) chopped green onions with the second addition of cheese in step 4.

You can use $2/3$ cup (150 mL) diced cooked chicken or turkey in place of the canned chicken.

♦ **16-oz (500 mL) mug**

1	can (5 oz/142 g) water-packed chunk chicken, drained and flaked	1
1½ tbsp	barbecue sauce	22 mL
½ cup	instant potato flakes	125 mL
⅛ tsp	salt	0.5 mL
Pinch	ground black pepper	Pinch
½ cup	water	125 mL
¼ cup	milk	60 mL
2 tsp	butter	10 mL
4 tbsp	shredded Cheddar cheese, divided	60 mL
⅓ cup	drained canned corn kernels	75 mL

Suggested Accompaniments

Ready-to-eat real bacon bits; sliced or chopped green onions

1. In a small bowl, combine chicken and barbecue sauce.
2. In the mug, use a fork to whisk potato flakes, salt, pepper, water and milk until blended. Add butter. Microwave on High for 60 seconds. Stir. Microwave on High for 60 to 75 seconds (checking at 60) or until thickened but not dry.
3. Stir in half the cheese. Spoon in chicken mixture, then spoon corn over chicken. Microwave on High for 45 to 60 seconds or until very warm.
4. Sprinkle with remaining cheese. Microwave on High for 20 seconds. Serve with any of the suggested accompaniments, as desired.

Prep Ahead Option

Combine the chicken and barbecue sauce in a small airtight container; cover and refrigerate. Measure the potato flakes, salt and pepper into the mug; cover and store at room temperature. Measure the water, milk and butter into a small airtight container; cover and refrigerate. Measure the cheese and corn into separate airtight containers; cover and refrigerate until ready to use.

Chicken Club Mug

Step aside, sandwich; this mug version of the chicken club might just be the beginning of a new tradition in your kitchen.

Tips

Look for ready-to-eat real bacon bits where salad dressings and croutons are shelved in the grocery store, or near the regular bacon in the packaged meat or deli department.

You can use 1/3 cup (75 mL) canned diced tomatoes with juice in place of the plum tomato.

♦ **16-oz (500 mL) mug**

1	can (5 oz/142 g) water-packed chunk chicken, drained and flaked	1
2 tbsp	ready-to-eat real bacon bits	30 mL
2 tbsp	light Alfredo sauce	30 mL
1/4 tsp	Dijon mustard (optional)	1 mL
4	garlic-seasoned or plain croutons, coarsely crushed	4
1	small plum (Roma) tomato, diced	1
1/2 cup	shredded iceberg lettuce	125 mL

Suggested Accompaniments

Diced avocado or prepared guacamole; grated Parmesan or crumbled blue cheese; chopped green onions

1. In the mug, combine chicken, bacon, Alfredo sauce and mustard (if using).
2. Microwave on High for 75 to 90 seconds (checking at 75) or until warmed through. Top with croutons, tomato, lettuce and any of the suggested accompaniments, as desired.

Variation

- **Crab Club Mug:** Replace the chicken with a 4- to 5-oz (114 to 142 g) can lump crabmeat, drained and flaked.

> **Prep Ahead Option**
> Combine the chicken, bacon, Alfredo sauce and mustard (if using) in the mug; cover and refrigerate. Measure the croutons, tomato and lettuce into separate small airtight containers; cover and refrigerate until ready to use.

King Ranch Chicken Casserole

If states and provinces had official casseroles, the clear choice for Texas would be King Ranch casserole. The origins are murky, but most sources indicate that it was a Junior League creation from the 1960s. A cross between chilaquiles and a Tex-Mex take on chicken à la king, it's always a hit. This mug riff is no exception.

Tip

You can use ½ cup (125 mL) coarsely crushed tortilla chips in place of the corn tortilla.

♦ **12- to 16-oz (375 to 500 mL) mug**

1	can (5 oz/142 g) water-packed chunk chicken, drained and flaked	1
1	5- to 6-inch (12.5 to 15 cm) corn tortilla, torn into small pieces	1
⅓ cup	light Alfredo sauce	75 mL
¼ cup	chunky salsa	60 mL
¼ tsp	chili powder or ground cumin	1 mL
⅓ cup	shredded Monterey Jack, pepper Jack or Cheddar cheese	75 mL

1. In the mug, combine chicken, tortilla, Alfredo sauce, salsa and chili powder until blended.

2. Microwave on High for 1½ to 2 minutes or until very hot. Sprinkle with cheese. Let stand for 1 minute or until cheese is melted.

Variation

- **Vegetarian Ranch Casserole:** Replace the chicken with ⅔ cup (150 mL) rinsed drained canned white beans (such as great Northern or cannellini) or diced tempeh.

Prep Ahead Option

Measure the chicken, tortilla, Alfredo sauce, salsa and chili powder into the mug; cover and refrigerate. Measure the cheese into a small airtight container; cover and refrigerate until ready to use.

Chicken and Broccoli Casserole

This mug meal takes everyday frozen broccoli and canned chicken and, with little effort — and no tricks — turns them into something special and delicious.

Tips

You can use ²/₃ cup (150 mL) cooked brown rice in place of the instant brown rice. Cook the broccoli in step 1 (without the rice) for 1¹/₂ to 2 minutes or until heated through, then drain off excess liquid. Add the rice with the chicken and increase the cooking time in step 2 by 30 seconds.

Opt for bags, as opposed to boxes, of frozen chopped broccoli, as it is easier to remove small amounts at a time.

◆ 16-oz (500 mL) mug

¹/₃ cup	instant brown rice	75 mL
²/₃ cup	water	150 mL
³/₄ cup	frozen chopped broccoli	175 mL
¹/₂	can (5 oz/142 g) water-packed chunk chicken, drained and flaked	¹/₂
¹/₃ cup	shredded Cheddar cheese	75 mL
¹/₄ cup	cottage cheese	60 mL
¹/₄ tsp	garlic powder (optional)	1 mL
¹/₄ tsp	dried Italian seasoning (optional)	1 mL
	Salt and ground black pepper	

1. In the mug, combine rice and water. Place broccoli on top. Cover with a small plate or saucer. Microwave on High for 5 to 6 minutes or until almost all of the water is absorbed. Remove from oven and let stand, covered, for 1 minute to absorb the remaining water.

2. Stir in chicken, Cheddar, cottage cheese, garlic powder (if using) and Italian seasoning (if using). Microwave, uncovered, on High for 45 to 75 seconds or until heated through. Let stand for 30 seconds. Season to taste with salt and pepper.

Variations

- **Chicken and Vegetable Casserole:** Replace the broccoli with drained canned mixed vegetables.

- **Chicken, Tomato and Goat Cheese Casserole:** Replace the broccoli with ¹/₂ cup (125 mL) drained canned diced tomatoes with Italian seasoning. Replace the Cheddar cheese with ¹/₄ cup (60 mL) crumbled goat cheese.

- **White Bean and Broccoli Casserole:** Replace the chicken with ¹/₂ cup (125 mL) rinsed drained canned white beans (such as cannellini or great Northern).

Prep Ahead Option

Measure the rice into the mug; cover and store at room temperature. Measure the broccoli into a small airtight container; cover and refrigerate. Measure the chicken, Cheddar, cottage cheese, garlic powder (if using) and Italian seasoning (if using) into a small airtight container; cover and refrigerate until ready to use.

Primavera Chicken and Vegetable Mug

This so-easy supper is a balanced blend of tender-crisp snap peas, hearty chicken and white beans, and piquant pesto. The sum total is mug meal satisfaction.

Tips

An equal amount of frozen green peas can be used in place of the sugar snap peas. Reduce the cooking time in step 1 to 60 seconds.

You can use $\frac{1}{3}$ cup (75 mL) canned diced tomatoes with juice in place of the plum tomato.

Canned chickpeas can be used in place of the white beans.

Freeze the remaining beans in a small sealable freezer bag. You can freeze the entire amount in one bag, or portion out $\frac{2}{3}$ cup (150 mL) per bag so that the beans are recipe-ready. Be sure to label the bag with the contents. Store for up to 3 months. Defrost in the refrigerator or microwave before using.

♦ **16-oz (500 mL) mug**

$\frac{1}{2}$ cup	frozen sugar snap peas	125 mL
1	small plum (Roma) tomato, diced	1
$\frac{1}{2}$	can (5 oz/142 g) water-packed chunk chicken, drained and flaked	$\frac{1}{2}$
$\frac{2}{3}$ cup	rinsed drained canned white beans (such as great Northern or cannellini)	150 mL
2 tbsp	basil pesto	30 mL

1. In the mug, microwave peas on High for $1\frac{1}{2}$ to 2 minutes or until heated through. Drain off excess liquid.

2. Stir in tomato, chicken, beans and pesto. Microwave on High for 45 to 60 seconds or until heated through.

Variation

- **Primavera Ham and Vegetable Mug:** Replace the chicken with $\frac{2}{3}$ cup (150 mL) diced ham.

Prep Ahead Option

Measure the peas into the mug; cover and refrigerate (decrease the cooking time in step 1 by 30 seconds). Measure the tomato, chicken, beans and pesto into a small airtight container; cover and refrigerate until ready to use.

Barbecued Chinese Chicken Lettuce Wraps

Ready-to-use Chinese hoisin sauce delivers a deep, round intensity to plain chicken, turning it into something sumptuous. Earthy mushrooms and a scattering of green onions ensure that each forkful is a hit.

Tips

If a frozen pepper and onion stir-fry blend isn't available, use ½ cup (125 mL) mixed sliced fresh bell peppers and onions and, in step 1, cook for about 2 minutes or until vegetables are tender-crisp.

Hoisin sauce is a thick Chinese sauce akin to American barbecue sauce. Look for it where soy sauce is shelved in the grocery store.

Prep Ahead Option

Measure the stir-fry blend into the mug; cover and refrigerate (decrease the cooking time in step 1 by 30 seconds). Measure the chicken, mushrooms and hoisin sauce into a small airtight container; cover and refrigerate. Place the lettuce leaves and green onions in a small airtight container; cover and refrigerate until ready to use.

♦ **16-oz (500 mL) mug**

½ cup	frozen sliced bell pepper and onion stir-fry blend	125 mL
1	can (5 oz/142 g) water-packed chunk chicken, drained and flaked	1
¼ cup	drained canned or jarred mushroom pieces	60 mL
2 tbsp	hoisin sauce	30 mL
2	large iceberg, romaine or butter lettuce leaves	2
1 tbsp	sliced green onions	15 mL

Suggested Accompaniments

Toasted or roasted chopped almonds, peanuts or cashews; crunchy chow mein noodles

1. In the mug, microwave stir-fry blend on High for 1½ to 2 minutes or until heated through. Drain off excess liquid.

2. Stir in chicken, mushrooms and hoisin sauce until blended. Microwave on High for 45 to 60 seconds or until warmed through.

3. Spoon half the chicken mixture into each lettuce leaf. Sprinkle with green onions and any of the suggested accompaniments, as desired.

Variations

- **Barbecued Chinese Shrimp or Crab Lettuce Wraps:** Replace the chicken with a 4-oz (114 g) can of small shrimp, drained, or a 4- to 5-oz (114 to 142 g) can of lump crabmeat, drained and flaked.

- **Barbecued Chinese Tempeh Lettuce Wraps:** Replace the chicken with ⅔ cup (150 mL) coarsely chopped tempeh.

Teriyaki Salmon Mug

A fresh cucumber pickle delivers sprightliness to robust salmon and teriyaki sauce in a quick Japanese-inspired mug that manages to be both substantial and refreshing.

Tip

Add the cucumbers to the vinegar mixture just a few minutes before serving the salmon; that way, they will remain crunchy. If left too long in the vinegar mixture, they will become soggy.

◆ **12- to 16-oz (375 to 500 mL) mug**

1/4 tsp	granulated sugar	1 mL
1/8 tsp	salt	0.5 mL
1 tsp	white, rice or cider vinegar	5 mL
1/2 cup	diced seeded peeled cucumber	125 mL
1 tbsp	sliced green onions	15 mL
1	can (5 oz/142 g) boneless salmon, drained and flaked	1
1 1/2 tbsp	teriyaki sauce	22 mL
1 1/2 tsp	toasted sesame seeds (optional)	7 mL

1. In a small bowl or cup, use a fork to whisk sugar, salt and vinegar until sugar is dissolved. Stir in cucumber and green onions.

2. In the mug, combine salmon and teriyaki sauce. Microwave on High for 75 to 90 seconds or until heated through. Top with the cucumber mixture. Sprinkle with sesame seeds, if using.

Variation

- **Teriyaki Chicken Mug:** Use an equal-size can of water-packed chunk chicken, drained and flaked, in place of the salmon.

Prep Ahead Option

Measure the sugar, salt and vinegar into a small airtight container; cover and refrigerate. Measure the cucumber and green onions into a small airtight container; cover and refrigerate. Measure the salmon and teriyaki sauce into the mug; cover and refrigerate. Measure the sesame seeds into an airtight container; cover and store at room temperature until ready to use.

So-Simple Salmon Cake

Don't bother with a frying pan; you can create a delectable salmon cake in your microwave, with a mug, in minutes. Consider mixing up a quick lemon mayonnaise — a spoonful of mayonnaise, a few drops of lemon juice and a drop of hot pepper sauce — to top the cake.

Tips

Crushed croutons lend a toasty flavor to the finished cake, but plain or Italian-seasoned bread crumbs can be used in their place.

You can use 1 tbsp (15 mL) chopped fresh herbs, such as basil, cilantro or parsley, in place of the green onions.

◆ **12- to 16-oz (375 to 500 mL) mug, sprayed with nonstick cooking spray**

1	large egg	1
$\frac{1}{8}$ tsp	salt	0.5 mL
$\frac{1}{8}$ tsp	garlic powder	0.5 mL
$\frac{1}{8}$ tsp	hot pepper sauce	0.5 mL
1	can (5 oz/142 g) boneless salmon, drained and flaked	1
3 tbsp	crushed plain or seasoned croutons	45 mL
2 tbsp	chopped drained jarred roasted red bell peppers (optional)	30 mL
$1\frac{1}{2}$ tbsp	finely chopped green onions	22 mL

1. In the mug, use a fork to whisk egg, salt, garlic powder and hot pepper sauce until blended. Stir in salmon, croutons, roasted peppers (if using) and green onion until blended. Gently press down in mug.

2. Microwave on High for 60 to 75 seconds or until just set and cake feels somewhat dry to the touch.

Variation

• **So-Simple Crab Cake:** Use a 4- to 5-oz (114 to 142 g) can of lump crabmeat, drained and flaked, in place of the salmon.

> **Prep Ahead Option**
> Prepare through step 1; cover and refrigerate until ready to use.

Tuna Crunch Casserole

With a creamy filling and a crispy potato chip topping, how could this hearty casserole for one be anything but wonderful? You'll definitely make it many times over.

Tip

Freeze the remaining vegetables in a small sealable freezer bag. You can freeze the entire amount in one bag or portion 1/3 cup (75 mL) per bag so that the vegetables are recipe-ready. Be sure to label the bag with the contents. Store for up to 3 months. Defrost in the refrigerator or microwave before using.

◆ **12- to 16-oz (375 to 500 mL) mug**

1	can (5 oz/142 g) water-packed chunk white tuna, drained and flaked	1
1/3 cup	drained canned mixed vegetables	75 mL
1/4 cup	light Alfredo sauce	60 mL
Pinch	ground black pepper	Pinch
1/3 cup	coarsely crushed potato chips	75 mL

1. In the mug, use a fork to combine tuna, vegetables, Alfredo sauce and pepper until blended.
2. Microwave on High for 75 to 90 seconds (checking at 75) or until heated through. Sprinkle with potato chips.

Variations

- **Creamy Crab Casserole:** Replace the tuna with a 4- to 5-oz (114 to 142 g) can of lump crabmeat, drained and flaked. Replace the vegetables with thawed frozen or canned corn. Add 1/4 tsp (1 mL) dried basil with the Alfredo sauce. Replace the potato chips with 3 tbsp (45 mL) crushed plain or seasoned croutons.

- **Tuna and Artichoke Casserole:** Replace the mixed vegetables with 1/4 cup (60 mL) coarsely chopped drained jarred marinated artichoke hearts.

Prep Ahead Option

Measure the tuna, vegetables, Alfredo sauce and pepper into the mug; cover and refrigerate. Measure the potato chips into a small airtight container; cover and store at room temperature until ready to use.

Tuna Niçoise Mug

Canned tuna — high in protein, low in cost, big on flavor — is an ideal pantry item for fast meals on the fly. Water-packed varieties have a large, moist and pleasantly firm flake. Combining tuna with briny olives, herb-infused tomatoes, potatoes and green beans evokes the warm regions of southern France.

Tips

Shredded hash browns, or diced hash browns with onions and peppers, can be used in place of the diced hash browns.

Freeze the remaining tomatoes in a small sealable freezer bag. You can freeze the entire amount in one bag, or portion out 1/2 cup (125 mL) per bag so that the tomatoes are recipe-ready. Be sure to label the bag with the contents. Store for up to 3 months. Defrost in the refrigerator or microwave before using.

♦ **16-oz (500 mL) mug**

1/2 cup	frozen diced hash brown potatoes	125 mL
1/2 cup	frozen cut green beans	125 mL
1/2	can (5 oz/142 g) water-packed chunk white tuna, drained and flaked	1/2
1/2 cup	canned diced tomatoes with Italian seasoning, with juice	125 mL
2 tbsp	sliced drained brine-cured olives (such as kalamata) or ripe olives	30 mL
1 tbsp	olive oil	15 mL
	Salt and ground black pepper	

Suggested Accompaniments

Chopped fresh parsley; lemon wedges

1. In the mug, microwave hash browns and green beans on High for 90 seconds or until heated through.
2. Stir in tuna, tomatoes, olives and oil. Microwave on High for 45 to 60 seconds or until heated through. Season to taste with salt and pepper. Serve with any of the suggested accompaniments, as desired.

Variation

- **Salmon Niçoise Mug:** Use an equal-size can of boneless salmon, drained and flaked, in place of the tuna.

Prep Ahead Option

Measure the hash browns and green beans into the mug; cover and refrigerate (decrease the cooking time in step 1 by 30 seconds). Measure the tuna, tomatoes, olives and oil into a small airtight container; cover and refrigerate until ready to use.

Crab, Corn and Tomato Mug

In this simple, fresh-tasting mugful, lemon juice, lemon zest and basil give the mix of crab, corn and tomatoes distinctive summer flair. But don't let that stop you from making it in the depths of winter; the flavors will transport you to warm, sunny shores.

Tips

If a frozen pepper and onion stir-fry blend isn't available, use ½ cup (125 mL) mixed sliced fresh bell peppers and onions and, in step 1, cook for about 2 minutes or until vegetables are tender-crisp.

If you have flavorful fresh tomatoes (including cherry tomatoes) on hand, chop them and use an equal amount in place of the canned tomatoes.

Freeze the remaining tomatoes in a small sealable freezer bag. You can freeze the entire amount in one bag, or portion out ⅔ cup (150 mL) per bag so that the tomatoes are recipe-ready. Be sure to label the bag with the contents. Store for up to 3 months. Defrost in the refrigerator or microwave before using.

◆ **12- to 16-oz (375 to 500 mL) mug**

½ cup	frozen corn kernels	125 mL
½ cup	frozen sliced bell pepper and onion stir-fry blend	125 mL
1	can (4 to 5 oz/114 to 142 g) lump crabmeat, drained and flaked	1
⅔ cup	canned diced tomatoes with Italian seasoning, with juice	150 mL
½ tsp	finely grated lemon zest (optional)	2 mL
2 tsp	freshly squeezed lemon juice	10 mL
1 tbsp	chopped fresh basil or parsley	15 mL
	Salt and ground black pepper	

1. In the mug, microwave corn and stir-fry blend on High for 1½ to 2 minutes or until heated through.
2. Stir in crab, tomatoes, lemon zest and lemon juice. Microwave on High for 45 to 60 seconds or until heated through. Stir in basil. Season to taste with salt and pepper.

Variation

- **Chicken, Corn and Tomato Mug:** Use an equal-size can of water-packed chunk chicken, drained and flaked, in place of the crab.

Prep Ahead Option

Measure the corn and stir-fry blend into the mug; cover and refrigerate (decrease the cooking time in step 1 by 30 seconds). Measure the crab, tomatoes, lemon zest and lemon juice into a small airtight container; cover and refrigerate. Measure the basil into a small airtight container; cover and refrigerate until ready to use.

Shrimp Cilantro

Here, pantry-friendly canned shrimp gets the fresh cilantro treatment. Enjoy directly from the mug or scoop the shrimp onto tortillas for handheld dinner perfection.

Tips

An equal amount (about ³⁄₄ cup/175 mL) of thawed frozen small or medium shrimp can be used in place of the canned shrimp.

Chopped fresh parsley can be used in place of the cilantro.

♦ **12- to 16-oz (375 to 500 mL) mug**

3 tbsp	salsa verde	45 mL
2 tsp	butter	10 mL
¹⁄₈ tsp	ground cumin	0.5 mL
1	can (4 oz/114 g) small or medium shrimp, drained	1
1 tbsp	chopped fresh cilantro	15 mL

Suggested Accompaniments

Crusty bread or warm tortillas (corn or flour); crumbled queso blanco or mild feta cheese

1. In the mug, microwave salsa, butter and cumin on High for 35 to 45 seconds or until butter is melted. Stir until blended.

2. Stir in shrimp and cilantro. Microwave on High for 30 to 40 seconds or until heated through. Serve with any of the suggested accompaniments, as desired.

Variations

- **Crab Cilantro:** Replace the shrimp with a 4- to 5-oz (114 to 142 g) can of lump crabmeat, drained and flaked.
- **Chicken Cilantro:** Replace the shrimp with a 5-oz (142 g) can of water-packed chunk chicken, drained and flaked.

> **Prep Ahead Option**
>
> Measure the salsa, butter and cumin into the mug; cover and refrigerate. Measure the shrimp and cilantro into a small airtight container; cover and refrigerate until ready to use.

Mediterranean Shrimp, Chickpeas and Peppers

Aromatic without being spicy, this shrimp and chickpea mug hits notes of earthy, briny, sweet and salty in each forkful.

Tips

If using a fresh lemon for the juice, consider finely grating the rind first to get ½ tsp (2 mL) lemon zest. Add the zest with the lemon juice.

White beans (such as cannellini or great Northern) can be used in place of the chickpeas.

Freeze the remaining chickpeas in a small sealable freezer bag. You can freeze the entire amount in one bag, or portion out ½ cup (125 mL) per bag so that the chickpeas are recipe-ready. Be sure to label the bag with the contents. Store for up to 3 months. Defrost in the refrigerator or microwave before using.

♦ 12- to 16-oz (375 to 500 mL) mug

½ cup	rinsed drained canned chickpeas	125 mL
3 tbsp	coarsely chopped drained jarred roasted red bell peppers	45 mL
2 tsp	olive oil	10 mL
1	can (4 oz/114 g) small or medium shrimp, drained	1
1 tbsp	chopped fresh parsley	15 mL
2 tsp	lemon juice	10 mL
	Salt and ground black pepper	
2 tbsp	crumbled feta cheese	30 mL

Suggested Accompaniments
Crusty bread, pita or pita chips

1. In the mug, combine chickpeas, roasted peppers and oil. Microwave on High for 60 to 90 seconds or until heated through.

2. Stir in shrimp. Microwave on High for 45 to 60 seconds or until heated through. Stir in parsley and lemon juice. Season to taste with salt and pepper. Sprinkle with feta. Serve with a suggested accompaniment, if desired.

Variations

- **Mediterranean Chickpeas and Peppers:** Omit the shrimp and increase the chickpeas to 1 cup (250 mL).

- **Mediterranean Chicken, Chickpeas and Peppers:** Replace the shrimp with a 5-oz (142 g) can of water-packed chunk chicken, drained and flaked.

Prep Ahead Option
Measure the chickpeas, roasted peppers and oil into the mug; cover and refrigerate. Measure the shrimp into a small airtight container; cover and refrigerate. Measure the parsley and lemon juice into a small airtight container; cover and refrigerate. Measure the feta into a small airtight container; cover and refrigerate until ready to use.

Shrimp, Sausage and Brown Rice Jambalaya

This ultra-quick riff on a New Orleans favorite gets an added layer of flavor from green chile-spiked tomatoes.

Tips

You can use 1 cup (250 mL) cooked brown rice in place of the instant rice. Omit step 1 and add the cooked rice with the tomatoes. Increase the cooking time in step 2 by 30 to 45 seconds.

Choose either regular or reduced-fat smoked sausage.

Freeze the remaining tomatoes in a small sealable freezer bag. Be sure to label the bag with the contents. Store for up to 3 months. Defrost in the refrigerator or microwave before using.

♦ **16-oz (500 mL) mug**

½ cup	instant brown rice	125 mL
½ cup	water	125 mL
½	can (10 oz/284 mL) diced tomatoes with green chiles, with juice	½
⅓ cup	drained canned or thawed frozen cooked tiny shrimp	75 mL
⅓ cup	diced cooked smoked sausage	75 mL
⅛ tsp	dried thyme (optional)	0.5 mL
	Salt and ground black pepper	

Suggested Accompaniment
Sliced green onions

1. In the mug, combine rice and water. Cover with a small plate or saucer. Microwave on High for 5 to 6 minutes or until almost all the water has been absorbed. Remove from oven and let stand, covered, for 1 minute to absorb remaining water.

2. Stir in tomatoes, shrimp, sausage and thyme (if using). Microwave, uncovered, on High for 60 to 90 seconds or until heated through. Garnish with green onions, if desired.

Variations
- **Shrimp Jambalaya:** Omit the sausage and increase the shrimp to ⅔ cup (150 mL).
- **Sausage Jambalaya:** Omit the shrimp and increase the sausage to ⅔ cup (150 mL).

> **Prep Ahead Option**
> Measure the rice into the mug; cover and store at room temperature. Measure the tomatoes, shrimp, sausage and thyme (if using) into a small airtight container; cover and refrigerate until ready to use.

Pasta and Grains

Pick-Your-Sauce Spaghetti

Chances are, you have at least one sauce option in your refrigerator or pantry to make an instant meal, whether it's salsa, marinara sauce, hummus or butter. Pick-Your-Sauce Spaghetti is healthy, delicious and a heck of a lot faster (and cheaper) than fast food!

Tip

If using broken spaghetti, break into 1- to 1½-inch (2.5 to 4 cm) pieces for best results.

Prep Ahead Option

Measure the spaghetti and salt into the mug; cover and store at room temperature. Measure the sauce into a small airtight container; cover and refrigerate until ready to use.

◆ **16-oz (500 mL) mug**

½ cup	cut or broken spaghetti	125 mL
Pinch	salt	Pinch
⅔ cup	water	150 mL
	Sauce of choice (see suggestions below)	
	Salt and ground black pepper	

Sauce Suggestions

2 tbsp	marinara sauce	30 mL
2 tbsp	Alfredo sauce	30 mL
1½ tbsp	basil pesto	22 mL
3 tbsp	salsa	45 mL
3 tbsp	cottage cheese or ricotta cheese	45 mL
1½ tbsp	olive tapenade	22 mL
1 tbsp	teriyaki sauce	15 mL
1 tbsp	butter or olive oil	15 mL
2 tbsp	hummus	30 mL
¼ cup	canned diced tomatoes (or diced tomatoes with green chiles), with juice	60 mL

Suggested Accompaniments

Grated, shredded or crumbled cheese (Parmesan, Cheddar, feta); chopped fresh herbs (chives, basil, parsley, cilantro)

1. In the mug, combine spaghetti, salt and water. Place in the microwave atop a doubled paper towel. Microwave on High for 2 minutes. Stir. Microwave on High for 3 minutes. If the mixture appears dry, add 1 tbsp (15 mL) water to the mug. Microwave for 1½ to 2 minutes or until spaghetti is tender.

2. Stir in sauce of choice. Microwave on High for 15 to 45 seconds (checking at 15) or until heated through. Let stand for 30 seconds, then stir. Season to taste with salt and pepper. Serve with any of the suggested accompaniments, as desired.

Macaroni and Cheese

If there is a more quintessential comfort food than macaroni and cheese, I don't know about it. Here, I've stripped away all the time-consuming steps, as well as all the artificial ingredients in the boxed varieties. The result is a perfect mug of delicious goodness.

Tips

Add ¼ tsp (1 mL) of your favorite dried herbs or herb blend (basil, oregano, Italian seasoning) with the cheeses.

Crushed potato chips or tortilla chips can be used in place of the croutons.

To crush croutons, place them in a small sealable plastic bag. Seal, then pound the croutons with a heavy object (such as a can, mallet or book) until crushed.

Prep Ahead Option

Measure the macaroni and salt into the mug; cover and store at room temperature. Measure the Cheddar, Parmesan, milk and mustard (if using) into a small airtight container; cover and refrigerate. If using croutons, crush them and store in the bag at room temperature until ready to use.

♦ **16-oz (500 mL) mug**

½ cup	elbow macaroni	125 mL
⅛ tsp	salt	0.5 mL
⅔ cup	water	150 mL
2 tbsp	shredded sharp (old) Cheddar cheese	30 mL
1 tbsp	grated Parmesan cheese	15 mL
2 tbsp	milk or half-and-half (10%) cream	30 mL
¼ tsp	Dijon or yellow mustard (optional)	1 mL
	Salt and ground black pepper	
2	garlic croutons, crushed (optional)	2

1. In the mug, combine macaroni, salt and water. Place in the microwave atop a doubled paper towel. Microwave on High for 2 minutes. Stir. Microwave on High for 3 minutes. If the mixture appears dry, add 1 tbsp (15 mL) water to the mug. Microwave for 1½ to 2 minutes or until macaroni is tender.

2. Stir in Cheddar, Parmesan, milk and mustard (if using) until cheeses are melted. Microwave on High for 15 to 30 seconds (checking at 15) or until heated through. Let stand for 1 minute, then stir. Season to taste with salt and pepper. If desired, sprinkle with croutons.

Variations

- **Bacon Cheddar Mac:** Add 1 tbsp (15 mL) ready-to-eat real bacon bits with the cheeses.

- **Tex-Mex Mac:** Reduce the milk to 1 tbsp (15 mL) and add 1 tbsp (15 mL) salsa and ¼ tsp (1 mL) ground cumin or chili powder with the cheeses.

- **Gluten-Free Mac and Cheese:** Use quinoa macaroni in place of the regular macaroni and decrease the final cooking time in step 1 by 30 seconds. Omit the croutons or use gluten-free croutons.

Unstuffed Shells with Cheese and Spinach

This cheese-enriched pasta tastes truly indulgent, yet it's loaded with good-for-you ingredients: spinach, tomatoes and protein-packed ricotta cheese.

Tips

Other frozen chopped greens (such as kale or mustard greens) or frozen chopped broccoli may be used in place of the spinach.

Add ¼ tsp (1 mL) of your favorite dried herbs or herb blend (basil, oregano, Italian seasoning) with the cheeses.

Cottage cheese can be used in place of the ricotta cheese.

Freeze the remaining tomatoes in a small sealable freezer bag. You can freeze the entire amount in one bag, or portion out ½ cup (125 mL) per bag so that the tomatoes are recipe-ready. Be sure to label the bag with the contents. Store for up to 3 months. Defrost in the refrigerator or microwave before using.

♦ 16-oz (500 mL) mug

1 cup	frozen chopped spinach	250 mL
½ cup	small shell pasta	125 mL
⅛ tsp	salt	0.5 mL
⅔ cup	water	150 mL
½ cup	canned diced tomatoes with Italian seasoning, with juice	125 mL
⅓ cup	ricotta cheese	75 mL
1 tbsp	grated Parmesan cheese	15 mL
	Salt and ground black pepper	

1. In the mug, microwave spinach on High for 1 to 2 minutes or until thawed and warm. Using the tines of a fork, press down firmly on the spinach and drain off excess liquid. Transfer spinach to a small plate or bowl.

2. In the mug, combine shells, salt and water. Place in the microwave atop a doubled paper towel. Microwave on High for 2 minutes. Stir. Microwave on High for 3 minutes. If the mixture appears dry, add 1 tbsp (15 mL) water to the mug. Microwave for 1½ to 2 minutes or until shells are tender.

3. Stir in spinach, tomatoes, ricotta and Parmesan. Microwave on High for 30 to 45 seconds or until heated through. Let stand for 1 minute. Season to taste with salt and pepper.

Variation

- **Gluten-Free Unstuffed Shells:** Use quinoa macaroni in place of the shells and decrease the final cooking time in step 2 by 30 seconds.

Prep Ahead Option

Measure the spinach into the mug; cover and refrigerate (decrease the cooking time in step 1 to 30 seconds). Measure the shells and salt into a small airtight container; cover and store at room temperature. Measure the tomatoes, ricotta and Parmesan into a small airtight container; cover and refrigerate until ready to use.

Puttanesca Pasta

In Italian, a *puttanesca* is a "lady of the night," which is why this pantry-friendly pasta dish is spicy, strong and gutsy.

Tips

Try adding 1 tbsp (15 mL) chopped fresh parsley just before serving.

Freeze the remaining tomatoes in a small sealable freezer bag. You can freeze the entire amount in one bag, or portion out ½ cup (125 mL) per bag so that the tomatoes are recipe-ready. Be sure to label the bag with the contents. Store for up to 3 months. Defrost in the refrigerator or microwave before using.

♦ **16-oz (500 mL) mug**

½ cup	ditalini or elbow macaroni	125 mL
⅛ tsp	salt	0.5 mL
⅔ cup	water	150 mL
½ cup	canned diced tomatoes with Italian seasoning, with juice	125 mL
1 tbsp	chopped pitted drained brined-cured olives	15 mL
1 tsp	drained capers (optional)	5 mL
1 tsp	olive oil	5 mL
Pinch	cayenne pepper	Pinch
	Salt	

1. In the mug, combine ditalini, salt and water. Place in the microwave atop a doubled paper towel. Microwave on High for 2 minutes. Stir. Microwave on High for 3 minutes. If the mixture appears dry, add 1 tbsp (15 mL) water to the mug. Microwave for 1½ to 2 minutes or until ditalini is tender.

2. Stir in tomatoes, olives, capers (if using), oil and cayenne. Microwave on High for 30 to 45 seconds or until heated through. Let stand for 1 minute, then stir. Season to taste with salt.

Variations

• **Muffuletta Pasta:** Omit the capers and increase the olives to 2 tbsp (30 mL). Add 3 tbsp (45 mL) chopped cooked smoked sausage or ham with the olives. Add 1 tbsp (15 mL) chopped fresh parsley with the salt.

• **Gluten-Free Puttanesca Pasta:** Use quinoa macaroni in place of the ditalini and decrease the final cooking time in step 1 by 30 seconds.

Prep Ahead Option

Measure the ditalini and salt into the mug; cover and store at room temperature. Measure the tomatoes, olives, capers (if using), oil and cayenne into a small airtight container; cover and refrigerate until ready to use.

Pumpkin, Sage and Parmesan Pasta

Sage and Parmesan coax out the savory side of ready-to-use pumpkin, leading to one of the best (and easiest) fall pasta sauces ever.

Tips

Canned butternut squash purée or thawed frozen winter squash purée may be used in place of the pumpkin.

Freeze the remaining pumpkin in a small sealable freezer bag. You can freeze the entire amount in one bag, or portion out 1/4 cup (60 mL) per bag so that the pumpkin is recipe-ready. Be sure to label the bag with the contents. Store for up to 3 months. Defrost in the refrigerator or microwave before using.

♦ 16-oz (500 mL) mug

1/2 cup	ditalini or elbow macaroni	125 mL
1/8 tsp	salt	0.5 mL
2/3 cup	water	150 mL
1/4 cup	pumpkin purée (not pie filling)	60 mL
2 tbsp	half-and-half (10%) cream or milk	30 mL
4 tsp	grated Parmesan cheese, divided	20 mL
1/8 tsp	dry rubbed sage or dried thyme	0.5 mL
	Salt and ground black pepper	

1. In the mug, combine ditalini, salt and water. Place in the microwave atop a doubled paper towel. Microwave on High for 2 minutes. Stir. Microwave on High for 3 minutes. If the mixture appears dry, add 1 tbsp (15 mL) water to the mug. Microwave for $1\frac{1}{2}$ to 2 minutes or until ditalini is tender.

2. Stir in pumpkin, cream, 3 tsp (15 mL) Parmesan and sage until blended. Microwave on High for 30 to 45 seconds or until heated through. Let stand for 1 minute, then stir. Season to taste with salt and pepper. Sprinkle with remaining Parmesan.

Variations

- **Gluten-Free Pumpkin Pasta:** Use quinoa macaroni in place of the ditalini and decrease the final cooking time in step 1 by 30 seconds.

- **Pumpkin Goat Cheese Pasta:** Replace the sage with an equal amount of crumbled dried rosemary. Replace the Parmesan with 2 tbsp (30 mL) crumbled goat cheese.

Prep Ahead Option

Measure the ditalini and salt into the mug; cover and store at room temperature. Measure the pumpkin, cream, 3 tsp (15 mL) Parmesan and sage into a small airtight container; cover and refrigerate. Measure the remaining Parmesan into a small airtight container; cover and refrigerate until ready to use.

Hummus Pasta

Ready-to-use hummus, enhanced with lemon juice, cumin, and a sprinkle of fresh herbs, becomes a hearty vegetarian meal in this delicious pasta.

Tips

If using broken spaghetti, break into 1- to 1½-inch (2.5 to 4 cm) pieces for best results.

Prepared hummus is available in multiple flavor variations; use any flavor you like to vary the taste.

For extra flavor, add ½ tsp (2 mL) finely grated lemon zest. Be sure to zest the lemon before juicing.

♦ **16-oz (500 mL) mug**

½ cup	cut or broken spaghetti	125 mL
⅛ tsp	salt	0.5 mL
⅔ cup	water	150 mL
2 tbsp	hummus	30 mL
1½ tsp	lemon juice	7 mL
¼ tsp	ground cumin	1 mL
	Salt and ground black pepper	
1 tbsp	chopped fresh cilantro or parsley	15 mL

1. In the mug, combine spaghetti, salt and water. Place in the microwave atop a doubled paper towel. Microwave on High for 2 minutes. Stir. Microwave on High for 3 minutes. If the mixture appears dry, add 1 tbsp (15 mL) water to the mug. Microwave for 1½ to 2 minutes or until spaghetti is tender.

2. Stir in hummus, lemon juice and cumin until blended. Microwave on High for 15 to 30 seconds or until heated through. Let stand for 1 minute, then stir. Season to taste with salt and pepper. Stir in cilantro.

Variations

- **Gluten-Free Hummus Pasta:** Use quinoa macaroni in place of the regular macaroni and decrease the final cooking time in step 1 by 30 seconds.

- **Roasted Pepper Hummus Pasta:** Replace the cumin with an equal amount of smoked paprika and add 3 tbsp (45 mL) drained chopped jarred roasted red bell peppers.

Prep Ahead Option

Measure the spaghetti and salt into the mug; cover and store at room temperature. Measure the hummus, lemon juice, cumin and cilantro (if using) into a small airtight container; cover and refrigerate until ready to use.

Spinach, Chickpea and Feta Pasta

The salty, creamy, slightly briny flavor of feta adds an assertive edge to this Greek-inspired pasta, though milder cheeses (such as shredded Monterey Jack or Swiss) are also fine.

Tips

Opt for bags, as opposed to boxes, of frozen chopped spinach, as it is easier to remove small amounts at a time.

Add 1/4 tsp (1 mL) of your favorite dried herbs or herb blend (basil, oregano, Italian seasoning) with the feta.

Freeze the remaining tomatoes and chickpeas in separate small sealable freezer bags. You can freeze the entire amount in one bag, or portion out 1/2 cup (125 mL) per bag (for the tomatoes) or 1/3 cup (75 mL) per bag (for the chickpeas) so that they are recipe-ready. Be sure to label the bags with the contents. Store for up to 3 months. Defrost in the refrigerator or microwave before using.

To make this recipe gluten-free, use quinoa macaroni in place of the ditalini and decrease the final cooking time in step 1 by 30 seconds.

◆ **16-oz (500 mL) mug**

1 cup	frozen chopped spinach	250 mL
1/2 cup	ditalini or elbow macaroni	125 mL
1/8 tsp	salt	0.5 mL
2/3 cup	water	150 mL
1/2 cup	canned diced tomatoes with Italian seasoning, with juice	125 mL
1/3 cup	rinsed drained canned chickpeas	75 mL
2 tbsp	crumbled feta cheese	30 mL
	Salt and ground black pepper	

1. In the mug, microwave spinach on High for 1 to 2 minutes or until thawed and warm. Using the tines of a fork, press down firmly on the spinach and drain off excess liquid. Transfer to a small plate or bowl.

2. In the mug, combine ditalini, salt and water. Place in the microwave atop a doubled paper towel. Microwave on High for 2 minutes. Stir. Microwave on High for 3 minutes. If the mixture appears dry, add 1 tbsp (15 mL) water to the mug. Microwave for 1 1/2 to 2 minutes or until ditalini is tender.

3. Stir in spinach, tomatoes and chickpeas. Microwave on High for 60 to 90 seconds or until heated through. Let stand for 1 minute, then stir in feta. Season to taste with salt and pepper.

Variation

- **Spinach, Chicken and Feta Pasta:** Use an equal amount of diced cooked chicken breast (or canned water-packed chunk chicken, drained and flaked) in place of the chickpeas.

Prep Ahead Option

Measure the spinach into the mug; cover and refrigerate (decrease the cooking time in step 1 to 30 seconds). Measure the ditalini and salt into a small airtight container; cover and store at room temperature. Measure the tomatoes and chickpeas into a small airtight container; cover and refrigerate. Measure the feta into a small airtight container; cover and refrigerate until ready to use.

Pasta with White Beans, Broccoli and Parmesan

White beans and broccoli seem like something new in this hearty, satisfyingly chunky vegetarian pasta dolled up with Parmesan and lemon juice.

Tips

Opt for bags, as opposed to boxes, of frozen chopped broccoli, as it is easier to remove small amounts at a time.

Add ¼ tsp (1 mL) of your favorite dried herbs or herb blend (basil, oregano, Italian seasoning) with the Parmesan.

Freeze the remaining beans in a small sealable freezer bag. You can freeze the entire amount in one bag, or portion out ⅓ cup (75 mL) per bag so that the beans are recipe-ready. Be sure to label the bag with the contents. Store for up to 3 months. Defrost in the refrigerator or microwave before using.

♦ **16-oz (500 mL) mug**

½ cup	ditalini or elbow macaroni	125 mL
⅛ tsp	salt	0.5 mL
⅔ cup	water	150 mL
½ cup	frozen chopped broccoli	125 mL
⅓ cup	rinsed drained canned white beans (such as great Northern or cannellini)	75 mL
2 tsp	olive oil or butter	10 mL
1 tsp	lemon juice	5 mL
1½ tbsp	grated Parmesan cheese	22 mL
	Salt and ground black pepper	

1. In the mug, combine ditalini, salt and water. Place in the microwave atop a doubled paper towel. Microwave on High for 2 minutes. Stir. Microwave on High for 3½ minutes.

2. Stir in broccoli. And 1 tbsp (15 mL) water if mixture appears dry. Microwave on High for 1 to 1½ minutes.

3. Stir in beans, oil and lemon juice. Microwave on High for 45 to 60 seconds or until heated through. Let stand for 1 minute, then stir in Parmesan. Season to taste with salt and pepper.

Variations

- **Gluten-Free Mac and Cheese:** Use quinoa macaroni in place of the ditalini and decrease the final cooking time in step 1 by 30 seconds.

Prep Ahead Option

Measure the ditalini and salt into the mug; cover and store at room temperature. Measure the broccoli into a small airtight container; cover and refrigerate. Measure the beans, oil and lemon juice into a small airtight container; cover and refrigerate. Measure the Parmesan into a small airtight container; cover and refrigerate until ready to use.

Cheeseburger Noodles

The term "comfort food" might have been coined for this mug of melting Cheddar cheese surrounding hearty beef and noodles. The traditional cheeseburger accompaniments of ketchup, mustard and relish make the dish.

Tips

Add ¼ tsp (1 mL) of your favorite dried herbs or herb blend (basil, oregano, Italian seasoning) with the mustard.

Freeze the remaining tomatoes in a small sealable freezer bag. You can freeze the entire amount in one bag, or portion out ⅓ cup (75 mL) per bag so that the tomatoes are recipe-ready. Be sure to label the bag with the contents. Store for up to 3 months. Defrost in the refrigerator or microwave before using.

To make this recipe gluten-free, use quinoa macaroni in place of the regular macaroni and decrease the final cooking time in step 2 by 30 seconds. Check the packaging to make sure the meatballs and ketchup are gluten-free.

◆ 16-oz (500 mL) mug

2	frozen cooked beef meatballs	2
½ cup	elbow macaroni	125 mL
⅔ cup	water	150 mL
⅓ cup	canned diced tomatoes, with juice	75 mL
3 tbsp	shredded sharp (old) Cheddar cheese	45 mL
1 tsp	ketchup	5 mL
1 tsp	sweet pickle relish (optional)	5 mL
¼ tsp	Dijon or yellow mustard (optional)	1 mL
1 tbsp	chopped green onions (optional)	15 mL

1. In the mug, microwave meatballs on High for 1 to 2 minutes or until completely warmed through. Transfer to a small bowl and break apart with a fork.

2. In the mug, combine macaroni and water. Place in the microwave atop a doubled paper towel. Microwave on High for 2 minutes. Stir. Microwave on High for 3 minutes. If the mixture appears dry, add 1 tbsp (15 mL) water to the mug. Microwave for 1½ to 2 minutes or until macaroni is tender.

3. Stir in crumbled meatballs, tomatoes, cheese, ketchup, relish (if using) and mustard (if using) until cheese is melted. Microwave on High for 45 to 60 seconds or until heated through. Let stand for 1 minute, then stir. If desired, sprinkle with green onions.

Variation

- **Vegan Cheeseburger Noodles:** Use vegan meatballs in place of the beef meatballs and non-dairy shredded Cheddar-style cheese in place of the Cheddar cheese.

Prep Ahead Option

Place the meatballs in the mug; cover and refrigerate (decrease the cooking time in step 1 to 30 to 45 seconds). Measure the macaroni into a small airtight container; cover and store at room temperature. Measure the tomatoes, cheese, ketchup, relish (if using) and mustard (if using) into a small airtight container; cover and refrigerate. If using green onions, measure them into a small airtight container; cover and refrigerate until ready to use.

Three-Cheese Spaghetti Pie

Perfect when you're famished, this pasta mug "pie" — spaghetti, meatballs and three kinds of cheese — won't disappoint. You'll be deliciously rewarded for your (minimal) effort.

Tips

If using broken spaghetti, break into 1- to 1½-inch (2.5 to 4 cm) pieces for best results.

Add ¼ tsp (1 mL) of your favorite dried herbs or herb blend (basil, oregano, Italian seasoning) with the mozzarella.

Prep Ahead Option

Measure the meatballs into the mug; cover and refrigerate (decrease the cooking time in step 1 to 30 to 45 seconds). Measure the spaghetti into a small airtight container; cover and store at room temperature. Measure the marinara, cottage cheese and Parmesan into a small airtight container; cover and refrigerate. Measure the mozzarella into a small airtight container; cover and refrigerate until ready to use.

♦ **16-oz (500 mL) mug**

2	frozen cooked beef meatballs	2
½ cup	cut or broken spaghetti	125 mL
⅔ cup	water	150 mL
⅓ cup	marinara sauce	75 mL
¼ cup	cottage cheese	60 mL
1 tbsp	grated Parmesan cheese	15 mL
¼ cup	shredded mozzarella or Italian-blend cheese	60 mL

1. In the mug, microwave meatballs on High for 1 to 2 minutes or until completely warmed through. Transfer to a small bowl and break apart with a fork.

2. In the mug, combine spaghetti and water. Place in the microwave atop a doubled paper towel. Microwave on High for 2 minutes. Stir. Microwave on High for 3 minutes. If the mixture appears dry, add 1 tbsp (15 mL) water to the mug. Microwave for 1½ to 2 minutes or until spaghetti is tender.

3. Stir in crumbled meatballs, marinara, cottage cheese and Parmesan until blended. Sprinkle with mozzarella. Microwave on High for 30 to 45 seconds or until hot and cheese is melted. Let stand for 1 minute before eating.

Variations

- **Vegan Spaghetti Pie:** Use vegan meatballs in place of the beef meatballs and non-dairy shredded mozzarella-style cheese in place of the mozzarella cheese. Use ¼ cup (60 mL) mashed drained soft silken tofu in place of the cottage cheese. Omit the Parmesan.

- **Gluten-Free Spaghetti Pie:** Use quinoa spaghetti, broken in 1-inch (5 cm) lengths, in place of the regular spaghetti and decrease the final cooking time in step 2 by 30 seconds. Check the packaging to make sure that the meatballs and marinara sauce are gluten-free.

Bacon and Egg Spaghetti

A bit of bacon and an egg will quickly enliven the box of spaghetti parked in your pantry. Add nutty Parmesan for a satisfying, inexpensive meal.

Tips

If using broken spaghetti, break into 1- to 1½-inch (2.5 to 4 cm) pieces for best results.

Look for ready-to-eat real bacon bits where salad dressings and croutons are shelved in the grocery store, or near the regular bacon in the packaged meat or deli department.

Add ¼ tsp (1 mL) of your favorite dried herbs or herb blend (basil, oregano, Italian seasoning) with the Parmesan.

◆ **16-oz (500 mL) mug**

½ cup	cut or broken spaghetti	125 mL
⅛ tsp	salt	0.5 mL
⅔ cup	water	150 mL
1	large egg	1
1 tbsp	ready-to-eat real bacon bits	15 mL
1 tbsp	grated Parmesan cheese	15 mL
1 tsp	olive oil	5 mL
	Salt and ground black pepper	

1. In the mug, combine spaghetti, salt and water. Place in the microwave atop a doubled paper towel. Microwave on High for 2 minutes. Stir. Microwave on High for 3 minutes. If the mixture appears dry, add 1 tbsp (15 mL) water to the mug. Microwave for 1½ to 2 minutes or until spaghetti is tender.

2. Using a fork, quickly stir in egg, bacon, Parmesan and oil until pasta is coated. Microwave on High for 15 to 45 seconds (checking at 15) or until egg no longer appears wet and is just set. Let stand for 1 minute. Season to taste with salt and pepper.

Variation

- **Gluten-Free Bacon and Egg Spaghetti:** Use quinoa spaghetti, broken into 1-inch (2.5 cm) pieces, in place of the regular spaghetti and decrease the final cooking time in step 1 by 30 seconds.

Prep Ahead Option

Measure the spaghetti and salt into the mug; cover and store at room temperature. Measure the egg, bacon, Parmesan and oil into a small airtight container; cover and refrigerate until ready to use.

Bacon, Goat Cheese and Butternut Squash Pasta

This colorful pasta tastes like it took tremendous effort, but is actually quite simple to put together. The essential tricks include precut butternut squash (bye-bye butcher knife) and ready-to-eat real bacon bits.

Tips

Look for bags of ready-to-use diced butternut squash in the produce section. Leftover squash can be frozen in airtight containers or plastic bags for up to 3 months.

Look for ready-to-eat real bacon bits where salad dressings and croutons are shelved in the grocery store, or near the regular bacon in the packaged meat or deli department.

♦ **16-oz (500 mL) mug**

½ cup	ditalini or elbow macaroni	125 mL
¼ cup	ready-to-use fresh or frozen diced butternut squash	60 mL
⅛ tsp	salt	0.5 mL
¾ cup	water	175 mL
2 tbsp	crumbled goat cheese	30 mL
1 tbsp	ready-to-eat real bacon bits	15 mL
	Salt and ground black pepper	

1. In the mug, combine ditalini, squash, salt and water. Place in the microwave atop a doubled paper towel. Microwave on High for 2 minutes. Stir. Microwave on High for 3 minutes. If the mixture appears dry, add 1 tbsp (15 mL) water to the mug. Microwave for 1½ to 2 minutes or until ditalini and squash are tender.

2. Stir in goat cheese and bacon until cheese is melted. Microwave on High for 15 to 30 seconds or until heated through. Let stand for 1 minute, then stir. Season to taste with salt and pepper.

Variations

- **Gluten-Free Bacon, Goat Cheese and Butternut Squash Pasta:** Use quinoa macaroni in place of the ditalini and decrease the final cooking time in step 1 by 30 seconds.

> **Prep Ahead Option**
> Combine the macaroni, squash and salt in the mug; cover and refrigerate. Measure the goat cheese and bacon into a small airtight container; cover and refrigerate until ready to use.

Antipasto Pasta

Taking a cue from Italian antipasto platters, this piquant pasta is tossed with seasoned tomatoes, white beans, salami and cheese, then further enlivened with briny olives and fresh parsley.

Tips

Add ¼ tsp (1 mL) of your favorite dried herbs or herb blend (basil, oregano, Italian seasoning) with the cheese.

Freeze the remaining tomatoes and chickpeas in separate small sealable freezer bags. You can freeze the entire amount in one bag, or portion out ⅓ cup (75 mL) per bag so that the tomatoes and chickpeas are recipe-ready. Be sure to label the bags with the contents. Store for up to 3 months. Defrost in the refrigerator or microwave before using.

♦ **16-oz (500 mL) mug**

½ cup	ditalini or elbow macaroni	125 mL
⅔ cup	water	150 mL
⅓ cup	canned diced tomatoes with Italian seasoning, with juice	75 mL
⅓ cup	rinsed drained canned chickpeas or white beans (such as cannellini or navy)	75 mL
2 tbsp	chopped salami	30 mL
1 tbsp	sliced drained brine-cured or ripe olives	15 mL
1 tbsp	olive oil	15 mL
1 tbsp	diced or crumbled cheese (such as mozzarella, goat cheese or feta)	15 mL
1 tbsp	chopped fresh parsley	15 mL
	Salt and ground black pepper	

1. In the mug, combine ditalini and water. Place in the microwave atop a doubled paper towel. Microwave on High for 2 minutes. Stir. Microwave on High for 3 minutes. If the mixture appears dry, add 1 tbsp (15 mL) water to the mug. Microwave for 1½ to 2 minutes or until ditalini is tender.

2. Stir in tomatoes, chickpeas, salami, olives and oil. Microwave on High for 30 to 45 seconds or until heated through. Let stand for 1 minute, then stir in cheese and parsley. Season to taste with salt and pepper.

Variation

• **Gluten-Free Antipasto Pasta:** Use quinoa macaroni in place of the ditalini and decrease the final cooking time in step 1 by 30 seconds.

Prep Ahead Option

Measure the ditalini into the mug; cover and store at room temperature. Measure the tomatoes, chickpeas, salami, olives and oil into a small airtight container; cover and refrigerate. Measure the cheese and parsley into a small container; cover and refrigerate until ready to use.

Sausage and Pepper Pasta

Here's a substantial, pasta-style spin on an Italian sausage and peppers sandwich, rich with marinara sauce and two kinds of cheese.

Tips

If a frozen pepper and onion stir-fry blend isn't available, use ⅔ cup (150 mL) mixed sliced fresh bell peppers and onions and, in step 3, cook for about 2 minutes or until vegetables are tender-crisp.

Add ¼ tsp (1 mL) dried Italian seasoning with the cheeses.

Prep Ahead Option

Place the sausages in the mug; cover and refrigerate (decrease the cooking time in step 1 to 30 seconds). Measure the ditalini and salt into a small airtight container; cover and store at room temperature. Measure the stir-fry blend into a small airtight container; cover and refrigerate (decrease the cooking time in step 3 by 30 seconds). Measure the marinara sauce, Italian-blend cheese and Parmesan into a small airtight container; cover and refrigerate until ready to use.

♦ **16-oz (500 mL) mug**

2	frozen cooked breakfast sausage links	2
½ cup	ditalini or elbow macaroni	125 mL
⅛ tsp	salt	0.5 mL
⅔ cup	water	150 mL
⅔ cup	frozen sliced bell pepper and onion stir-fry blend	150 mL
⅓ cup	marinara sauce	75 mL
2 tbsp	shredded Italian-blend or mozzarella cheese	30 mL
1 tbsp	grated Parmesan cheese	15 mL
	Salt and ground black pepper	

1. In the mug, microwave sausages on High for 60 to 75 seconds or until heated through. Transfer to a small bowl and break apart with a fork.

2. In the mug, combine ditalini, salt and water. Place in the microwave atop a doubled paper towel. Microwave on High for 2 minutes. Stir. Microwave on High for 3 minutes. If the mixture appears dry, add 1 tbsp (15 mL) water to the mug. Microwave for 1½ to 2 minutes or until ditalini is tender.

3. Stir in stir-fry blend. Microwave on High for 1½ to 2 minutes or until heated through.

4. Stir in sausages, marinara sauce, Italian-blend cheese and Parmesan. Microwave on High for 30 to 45 seconds or until heated through. Let stand for 1 minute, then stir. Season to taste with salt and pepper.

Variation

- **Gluten-Free Sausage and Pepper Pasta:** Use quinoa macaroni in place of the ditalini and decrease the final cooking time in step 2 by 30 seconds.

Chicken Noodle Mug

Is there anything more comforting than the combination of chicken and noodles? It's doubtful. Here, most of the broth is absorbed into the spaghetti noodles, leading to a stick-to-the-ribs, pasta-style version of the classic soup.

Tips

If using broken spaghetti, break into 1- to 1½-inch (2.5 to 4 cm) pieces for best results.

Add ¼ tsp (1 mL) of your favorite dried herbs or herb blend (basil, oregano, Italian seasoning) with the peas and carrots.

♦ **16-oz (500 mL) mug**

½ cup	cut or broken spaghetti	125 mL
¾ cup	chicken broth	175 mL
1	can (5 oz/142 g) water-packed chunk chicken, drained and flaked	1
⅓ cup	frozen peas and carrots	125 mL
	Salt and ground black pepper	

1. In the mug, combine spaghetti and broth. Place in the microwave atop a doubled paper towel. Microwave on High for 2 minutes. Stir. Microwave on High for 3 minutes. If the mixture appears dry, add 1 tbsp (15 mL) water to the mug. Microwave for 1½ to 2 minutes or until spaghetti is tender.

2. Stir in chicken and peas and carrots. Microwave on High for 60 to 90 seconds or until heated through. Let stand for 1 minute, then stir. Season to taste with salt and pepper.

Variation

- **Gluten-Free Chicken Noodle Mug:** Use quinoa spaghetti, broken into 1-inch (2.5 cm) pieces, in place of the regular spaghetti and decrease the final cooking time in step 1 by 30 seconds.

> **Prep Ahead Option**
> Measure the spaghetti into the mug; cover and store at room temperature. Measure the broth into a small airtight container; cover and refrigerate. Measure the chicken and peas and carrots into a small container; cover and refrigerate until ready to use (decrease the cooking time in step 2 by 30 seconds).

Salmon and Dill Orzo

Just a sprinkle of lemon zest, lemon juice and dill beautifully highlights the flavor of the salmon in this dish.

Tip

Store the remaining drained salmon in a small airtight container or freezer bag in the freezer for up to 3 months.

♦ **16-oz (500 mL) mug**

$1/3$ cup	orzo or other small pasta	75 mL
$1/8$ tsp	salt	0.5 mL
$2/3$ cup	water	150 mL
$1/2$	can (5 oz/142 g) boneless salmon, drained and flaked	$1/2$
$1/2$ tsp	dried dillweed	2 mL
1 tbsp	olive oil	15 mL
$1/2$ tsp	finely grated lemon zest	2 mL
2 tsp	freshly squeezed lemon juice	10 mL
	Salt and ground black pepper	

1. In the mug, combine orzo, salt and water. Place in the microwave atop a doubled paper towel. Microwave on High for 2 minutes. Stir. Microwave on High for 3 minutes. If the mixture appears dry, add 1 tbsp (15 mL) water to the mug. Microwave for $1^1/2$ to 2 minutes or until orzo is tender.

2. Stir in salmon, dill and oil. Microwave on High for 30 to 60 seconds or until heated through. Stir in lemon zest and lemon juice. Let stand for 1 minute, then stir. Season to taste with salt and pepper.

Variation

• **Dilled Shrimp Orzo:** Use $1/3$ cup (75 mL) drained canned small shrimp in place of the salmon.

Prep Ahead Option

Measure the orzo and salt into the mug; cover and store at room temperature. Measure the salmon, dill and oil into a small airtight container; cover and refrigerate. Measure the lemon zest and lemon juice into a small airtight container; cover and refrigerate until ready to use.

Cheesy Tuna Pasta Casserole

Even those who prefer their tuna in salads and sandwiches will be won over by this home-style preparation.

Tips

Add ¼ tsp (1 mL) of your favorite dried herbs or herb blend (dill, basil, oregano, Italian seasoning) with the cheese.

Crushed potato chips or tortilla chips can be used in place of the crushed croutons.

To crush croutons, place them in a small sealable plastic bag. Seal, then pound the croutons with a heavy object (such as a can, mallet or book) until crushed.

Store the remaining drained tuna in a small airtight container or freezer bag in the freezer for up to 3 months.

◆ 16-oz (500 mL) mug

⅓ cup	small shell pasta or elbow macaroni	75 mL
⅛ tsp	salt	0.5 mL
⅔ cup	water	150 mL
⅓ cup	frozen peas and carrots	75 mL
½	can (6 oz/170 g) water-packed chunk white tuna, drained and flaked	½
2 tbsp	shredded Cheddar cheese	30 mL
2 tbsp	Alfredo sauce	30 mL
	Salt and ground black pepper	
2	garlic croutons, crushed (optional)	2

1. In the mug, combine shells, salt and water. Place in the microwave atop a doubled paper towel. Microwave on High for 2 minutes. Stir. Microwave on High for 3 minutes. If the mixture appears dry, add 1 tbsp (15 mL) water to the mug. Microwave for 1½ to 2 minutes or until shells are tender.

2. Stir in peas and carrots. Microwave on High for 45 to 75 seconds or until heated through.

3. Stir in tuna, Cheddar and Alfredo sauce until cheese is melted. Microwave on High for 30 seconds. Let stand for 1 minute, then stir. Season to taste with salt and pepper. If desired, sprinkle with croutons.

Variations

- **Cheesy Chicken Pasta Casserole:** Use ⅓ cup (75 mL) diced cooked chicken breast in place of the tuna.

- **Gluten-Free Tuna Casserole:** Use quinoa macaroni in place of the regular macaroni and decrease the final cooking time in step 1 by 30 seconds. Omit the crouton topping or use gluten-free croutons.

Prep Ahead Option

Measure the shells and salt into the mug; cover and store at room temperature. Measure the peas and carrots into a small airtight container; cover and refrigerate (decrease the cooking time in step 2 by 15 seconds). Measure the tuna, Cheddar and Alfredo sauce into a small airtight container; cover and refrigerate. If using croutons, crush them (see tip, at left) and store in the bag at room temperature until ready to use.

Tuna Pasta with Capers and Lemon

Tuna is often tossed with mayonnaise and pickle relish, but switching things up with olive oil and lemon — not to mention briny capers and fresh parsley — turns a workhorse into a thoroughbred.

Tips

Add $1/4$ tsp (1 mL) of your favorite dried herbs or herb blend (dill, basil, oregano, Italian seasoning) with the tuna.

Store the remaining drained tuna in a small airtight container or freezer bag in the freezer for up to 3 months.

♦ **16-oz (500 mL) mug**

$1/3$ cup	orzo or other small pasta	75 mL
$1/8$ tsp	salt	0.5 mL
$2/3$ cup	water	150 mL
$1/2$	can (6 oz/170 g) water-packed chunk white tuna, drained and flaked	$1/2$
1 tbsp	olive oil	15 mL
2 tsp	drained capers	10 mL
$1/2$ tsp	finely grated lemon zest	2 mL
2 tsp	freshly squeezed lemon juice	10 mL
	Salt and ground black pepper	
1 tbsp	chopped fresh parsley (optional)	15 mL

1. In the mug, combine orzo, salt and water. Place in the microwave atop a doubled paper towel. Microwave on High for 2 minutes. Stir. Microwave on High for 3 minutes. If the mixture appears dry, add 1 tbsp (15 mL) water to the mug. Microwave for $1^1/_2$ to 2 minutes or until orzo is tender.

2. Stir in tuna, oil, capers, lemon zest and lemon juice. Microwave on High for 45 to 75 seconds or until heated through. Let stand for 1 minute, then stir. Season to taste with salt and pepper. If desired, stir in parsley.

Variations

- **Chicken Pasta with Capers and Lemon:** Use half a 5-oz (142 g) can of water-packed chunk chicken, drained and flaked, in place of the tuna.

- **Gluten-Free Tuna Pasta with Capers and Lemon:** Use quinoa macaroni in place of the regular macaroni and decrease the final cooking time in step 1 by 30 seconds.

Prep Ahead Option

Measure the orzo and salt into the mug; cover and store at room temperature. Measure the tuna, oil, capers, lemon zest and lemon juice into a small airtight container; cover and refrigerate. If using parsley, measure it into a small airtight container; cover and refrigerate until ready to use.

Miso Noodles

Miso adds a meaty umami boost to this vegetarian, tofu-enriched noodle mug.

Tip

If using broken spaghetti, break into 1- to 1½-inch (2.5 to 4 cm) pieces for best results.

♦ **16-oz (500 mL) mug**

½ cup	cut or broken spaghetti	125 mL
¾ cup	water	175 mL
⅓ cup	diced firm or extra-firm tofu	75 mL
2 tbsp	thinly sliced green onions	30 mL
1½ tbsp	mirin or cooking sherry	22 mL
2½ tsp	miso paste	12 mL

1. In the mug, combine spaghetti and water. Place in the microwave atop a doubled paper towel. Microwave on High for 2 minutes. Stir. Microwave on High for 3 minutes. If the mixture appears dry, add 1 tbsp (15 mL) water to the mug. Microwave for 1½ to 2 minutes or until spaghetti is tender.

2. Stir in tofu, green onions, mirin and miso. Microwave on High for 15 to 30 seconds or until heated through. Let stand for 1 minute, then stir.

Variations

- **Miso Bok Choy Noodles:** Add ½ cup (125 mL) thinly sliced bok choy during the last minute of the pasta's cook time.

- **Miso Chicken Noodles:** Replace the tofu with half a 5-oz (142 g) can of water-packed chunk chicken, drained and flaked.

> **Prep Ahead Option**
> Measure the spaghetti into the mug; cover and store at room temperature. Measure the tofu, green onions, mirin and miso into a small airtight container; cover and refrigerate until ready to use.

Sesame Noodles

Aromatic sesame oil and a splash of hot pepper sauce give these Asian-inspired noodles full, deep flavor and a hint of heat. Rich with umami, they are near-instant satisfaction.

Tips

If using broken spaghetti, break into 1- to 1$\frac{1}{2}$-inch (2.5 to 4 cm) pieces for best results.

Try adding 2 tbsp (30 mL) chopped green onions with the soy sauce.

Consider sprinkling the finished noodles with 1 tsp (5 mL) toasted sesame seeds. Look for toasted sesame seeds where Asian ingredients are shelved.

For a piquant touch, add $\frac{1}{4}$ tsp (1 mL) ground ginger with the garlic powder.

For a higher-protein meal, add up to $\frac{1}{3}$ cup (75 mL) diced cooked chicken, diced deli roast beef, diced tempeh or drained canned tiny shrimp.

♦ **16-oz (500 mL) mug**

$\frac{1}{2}$ cup	cut or broken spaghetti	125 mL
Pinch	salt	Pinch
$\frac{2}{3}$ cup	water	150 mL
1$\frac{1}{2}$ tsp	granulated sugar	7 mL
$\frac{1}{4}$ tsp	garlic powder	1 mL
1 tbsp	soy sauce	15 mL
1$\frac{1}{2}$ tsp	toasted sesame oil	7 mL
1 tsp	white or cider vinegar	5 mL
$\frac{1}{8}$ tsp	hot pepper sauce	0.5 mL

1. In the mug, combine spaghetti, salt and water. Place in the microwave atop a doubled paper towel. Microwave on High for 2 minutes. Stir. Microwave on High for 3 minutes. If the mixture appears dry, add 1 tbsp (15 mL) water to the mug. Microwave for 1$\frac{1}{2}$ to 2 minutes or until spaghetti is tender.

2. Stir in sugar, garlic powder, soy sauce, oil, vinegar and hot pepper sauce. Microwave on High for 10 to 20 seconds or until heated through. Let stand for 1 minute, then stir.

Variations

- **Gluten-Free Sesame Noodles:** Use quinoa spaghetti, broken into 1-inch (2.5 cm) pieces, in place of the regular spaghetti and decrease the final cooking time in step 1 by 30 seconds. Use gluten-free soy sauce.

Prep Ahead Option

Measure the spaghetti and salt into the mug; cover and store at room temperature. Measure the sugar, garlic powder, soy sauce, oil, vinegar and hot pepper sauce into a small airtight container; cover and refrigerate until ready to use.

Brown Rice with Edamame and Pineapple

Here, the light, tropical combination of pineapple and brown rice is given texture and heft with the additions of edamame and cashews, turning it into a flavorful main course mug.

Tips

You can use $2/3$ cup (150 mL) cooked brown rice (or any other cooked grain, such as quinoa, barley or bulgur) in place of the instant brown rice. In step 1, microwave the edamame in the water on High for 5 to 6 minutes or until heated through. Drain. Add the cooked rice with the pineapple in step 2. Increase the cooking time by 45 to 60 seconds.

Chopped roasted peanuts or almonds can be used in place of the cashews.

◆ 16-oz (500 mL) mug

$1/2$ cup	instant brown rice	125 mL
$2/3$ cup	water	150 mL
$1/3$ cup	frozen shelled edamame	75 mL
$1/4$ cup	diced fresh or drained canned pineapple	60 mL
1 tbsp	teriyaki sauce	15 mL
	Hot pepper sauce	
2 tbsp	chopped cashews	30 mL

Suggested Accompaniments

Sliced green onions; chopped fresh mint or cilantro

1. In the mug, combine rice and water. Place edamame on top. Cover with a small plate or saucer. Microwave on High for 5 to 6 minutes or until almost all of the water has been absorbed. Remove from oven and let stand, covered, for 1 minute to absorb the remaining water.

2. Stir in pineapple and teriyaki sauce. Microwave, uncovered, on High for 30 to 45 seconds or until pineapple is heated through. Let stand for 30 seconds. Stir, then season to taste with hot pepper sauce. Sprinkle with cashews and any of the suggested accompaniments, as desired.

> **Prep Ahead Option**
> Measure the rice and edamame into the mug; cover and refrigerate. Measure the pineapple and teriyaki sauce into a small airtight container; cover and refrigerate. Measure the cashews into a small airtight container; cover and store at room temperature until ready to use.

Hoppin' John

Hoppin' John is a classic dish from the American South, traditionally served on New Year's Day to bring good luck in the coming year. Although countless variations exist, the core ingredients remain constant: rice, black-eyed peas, smoked pork (ham, bacon or smoked sausage) and onions. It is pure comfort food.

Tips

Try adding $1/8$ tsp (0.5 mL) dried thyme with the tomatoes.

An equal amount of thick and chunky salsa can be used in place of the tomatoes with chiles.

Look for ready-to-eat real bacon bits where salad dressings and croutons are shelved in the grocery store, or near the regular bacon in the packaged meat or deli department.

Freeze the remaining black-eyed peas and tomatoes in separate small sealable freezer bags. You can freeze the entire amount in one bag, or portion out $1/2$ cup (125 mL) per bag (for the peas) or $1/3$ cup (75mL) per bag (for the tomatoes) so that they are recipe-ready. Be sure to label the bags with the contents. Store for up to 3 months. Defrost in the refrigerator or microwave before using.

◆ 16-oz (500 mL) mug

$1/2$ cup	instant brown rice	125 mL
$2/3$ cup	water	150 mL
$1/2$ cup	rinsed drained canned black-eyed peas	125 mL
$1/3$ cup	canned diced tomatoes with green chiles, with juice	75 mL
2 tbsp	chopped green onions	30 mL
1 tbsp	ready-to-eat real bacon bits	15 mL
	Salt and hot pepper sauce	

1. In the mug, combine rice and water. Cover with a small plate or saucer. Microwave on High for 5 to 6 minutes or until almost all of the water has been absorbed. Remove from oven and stir in peas. Let stand, covered, for 1 minute to absorb the remaining water.

2. Stir in tomatoes, green onions and bacon. Microwave, uncovered, on High for 20 to 30 seconds or until heated through. Let stand for 30 seconds, then stir. Season to taste with salt and hot pepper sauce.

Variation

- **Vegetarian Hoppin' John:** Omit the bacon. If desired, add a dash of liquid smoke with the peas.

Prep Ahead Option

Measure the rice into the mug; cover and refrigerate. Measure the peas into a small airtight container; cover and refrigerate. Measure the tomatoes, green onions and bacon into a small airtight container; cover and refrigerate until ready to use.

Paella

Paella, one of the ultimate comfort foods of Spain, gets assembled in a mug for this simplified revamp of a classic.

Tips

You can use $2/3$ cup (150 mL) cooked brown rice (or any other cooked grain, such as quinoa, barley or bulgur) in place of the instant brown rice. In step 1, microwave the pepper and onion blend for $1\frac{1}{2}$ to 2 minutes or until heated through. Add the peas and microwave for 20 to 30 seconds or until heated through. Drain off excess liquid. Stir in the rice with the shrimp and increase the cooking time in step 2 by 30 to 45 seconds.

Try adding $\frac{1}{8}$ tsp (0.5 mL) dried oregano and/or $\frac{1}{4}$ tsp (1 mL) smoked paprika with the marinara sauce.

If a frozen pepper and onion blend isn't available, use $\frac{1}{3}$ cup (75 mL) mixed chopped fresh bell peppers and onions.

◆ 16-oz (500 mL) mug

$\frac{1}{2}$ cup	instant brown rice	125 mL
$2/3$ cup	water	150 mL
$\frac{1}{3}$ cup	frozen chopped bell pepper and onion blend	75 mL
2 tbsp	frozen petite green peas	30 mL
$\frac{1}{4}$ cup	drained canned small shrimp	60 mL
2 tbsp	diced or chopped ham	30 mL
2 tbsp	marinara sauce	30 mL
	Salt and ground black pepper	
	Chopped fresh parsley (optional)	

1. In the mug, combine rice and water. Place pepper and onion blend on top. Cover with a small plate or saucer. Microwave on High for 5 to 6 minutes or until almost all of the water has been absorbed. Remove from oven and stir in peas. Let stand, covered, for 1 minute to absorb the remaining water.

2. Stir in shrimp, ham and marinara sauce. Microwave, uncovered, on High for 45 to 60 seconds or until heated through. Let stand for 30 seconds, then stir. Season to taste with salt and pepper. Sprinkle with parsley, if desired.

Prep Ahead Option

Measure the rice into the mug; cover and store at room temperature. Measure the pepper and onion blend into a small airtight container; cover and refrigerate. Measure the peas into a small airtight container; cover and refrigerate. Measure the shrimp, ham and marinara sauce into a small airtight container; cover and refrigerate until ready to use.

Brown Rice Risotto

You'll love the satisfying simplicity of this quick dish, especially the contrast of rustic brown rice against the risotto's Parmesan-amplified creaminess.

Tips

You can use $2/3$ cup (150 mL) cooked brown rice (or any other cooked grain, such as quinoa, barley or bulgur) in place of the instant brown rice. Add the rice and 1 tbsp (15 mL) broth to the onion mixture after step 1 and microwave for 60 seconds. Cover and let stand for 1 minute, then proceed with step 3.

An equal amount of evaporated milk can be used in place of the cream.

Finely chopped green onion can be used in place of the chopped onion.

♦ **16-oz (500 mL) mug**

1 tbsp	chopped onion	15 mL
2 tsp	butter	10 mL
$1/2$ cup	instant brown rice	125 mL
$2/3$ cup	ready-to-use chicken or vegetable broth	150 mL
2 tbsp	half-and-half (10%) cream or heavy or whipping (35%) cream	30 mL
2 tbsp	grated Parmesan cheese, divided	30 mL
	Salt and ground black pepper	

1. In the mug, microwave onion and butter on High for $1/2$ to 2 minutes or until onion is softened.

2. Add rice and broth. Cover with a small plate or saucer. Microwave on High for 5 to 6 minutes or until almost all of the broth has been absorbed. Remove from oven and let stand, covered, for 1 minute to absorb the remaining broth.

3. Stir in cream and $1^{1}/_{2}$ tbsp (22 mL) Parmesan. Microwave, uncovered, on High for 30 to 45 seconds or until heated through. Let stand for 1 minute. Season to taste with salt and pepper. Sprinkle with remaining Parmesan.

> **Prep Ahead Option**
>
> Measure the onion and butter into the mug; cover and refrigerate. Measure the rice and broth into a small airtight container; cover and refrigerate. Measure the cream and $1^{1}/_{2}$ tbsp (22 mL) Parmesan into a small airtight container; cover and refrigerate. Measure the remaining Parmesan into a small airtight container; cover and refrigerate until ready to use.

Mushroom Barley Risotto

Even barley skeptics will enjoy this textural dish full of buttery mushrooms, herbs and Parmesan cheese.

Tips

Look for quick-cooking barley near the rice or near the soups at the supermarket. If you can't find it, you can use ⅔ cup (150 mL) cooked pearl barley. Reduce the broth to 1½ tbsp (22 mL) and decrease the cooking time in step 2 to 1½ minutes.

You can use an equal amount of instant brown rice in place of the quick-cooking barley.

An equal amount of water, plus ⅛ tsp (0.5 mL) salt, can be used in place of the broth.

You can use ¼ cup (60 mL) drained canned mushroom pieces in place of the fresh mushrooms.

♦ 16-oz (500 mL) mug

1	green onion, chopped, green and white parts separated	1
½ cup	chopped mushrooms	125 mL
2 tsp	butter	10 mL
¼ cup	quick-cooking barley	60 mL
¼ tsp	dried Italian seasoning	1 mL
⅔ cup	ready-to-use beef, chicken or vegetable broth	150 mL
1 tbsp	grated Parmesan cheese	15 mL

1. In the mug, combine white part of green onion, mushrooms and butter. Microwave on High for 1 minute or until tender.
2. Stir in barley, Italian seasoning and broth. Microwave on High for 4 minutes. Stir. Microwave on High for 4 to 5 minutes or until barley is tender (some liquid will remain). Cover with a small plate or saucer and let stand for 2 minutes. Stir in Parmesan and green part of green onion.

Prep Ahead Option

Combine the white part of green onion, mushrooms and butter in the mug; cover and refrigerate. Measure the barley into a small airtight container; cover and store at room temperature. Measure the Italian seasoning and broth into a small airtight container; cover and refrigerate. Measure the Parmesan and green part of green onion into a small airtight container; cover and refrigerate until ready to use.

Tabbouleh

Studded with diced tomatoes and fragrant lemon zest, this speedy version of tabbouleh gets an added flavor amplification from fresh mint and parsley.

Tips

For best results, use bulgur that is labeled "light" or "fine." This means that the pieces of cracked wheat are smaller than other varieties of bulgur and cook more quickly than coarse varieties.

You can omit the mint and increase the chopped parsley to 2 tbsp (30 mL); alternatively, you can omit the parsley and increase the mint to 2 tbsp (30 mL).

♦ **16-oz (500 mL) mug**

1/2 cup	water	125 mL
1/4 cup	cracked wheat bulgur	60 mL
1/4 tsp	salt	1 mL
1/2 cup	chopped or diced tomato	125 mL
1/4 tsp	ground cumin	1 mL
1/2 tsp	finely grated lemon zest	2 mL
1 tbsp	freshly squeezed lemon juice	15 mL
1 tbsp	olive oil	15 mL
1 tbsp	chopped fresh parsley	15 mL
1 tbsp	chopped fresh mint	15 mL
	Salt and ground black pepper	

1. In the mug, microwave water on High for 2 to 3 minutes or until boiling.

2. Stir in bulgur and salt. Cover with a small plate or saucer. Microwave on High for 5 to 6 minutes or until most of the liquid is absorbed. Remove from oven and let stand, covered, for 20 minutes or until water is completely absorbed.

3. Stir in tomato, cumin, lemon zest, lemon juice and oil. Refrigerate for at least 5 minutes. Stir in parsley and mint. Season to taste with salt and pepper.

Variation

- **Spiced Raisin Tabbouleh:** Omit the tomato and add 1 1/2 tbsp (22 mL) raisins with the bulgur. Add 1/8 tsp (0.5 mL) ground cinnamon with the cumin.

Prep Ahead Option

Measure the bulgur and salt into a small airtight container; cover and store at room temperature. Measure the tomato, cumin, lemon zest, lemon juice and oil into a small airtight container; cover and refrigerate. Measure the parsley and mint into a small airtight container; cover and refrigerate until ready to use.

Mediterranean Chickpea Couscous

This vegetarian mugful will bowl you over with its layers of flavor. Herbed couscous serves as a light and fluffy base for toothsome chickpeas, sweet sun-dried tomatoes, bright lemon juice and nutty Parmesan cheese.

Tips

Either regular or whole wheat couscous can be used in the dish.

Freeze the remaining chickpeas in a small sealable freezer bag. You can freeze the entire amount in one bag, or portion out 1/2 cup (125 mL) per bag so that the chickpeas are recipe-ready. Be sure to label the bag with the contents. Store for up to 3 months. Defrost in the refrigerator or microwave before using.

♦ **16-oz (500 mL) mug**

1/3 cup	ready-to-use chicken or vegetable broth	75 mL
1/2 cup	rinsed drained canned chickpeas	125 mL
1/4 cup	couscous	60 mL
1/2 tsp	dried Italian seasoning	2 mL
1 tbsp	chopped oil-packed sun-dried tomatoes	15 mL
1 tbsp	grated Parmesan cheese	15 mL
2 tsp	lemon juice	10 mL
	Salt and ground black pepper	

1. In the mug, microwave broth on High for 2 to 3 minutes or until boiling.

2. Stir in chickpeas, couscous and Italian seasoning. Cover with a small plate or saucer and let stand for 5 minutes.

3. Using a fork, fluff couscous mixture and stir in sun-dried tomatoes, Parmesan and lemon juice. Season to taste with salt and pepper.

Variations

- **Chickpea Couscous with Dates and Goat Cheese:** Replace the Italian seasoning with 1/4 tsp (1 mL) ground cinnamon. Omit the tomatoes and add 2 tbsp (30 mL) chopped dates with the chickpeas. Replace the Parmesan with 2 tbsp (30 mL) crumbled goat cheese.

- **Mediterranean Chicken Couscous:** Omit the chickpeas. Add half a 5-oz (142 g) can of water-packed chunk chicken, drained and flaked, with the sun-dried tomatoes.

Prep Ahead Option

Measure the broth into the mug; cover and refrigerate. Measure the chickpeas, couscous and Italian seasoning into a small airtight container; cover and refrigerate. Measure the sun-dried tomatoes, Parmesan and lemon juice into a small airtight container; cover and refrigerate until ready to use.

Mug Polenta

This velvety mug of cornmeal comfort can be topped with just about any savory bits and pieces you like — think cheeses, meats, herbs, sauces, vegetables — for a soul-satisfying meal in a hurry.

Tip

Stone-ground (aka coarse-grind) cornmeal produces a polenta with a thicker texture and fuller flavor than regular cornmeal. Look for it where regular cornmeal is shelved, or in the natural foods section of the supermarket.

◆ **16-oz (500 mL) mug**

¼ cup	yellow cornmeal (preferably stone-ground)	60 mL
1 cup	ready-to-use chicken or vegetable broth	250 mL
2 tbsp	milk	30 mL
1 tbsp	grated Parmesan cheese (optional)	15 mL
1 tbsp	butter	15 mL
	Salt and ground black pepper	

1. In the mug, combine cornmeal and broth. Place in the microwave atop a doubled paper towel. Microwave on High for 3 to 4 minutes or until bubbling.

2. Stir in milk. Microwave on High for 2 minutes. Stir. Microwave on High for 30 to 90 seconds or until thickened. Stir in Parmesan (if using) and butter until butter is melted. Season to taste with salt and pepper.

Variations

- **Blue Cheese and Bacon Polenta:** Top with 1 tbsp (15 mL) crumbled blue cheese and 1 tbsp (15 mL) ready-to-eat real bacon bits.

- **Marinara and Cheese Polenta:** Top with 2 tbsp (30 mL) marinara sauce and 2 tbsp (30 mL) shredded Italian-blend cheese or 1 tbsp (15 mL) grated Parmesan cheese.

- **Pesto Polenta:** Top with 1 tbsp (15 mL) basil pesto and 2 tbsp (30 mL) shredded Italian-blend cheese.

- **Double-Corn Polenta:** Add ¼ cup (60 mL) frozen corn kernels and ¼ tsp (1 mL) dried basil with the milk.

Prep Ahead Option

Measure the cornmeal into the mug; cover and store at room temperature. Measure the broth, milk, Parmesan (if using) and butter into separate small airtight containers; cover and refrigerate until ready to use.

Shrimp and Grits

Here, shrimp and salsa join forces with quick-cooking grits in a mug-style take on a Southern favorite.

♦ **12- to 16-oz (375 to 500 mL) mug**

3 tbsp	quick-cooking grits	45 mL
$^1/_2$ cup	milk	125 mL
$^1/_4$ cup	water	60 mL
1 tbsp	grated Parmesan cheese	30 mL
	Salt and ground black pepper	
1	can (4 oz/114 g) cooked tiny shrimp, drained	1
3 tbsp	thick and chunky salsa	45 mL
Pinch	dried thyme	Pinch

1. In the mug, combine grits, milk and water. Microwave on High for 60 to 90 seconds or until beginning to bubble at the edges. Stir. Microwave on High for 60 to 90 seconds (checking at 60) or until thickened and creamy. Stir in Parmesan. Let stand for 30 seconds. Season to taste with salt and pepper.

2. Meanwhile, in a small bowl or cup, combine shrimp, salsa and thyme. Spoon on top of grits. Microwave on High for 30 to 40 seconds or until heated through.

Variation

• **Smoked Sausage and Grits:** Replace the shrimp with $^2/_3$ cup (150 mL) diced cooked smoked sausage.

Prep Ahead Option

Measure the grits into the mug; cover and refrigerate. Measure the milk and water into a small airtight container; cover and refrigerate. Measure the Parmesan into a small airtight container; cover and refrigerate. Measure the shrimp, salsa and thyme into a small airtight container; cover and refrigerate until ready to use.

Primavera Quinoa Mug

This quinoa mug is so simple, and so good for you. Gluten-free, high in protein and low on the glycemic index, quinoa is one of the most nutritious items to have in the pantry. But all you really need to know is that this mix of quinoa, feta, vegetables and nuts is satisfying, energizing and very delicious.

Tips

Frozen asparagus pieces can be used in place of the fresh asparagus.

An equal amount of water, plus $\frac{1}{8}$ tsp (0.5 mL) salt, can be used in place of the broth.

Freeze the remaining chickpeas in a small sealable freezer bag. You can freeze the entire amount in one bag, or portion out $\frac{1}{2}$ cup (125 mL) per bag so that the chickpeas are recipe-ready. Be sure to label the bag with the contents. Store for up to 3 months. Defrost in the refrigerator or microwave before using.

◆ 16-oz (500 mL) mug

$\frac{1}{3}$ cup	quinoa, rinsed	75 mL
$\frac{2}{3}$ cup	ready-to-use chicken or vegetable broth	150 mL
$\frac{1}{2}$ cup	chopped asparagus	125 mL
$\frac{1}{2}$ cup	rinsed drained canned chickpeas	125 mL
2 tbsp	crumbled feta cheese	30 mL
1 tbsp	coarsely chopped roasted almonds	15 mL
1 tbsp	chopped fresh parsley or cilantro	15 mL
1 tbsp	olive oil	15 mL
2 tsp	white wine vinegar	10 mL
	Salt and ground black pepper	

1. In the mug, combine quinoa and broth. Microwave on High for 5 minutes. Stir. Microwave on High for 2 minutes.

2. Place asparagus on top of quinoa. Cover with a small plate or saucer. Microwave on High for 2 to 3 minutes or almost all of the water is absorbed.

3. Stir in chickpeas, feta, almonds, parsley, oil and vinegar. Let stand, covered, for 1 minute to warm through. Season to taste with salt and pepper.

Prep Ahead Option

Measure the quinoa and broth into the mug; cover and refrigerate. Measure the asparagus into a small airtight container; cover and refrigerate. Measure the chickpeas, feta, almonds, parsley, oil and vinegar into a small airtight container; cover and refrigerate until ready to use.

Loaded Quinoa Taco Mug

If you're hankering for a healthy version of Tex-Mex, look no further than this hearty mug. Nutty quinoa is the base for all of your favorite fillings and fixings, from black beans and chicken to salsa and cheese.

Tips

Pinto beans can be used in place of the black beans.

An equal amount of crumbled queso blanco can be used in place of the Cheddar cheese.

Freeze the remaining beans in a small sealable freezer bag. You can freeze the entire amount in one bag, or portion out ½ cup (125 mL) per bag so that the beans are recipe-ready. Be sure to label the bag with the contents. Store for up to 3 months. Defrost in the refrigerator or microwave before using.

♦ 16-oz (500 mL) mug

⅓ cup	quinoa, rinsed	75 mL
¼ tsp	ground cumin	1 mL
⅔ cup	ready-to-use chicken or vegetable broth	150 mL
½ cup	rinsed drained canned black beans	125 mL
⅓ cup	diced cooked chicken breast	75 mL
3 tbsp	salsa, divided	45 mL
2 tbsp	shredded Cheddar or Monterey Jack cheese	30 mL
1 tbsp	chopped fresh cilantro or green onions	15 mL

Suggested Accompaniment

Tortilla chips or warm corn or flour tortilla

1. In the mug, combine quinoa, cumin and broth. Microwave on High for 5 minutes. Stir. Microwave on High for 2 minutes. Cover with a small plate or saucer. Microwave on High for 2 to 3 minutes or almost all of the water is absorbed.

2. Stir in beans, chicken and 2 tbsp (30 mL) salsa. Cover and microwave on High for 30 to 60 seconds or until heated through. Let stand, covered, for 1 minute. Top with cheese, cilantro and remaining salsa. Serve with a suggested accompaniment, as desired.

Prep Ahead Option

Measure the quinoa, cumin and broth into the mug; cover and refrigerate. Measure the beans, chicken and 2 tbsp (30 mL) salsa into a small airtight container; cover and refrigerate. Measure the cheese and cilantro into a small airtight container; cover and refrigerate. Measure the remaining salsa into a small airtight container; cover and refrigerate until ready to use.

Snacks

Sesame Soy Edamame

Forgo potato chips and candy from the vending machine in favor of this so-simple and tasty edamame. As a bonus: a helping of protein (edamame is packed with it), which will energize you and stave off cravings for several more hours.

Tip

Look for toasted sesame seeds in small bottles in the Asian foods section of the supermarket.

♦ **12- to 16-oz (375 to 500 mL) mug**

1/2 cup	frozen shelled edamame	125 mL
1/2 cup	water	125 mL
2 tsp	soy sauce	10 mL
1/2 tsp	toasted sesame oil	2 mL
1/2 tsp	toasted sesame seeds (optional)	2 mL

1. In the mug, microwave edamame and water on High for 3 to 4 minutes (checking at 3 minutes, then every 15 seconds) or until edamame are tender but still firm. Drain and blot edamame with a paper towel, then return edamame to mug.
2. Add soy sauce and sesame oil, tossing to coat. Sprinkle with sesame seeds, if desired.

Prep Ahead Option

Measure the edamame into the mug; cover and refrigerate. Measure the soy sauce and sesame oil into a small airtight container; cover and refrigerate. If using sesame seeds, measure them into a small airtight container; cover and refrigerate until ready to use.

Crispy Cumin Chickpeas

Chickpeas tossed with olive oil, cumin and hot pepper sauce, then microwave-roasted until crispy, make an addictive snack.

Tips

Use any other spice or dried herb of choice (curry powder, Italian seasoning, garlic powder, dill, oregano) in place of the cumin.

Freeze the remaining chickpeas in a small sealable freezer bag. You can freeze the entire amount in one bag, or portion out ½ cup (125 mL) per bag so that the chickpeas are recipe-ready. Be sure to label the bag with the contents. Store for up to 3 months. Defrost in the refrigerator or microwave before using.

- ♦ **12- to 16-oz (375 to 500 mL) mug**
- ♦ **Plate lined with a paper towel**

½ cup	rinsed drained canned chickpeas	125 mL
⅛ tsp	ground cumin	0.5 mL
Pinch	salt	Pinch
1½ tsp	vegetable or olive oil	7 mL
⅛ tsp	hot pepper sauce	0.5 mL

1. In the mug, combine chickpeas, cumin, salt, oil and hot pepper sauce.

2. Microwave on High for 1 minute. Stir. Microwave on High for 2 to 3 minutes, stopping to stir every 30 seconds, until chickpeas have shrunk slightly and appear dry. Spread chickpeas on prepared plate and let cool completely.

Variation

- **Cinnamon Sugar Chickpeas:** Omit the cumin, salt and hot pepper sauce. When chickpeas are finished cooking, immediately toss with 2 tsp (10 mL) granulated sugar and ¼ tsp (1 mL) ground cinnamon.

> **Prep Ahead Option**
> Measure the chickpeas, cumin, salt, oil and hot pepper sauce into the mug; cover and refrigerate until ready to use.

Sugar and Spice Nuts

When you've had your fill of overly salty or sweet snacks from the supermarket, turn to this recipe. The lightly sweet and spicy nuts will satisfy and energize you in the most delicious way.

Tip

An equal amount of roasted seeds (sunflower seeds, green pumpkin seeds) can be used in place of the nuts.

♦ **12- to 16-oz (375 to 500 mL) mug**

♦ **Foil-covered plate, sprayed with nonstick cooking spray**

1 tbsp	packed brown sugar	15 mL
1/8 tsp	pumpkin pie spice	0.5 mL
1/2 tsp	water	2 mL
1/3 cup	roasted salted mixed nuts	75 mL

1. In the mug, combine brown sugar, pumpkin pie spice and water until blended. Stir in nuts until coated.

2. Microwave on High for 45 seconds. Stir. Microwave on High for 1 to 2 minutes (checking at 1 minute, then every 10 seconds) or until syrup begins to harden. Pour onto prepared plate, separating nuts with a fork. Let cool completely.

Variation

- **Cinnamon Sugar Nuts:** Replace the brown sugar with granulated sugar, and replace the pumpkin pie spice with ground cinnamon.

Prep Ahead Option

Combine the brown sugar, pumpkin pie spice and water in the mug; cover and store at room temperature. Measure the nuts into a small airtight container; cover and store at room temperature until ready to use.

Chili-Spiced Nuts

Subtly spiced and sweetened, this easy nut mix will spoil you for all other snacks. It makes a great pre- or post-workout snack, or an energizing nibble on the run.

Tips

A pinch of cayenne pepper can be used in place of the hot pepper sauce.

An equal amount of granulated sugar can be used in place of the brown sugar.

♦ **12- to 16-oz (375 to 500 mL) mug**

♦ **Foil-covered plate, sprayed with nonstick cooking spray**

2 tsp	butter	10 mL
1 tbsp	packed brown sugar	15 mL
Pinch	salt	Pinch
1/8 tsp	chili powder	0.5 mL
1 tsp	water	5 mL
Drop	hot pepper sauce	Drop
1/3 cup	pecan halves, walnut halves or almonds	75 mL

1. In the mug, microwave butter on High for 25 to 35 seconds or until melted.

2. Stir in brown sugar, salt, chili powder, water and hot pepper sauce. Microwave on High for 45 to 60 seconds or until sugar is melted and mixture bubbles.

3. Add nuts, tossing to coat. Microwave on High for 1 to 2 minutes (checking at 1 minute, then every 10 seconds) or until the coating feels dry. Pour onto prepared plate, separating nuts with a fork. Let cool completely.

Prep Ahead Option

Measure the butter into the mug; cover and refrigerate. Measure the brown sugar, salt, chili powder, water and hot pepper sauce into a small airtight container; cover and store at room temperature. Measure the nuts into a small airtight container; cover and store at room temperature until ready to use.

Parmesan Pepper Snack Mix

Loaded with lots of umami flavor (from the Parmesan cheese and Worcestershire sauce) and plenty of crunchy goodness, this quick mix will likely become your favorite mid-afternoon or midnight snack.

Tip

To cool the mix more quickly, spread on a large plate. It will be cool in about 5 to 10 minutes.

♦ **16-oz (500 mL) mug**

1½ tbsp	butter	22 mL
½ tsp	Worcestershire sauce or soy sauce	2 mL
⅛ tsp	ground black pepper	0.5 mL
⅛ tsp	garlic powder	0.5 mL
⅔ cup	rice, wheat or corn cereal squares (such as Chex)	150 mL
⅓ cup	broken stick pretzels	75 mL
2 tbsp	roasted salted peanuts	30 mL
1 tbsp	grated Parmesan cheese	15 mL

1. In the mug, microwave butter, Worcestershire sauce, pepper and garlic powder on High for 25 to 35 seconds or until butter is melted.

2. Add cereal, pretzels, peanuts and Parmesan, tossing to coat. Microwave on High for 1½ to 2 minutes, stopping to stir every 30 seconds, until mixture begins to toast. Let cool completely in mug.

Prep Ahead Option

Measure the butter, Worcestershire sauce, pepper and garlic powder into the mug; cover and refrigerate. Measure the cereal, pretzels, peanuts and Parmesan into a small airtight container; cover and store at room temperature until ready to use.

Chocolate Trail Mix Bark

A handful of this lightly sweet trail mix is just the nibble you need to tame your sweet tooth and deliver a delicious dose of quick energy.

Tips

An equal amount of coconut oil or vegetable oil can be used in place of the butter.

Either sweetened or unsweetened coconut can be used.

◆ **12- to 16-oz (375 to 500 mL) mug**

◆ **Small plate lined with waxed paper or parchment paper**

2 tbsp	semisweet chocolate chips	30 mL
1/2 tsp	butter	2 mL
1/4 cup	assorted raw, toasted or roasted nuts, coarsely chopped	60 mL
2 tbsp	raw or roasted sunflower seeds	30 mL
2 tbsp	chopped dried fruit (such as apricots, cranberries or raisins)	30 mL
1 tbsp	flaked or shredded coconut	15 mL

1. In the mug, microwave chocolate chips and butter on High for 30 seconds. Stir. Microwave in 10-second intervals, stopping to stir after each, until chocolate is melted and mixture is smooth.

2. Stir in nuts, seeds, dried fruit and coconut until well coated. Scoop mixture onto prepared plate, spreading slightly with back of spoon. Freeze for 10 to 15 minutes or until set. Break into bite-size pieces.

Variations

- **White Chocolate Trail Mix Bark:** Use white chocolate chips in place of the semisweet chocolate chips.

- **Peanut Butterscotch Bar:** Use butterscotch baking chips in place of the semisweet chocolate chips. Stir in 2 tsp (10 mL) creamy peanut butter after melting the chips.

> **Prep Ahead Option**
>
> Measure the chocolate chips and butter into the mug; cover and refrigerate. Measure the nuts, seeds, dried fruit and coconut into a small airtight container; cover and store at room temperature until ready to use.

Chewy Cranberry Granola Bar

Loaded with flavor and plenty of chewy goodness, this easy bar delivers great taste and portable energy for pennies. Vary it any which way: with spices, dried fruits, nuts or different sweeteners.

Tips

Granulated sugar can be used in place of the brown sugar.

An equal amount of coconut oil can be used in place of the butter.

Be sure to use crisp rice cereal, not puffed rice cereal, for the best results.

♦ **12- to 16-oz (375 to 500 mL) mug, sprayed with nonstick cooking spray**

♦ **Square of waxed paper or parchment paper**

2 tsp	packed brown sugar	10 mL
2 tsp	butter	10 mL
2 tsp	liquid honey or pure maple syrup	10 mL
1/4 cup	quick-cooking rolled oats	60 mL
2 tbsp	crisp rice cereal	30 mL
1 tbsp	dried cranberries	15 mL
Pinch	salt	Pinch
1/8 tsp	vanilla extract (optional)	0.5 mL

1. In the mug, microwave brown sugar, butter and honey on High for 45 to 60 seconds or until sugar is dissolved and mixture is bubbling. Stir until blended.

2. Stir in oats, cereal, cranberries, salt and vanilla (if using) until well coated. Scoop mixture into a mound onto waxed paper. Fold paper over the mound, pressing down very firmly to compact and form a bar shape. Freeze for 25 to 30 minutes or until set.

Variations

- **Gluten-Free Chewy Cranberry Granola Bar:** Use certified gluten-free oats and gluten-free crisp rice cereal.
- **Cinnamon Raisin Chewy Granola Bar:** Use raisins in place of the cranberries and add 1/8 tsp (0.5 mL) ground cinnamon with the salt.
- **Apricot Ginger Chewy Granola Bar:** Use chopped dried apricots in place of the cranberries and add 1/8 tsp (0.5 mL) ground ginger with the salt.

Prep Ahead Option

Measure the brown sugar, butter and honey into the mug; cover and refrigerate. Measure the oats, cereal, cranberries and salt into a small airtight container; cover and store at room temperature. Measure the vanilla (if using) into a small airtight container; cover and store at room temperature until ready to use.

Sweet-and-Sour Smoked Sausages

A favorite appetizer at potlucks and sports-watching parties, this sweet-and-sour sausage snack is just as easy to make and enjoy in a mug, anytime.

Tips

You can use ½ cup (125 mL) sliced cooked smoked sausages (cut crosswise, about ¼ inch/0.5 cm thick) in place of the miniature sausages.

An equal amount of ketchup, plus a dash of hot pepper sauce, can be used in place of the chili sauce.

♦ **12- to 16-oz (375 to 500 mL) mug**

1 tbsp	grape jelly	15 mL
1 tbsp	chili sauce	15 mL
6	cocktail-size cooked smoked sausages	6

1. In the mug, microwave grape jelly and chili sauce on High for 25 to 35 seconds or until jelly is melted. Stir until blended.

2. Add sausages. Microwave on High for 15 to 20 seconds or until sausages are hot. Toss to coat sausages in sauce.

Variation

• **Sweet-and-Sour Meatballs:** Microwave 3 frozen cooked beef meatballs in the mug for 1 to 2 minutes or until completely warmed through. Add grape jelly and chili sauce. Microwave on High for 15 to 20 seconds or until jelly is melted (it will take less time because the mug is hot). Toss to coat meatballs in sauce.

Prep Ahead Option

Measure the grape jelly and chili sauce into the mug; cover and refrigerate. Measure the sausages into a small airtight container; cover and refrigerate until ready to use.

Corn Chip Pie

Arguably an additional food group in the American South, corn chip "pie" is available at almost every football game, fair, parade or celebration. It's by no means fancy, but it is a tasty, filling snack in a pinch.

Tip

Any variety of prepared chili — vegetarian, con carne, turkey — can be used in this recipe.

♦ **12- to 16-oz (375 to 500 mL) mug**

½ cup	canned chili	125 mL
2 tbsp	shredded Monterey Jack or Cheddar cheese	30 mL
1 tbsp	chopped green onions	15 mL
½ cup	corn chips	125 mL

1. In the mug, microwave chili on High for 60 to 75 seconds or until heated through.

2. Sprinkle with cheese. Microwave on High for 15 to 20 seconds or until cheese is melted. Sprinkle with green onions and top with corn chips.

> **Prep Ahead Option**
> Measure the chili into the mug; cover and refrigerate. Measure the cheese and green onions into separate small airtight containers; cover and refrigerate. Measure the corn chips into a small airtight container; cover and store at room temperature until ready to use.

Chili Bean Queso

I predict you will make this yummy cheese dip again and again. It's free of the glowing artificial cheese typically used in queso dips.

Tips

Try adding 1 tbsp (15 mL) chopped green onions or fresh cilantro if you have them on hand.

Freeze the remaining beans in a small sealable freezer bag. You can freeze the entire amount in one bag, or portion out ¼ cup (60 mL) per bag so that the beans are recipe-ready. Be sure to label the bag with the contents. Store for up to 3 months. Defrost in the refrigerator or microwave before using.

♦ **12- to 16-oz (375 to 500 mL) mug**

3 tbsp	brick-style cream cheese (1½ oz/45 g)	45 mL
¼ cup	canned chili-seasoned pinto beans, with liquid	60 mL
3 tbsp	shredded sharp (old) Cheddar cheese	45 mL

Suggested Accompaniments

Breadsticks or crackers; tortilla chips or pita chips; assorted crudités (carrot sticks, celery sticks, radishes); pita wedges

1. In the mug, microwave cream cheese on High for 10 to 20 seconds or until warm and softened.
2. Stir in beans and Cheddar cheese. Microwave on High for 60 to 90 seconds or until heated through and cheese is melted. Serve with any of the suggested accompaniments, as desired.

Variation

- **Salsa Queso:** Replace the beans with an equal amount of salsa.

Prep Ahead Option

Measure the cream cheese into the mug; cover and refrigerate. Measure the beans and Cheddar cheese into a small airtight container; cover and refrigerate until ready to use.

Jalapeño Popper Dip

Here, pickled jalapeños team up with multiple cheeses in an irresistible dip that tastes just like jalapeño poppers.

Tips

1 tbsp (15 mL) minced fresh jalapeño can be used in place of the pickled jalapeños.

Consider adding 1 tbsp (15 mL) chopped green onions or cilantro leaves if you have them on hand.

◆ **12- to 16-oz (375 to 500 mL) mug**

3 tbsp	brick-style cream cheese (1½ oz/45 g)	45 mL
1½ tbsp	chopped pickled jalapeño peppers	22 mL
2 tbsp	shredded Cheddar cheese	30 mL
1 tbsp	grated Parmesan cheese	15 mL
1 tbsp	mayonnaise	15 mL
	Crushed plain or seasoned croutons (optional)	

1. In the mug, microwave cream cheese on High for 10 to 20 seconds or until warm and softened.
2. Stir in jalapeños, Cheddar, Parmesan and mayonnaise. Microwave on High for 45 to 60 seconds or until heated through. Sprinkle with croutons, if desired.

Variation

- **Chipotle Cheese Dip:** Replace the pickled jalapeños with 2 tbsp (30 mL) chipotle salsa.

> **Prep Ahead Option**
>
> Measure the cream cheese into the mug; cover and refrigerate. Measure the jalapeños, Cheddar, Parmesan and mayonnaise into a small airtight container; cover and refrigerate. If using croutons, measure them into a small airtight container; cover and store at room temperature until ready to use.

Loaded Tater Tot Dip

This delicious spin on loaded baked potatoes is destined to be a hit. It's just the right size to indulge in a bit of gooey, cheesy goodness without going overboard.

Tip

Look for ready-to-eat real bacon bits where salad dressings and croutons are shelved in the grocery store, or near the regular bacon in the packaged meat or deli department.

♦ **12- to 16-oz (375 to 500 mL) mug**

½ cup	frozen tater tots (about 7 or 8 whole tater tots)	125 mL
1 tbsp	ready-to-eat real bacon bits	15 mL
⅓ cup	light sour cream or plain Greek yogurt	75 mL
⅛ tsp	hot pepper sauce	0.5 mL
	Salt	
¼ cup	shredded sharp (old) Cheddar cheese	60 mL
1 tbsp	chopped green onions	15 mL

Suggested Accompaniments

Breadsticks or crackers; tortilla chips or pita chips; assorted crudités (red bell pepper strips, carrot sticks, celery sticks); pita wedges

1. In the mug, microwave tater tots on High for 1½ to 2 minutes or until hot. Break apart with a fork.

2. Stir in bacon, sour cream and hot pepper sauce. Season to taste with salt. Sprinkle with cheese. Microwave on High for 30 to 45 seconds or until cheese is melted. Sprinkle with green onions. Serve with any of the suggested accompaniments, as desired.

Prep Ahead Option

Measure the tater tots into the mug; cover and refrigerate (decrease the cooking time in step 1 by 30 seconds). Measure the bacon, sour cream and hot pepper sauce into a small airtight container; cover and refrigerate. Measure the cheese and green onions into separate small airtight containers; cover and refrigerate until ready to use.

Indian Yogurt Dip

Cooking the spices in the oil for a few seconds enhances their flavor, leading to a dip that tastes quite special despite its short list of ingredients and quick preparation time.

Tips

If you are not a fan of curry powder, use ³⁄₄ tsp (3 mL) ground cumin in its place.

Turn this into an instant meal by adding 1 cup (250 mL) rinsed drained canned chickpeas to the finished dip (be sure to use a 16-oz/500 mL mug). Eat straight from the mug as a salad or spoon into half a pita.

♦ **12- to 16-oz (375 to 500 mL) mug**

2 tbsp	finely chopped green onions	30 mL
1 tsp	curry powder	5 mL
¼ tsp	ground ginger	1 mL
Pinch	granulated sugar	Pinch
1 tsp	vegetable oil	5 mL
²⁄₃ cup	plain Greek yogurt	150 mL
1½ tbsp	chopped golden or dark raisins	22 mL
	Salt and ground black pepper	

Suggested Accompaniments

Breadsticks or crackers; tortilla chips or pita chips; assorted crudités (red bell pepper strips, carrot sticks, celery sticks); pita wedges

1. In the mug, combine green onions, curry powder, ginger, sugar and oil. Microwave on High for 15 to 20 seconds or until fragrant.

2. Stir in yogurt and raisins. Season to taste with salt and pepper. Serve with any of the suggested accompaniments, as desired.

Prep Ahead Option

Combine the green onions, curry powder, ginger, sugar and oil in the mug; cover and refrigerate. Measure the yogurt and raisins into a small airtight container; cover and refrigerate until ready to use.

Greek Yogurt Peanut Butter Dip

Here's a perfect option when you cannot decide between a snack or dessert. You'll be hard-pressed to find a more appealing (and healthy!) sweet snack than this one, reminiscent of cheesecake.

Tips

For best results, be sure to use Greek yogurt (which is very thick and creamy), not regular plain yogurt.

Any other creamy nut or seed butter (almond, cashew, sesame) can be used in place of the peanut butter.

♦ **12- to 16-oz (375 to 500 mL) mug**

1 tbsp	packed brown sugar or liquid honey	15 mL
1 tbsp	creamy peanut butter	15 mL
¾ cup	plain Greek yogurt	175 mL
¼ tsp	vanilla extract	1 mL
⅛ tsp	ground cinnamon	0.5 mL

Suggested Accompaniments

Apple wedges or grapes; pretzel sticks; graham crackers

1. In the mug, combine brown sugar and peanut butter until smooth. Microwave on High for 15 to 30 seconds or until peanut butter is melted.

2. Stir in yogurt, vanilla and cinnamon until blended and smooth. Serve with any of the suggested accompaniments, as desired.

Variation

- **PB&J Dip:** Omit the cinnamon. Spoon 1 tbsp (15 mL) raspberry preserves on top of the finished dip, then swirl it into the dip with the tip of knife.

Prep Ahead Option

Measure the brown sugar and peanut butter into the mug; cover and store at room temperature. Measure the yogurt, vanilla and cinnamon into a small airtight container; cover and refrigerate until ready to use.

Spicy Thai Peanut Dip

Snack time just got a little more exciting. Spicy, salty, tart and subtly sweet, this dip is the perfect way to enjoy a bevy of vegetables.

Tips

You can use $1/4$ tsp (1 mL) curry powder (any heat level) plus $1/4$ tsp (1 mL) ground ginger in place of the curry paste.

Any other creamy nut or seed butter (almond, cashew, sesame) can be used in place of the peanut butter.

♦ **12- to 16-oz (375 to 500 mL) mug**

$1/2$ tsp	packed brown sugar	2 mL
$1/2$ tsp	Thai curry paste (red, green or yellow)	2 mL
$1^{1}/_{2}$ tbsp	water	22 mL
1 tbsp	soy sauce	15 mL
3 tbsp	creamy peanut butter	45 mL
2 tsp	lime juice	10 mL

Suggested Accompaniments

Assorted crudités (red bell pepper strips, carrot sticks, celery sticks); pita wedges

1. In the mug, combine brown sugar, curry paste, water and soy sauce. Microwave on High for 45 to 60 seconds (checking at 45) or until sugar is dissolved and mixture is syrupy.
2. Stir in peanut butter and lime juice until blended and smooth. Serve warm or let cool to room temperature. Serve with any of the suggested accompaniments, as desired.

> **Prep Ahead Option**
> Measure the brown sugar, curry paste, water and soy sauce into the mug; cover and refrigerate. Measure the peanut butter and lime juice into a small airtight container; cover and refrigerate until ready to use.

Texas Caviar

Legendary Texan cook Helen Corbitt invented a simple, delicious black-eyed pea salad in 1940. It continues to be a popular appetizer, most often served with tortilla chips. It typically needs to marinate for several hours, but heating the dressing helps the peas absorb the flavors and slashes the marinating time to 15 minutes.

Tips

This salad also makes a delicious vegetarian filling for pitas, burritos and omelets — or just about anything else you can dream up.

Freeze the remaining black-eyed peas in a small sealable freezer bag. You can freeze the entire amount in one bag, or portion out 1/2 cup (125 mL) per bag so that the peas are recipe-ready. Be sure to label the bag with the contents. Store for up to 3 months. Defrost in the refrigerator or microwave before using.

♦ **12- to 16-oz (375 to 500 mL) mug**

1 tsp	granulated sugar	5 mL
1/2 tsp	chili powder	2 mL
1/4 tsp	garlic powder	1 mL
1 tbsp	extra virgin olive oil	15 mL
1 tbsp	freshly squeezed lime juice	15 mL
1/2 cup	rinsed drained canned black-eyed peas	125 mL
2 tbsp	chopped drained jarred roasted red bell peppers	30 mL
1 tbsp	chopped green onions	15 mL
1 tbsp	finely chopped fresh cilantro	15 mL
	Salt and ground black pepper	
	Tortilla chips or pita chips	

1. In the mug, combine sugar, chili powder, garlic powder, oil and lime juice. Microwave on High for 35 to 45 seconds or until hot.

2. Stir in peas and roasted peppers. Refrigerate for 15 minutes. Stir in green onions and cilantro.

3. Season to taste with salt and pepper. Serve with tortilla chips.

> **Prep Ahead Option**
> Prepare through step 2; cover and refrigerate. Measure the tortilla chips into a small airtight container; cover and store at room temperature until ready to use.

Warm White Bean Garlic Spread

You may appreciate white beans for their convenience and creaminess, but taste what happens when they're amped up with garlic powder, olive oil and lemon juice in this easy spread.

Tip

Freeze the remaining beans in a small sealable freezer bag. You can freeze the entire amount in one bag, or portion out 2/3 cup (150 mL), plus 2 tbsp (30 mL) reserved bean liquid, per bag so that the beans are recipe-ready. Be sure to label the bag with the contents. Store for up to 3 months. Defrost in the refrigerator or microwave before using.

Prep Ahead Option

Measure the bean liquid, beans, oil, lemon juice, garlic powder and hot pepper sauce into the mug; cover and refrigerate until ready to use.

♦ **12- to 16-oz (375 to 500 mL) mug**

2 tbsp	bean liquid (reserved from draining the beans)	30 mL
2/3 cup	rinsed drained canned white beans (such as cannellini or great Northern)	150 mL
1 tbsp	olive oil	15 mL
2 tsp	lemon juice	10 mL
1/4 tsp	garlic powder	1 mL
1/8 tsp	hot pepper sauce	0.5 mL
	Salt	
	Chopped fresh parsley (optional)	

Suggested Accompaniments

Breadsticks or crackers; tortilla chips or pita chips; assorted crudités (e.g., carrot sticks, celery sticks, radishes); pita bread triangles

1. In the mug, use a fork to mash bean liquid, beans, oil, lemon juice, garlic powder and hot pepper sauce until blended and a spreadable consistency.

2. Microwave on High for 30 to 45 seconds or until warm but not hot. Season to taste with salt. Sprinkle with parsley (if using). Serve with any of the suggested accompaniments, as desired.

Variations

- **Warm Parmesan White Bean Spread:** Omit the hot pepper sauce. Add 1 tbsp (15 mL) grated Parmesan cheese and 1/4 tsp (1 mL) dried basil or Italian seasoning with the beans. Season to taste with ground black pepper, along with the salt.

- **Warm White Bean and Goat Cheese Spread:** Omit the hot pepper sauce. Add 2 tbsp (30 mL) crumbled goat cheese and 1/8 tsp (0.5 mL) crumbled dried rosemary with the beans. Season to taste with ground black pepper, along with the salt.

Warm Tonnato Bean Spread

This piquant tuna spread is inspired by the creamy sauce for the Italian dish *vitello tonnato*. It makes a fantastic sandwich filling too.

Tips

Canned tuna packed in olive oil — typically imported from Italy — can be used in place of the water-packed tuna. Reserve the oil when draining and use for the 1 tbsp (15 mL) oil called for in the recipe.

Freeze the remaining beans in a small sealable freezer bag. You can freeze the entire amount in one bag, or portion out ¼ cup (60 mL) per bag so that the beans are recipe-ready. Be sure to label the bag with the contents. Store for up to 3 months. Defrost in the refrigerator or microwave before using.

♦ **12- to 16-oz (375 to 500 mL) mug**

¼ cup	rinsed drained canned white beans (such as cannellini or great Northern)	60 mL
½	can (5 oz/142 g) water-packed tuna, drained and flaked	½
1 tbsp	olive oil	15 mL
2 tsp	lemon juice	10 mL
1 tsp	roughly chopped drained capers	5 mL
⅛ tsp	garlic powder	0.5 mL
	Salt and ground black pepper	
	Chopped fresh parsley (optional)	

Suggested Accompaniments

Crackers or Melba toast rounds; vegetable sticks or crisp vegetable rounds (carrots, celery, cucumber, zucchini)

1. In the mug, use a fork to mash beans. Add tuna, olive oil, lemon juice, capers and garlic powder, mashing until blended. Season to taste with salt and pepper.
2. Microwave on High for 25 to 30 seconds or until just warmed through. Sprinkle with parsley, if desired. Serve with any of the suggested accompaniments, as desired.

> **Prep Ahead Option**
> Prepare through step 1; cover and refrigerate until ready to use.

Bubbling Deviled Crab Dip

Why wait for a party to enjoy this fantastic dip? Rich crab, creamy mayonnaise and a few key seasonings will turn any snack time into a mini celebration.

♦ **12- to 16-oz (375 to 500 mL) mug**

1/2	can (4 to 5 oz/114 to 142 g) lump crabmeat, drained and flaked	1/2
1 1/2 tbsp	mayonnaise	22 mL
1 tsp	lemon juice	5 mL
1/2 tsp	Dijon or brown mustard	2 mL
Dash	Worcestershire sauce	Dash
Dash	hot pepper sauce	Dash
	Chopped fresh parsley (optional)	

Suggested Accompaniments

Breadsticks or crackers; tortilla chips or pita chips; assorted crudités (red bell pepper strips, carrot sticks, celery sticks); pita wedges

1. In the mug, use a fork to combine crab, mayonnaise, lemon juice, mustard, Worcestershire sauce and hot pepper sauce.
2. Microwave on High for 45 to 60 seconds or until heated through. Sprinkle with parsley, if desired. Serve with any of the suggested accompaniments, as desired.

Variation

- **Deviled Shrimp Dip:** Use half a 4-oz (114 g) can of cooked tiny shrimp, drained, in place of the crab.

Prep Ahead Option

Prepare through step 1; cover and refrigerate until ready to use.

Desserts

Sugar Cookie

Simple is so often best: a few pantry staples, a mug, and you're done. Bring on the applause (and a glass of milk).

Tips

Don't be tempted to use a whole egg or an egg white in place of the egg yolk; the recipe will not turn out properly.

The egg white can be refrigerated in an airtight container for up to 2 days, or frozen for up to 2 months (thaw in the refrigerator).

♦ **12- to 16-oz (375 to 500 mL) mug**

1 tbsp	butter	15 mL
1	large egg yolk	1
2 tbsp	granulated sugar	30 mL
1/4 tsp	vanilla extract	1 mL
3 tbsp	all-purpose flour	45 mL
1/8 tsp	salt	0.5 mL
	Additional granulated sugar or colored sugar	

1. In the mug, microwave butter on High for 15 to 30 seconds or until melted. Using a fork, whisk in egg yolk, sugar and vanilla. Still using the fork, stir in flour and salt until very well blended. Smooth top with your fingertips or the back of a spoon. Sprinkle with additional sugar, if desired.

2. Microwave on High for 40 to 60 seconds (checking at 40) or until center is just set. Let cool slightly or entirely in mug. Eat directly from mug.

Variations

- **Gluten-Free Sugar Cookie:** Replace the all-purpose flour with an all-purpose gluten-free flour blend.
- **Lemon Cookie:** Replace the vanilla extract with 1/2 tsp (2 mL) finely grated lemon zest.
- **Brown Sugar Cookie:** Replace the granulated sugar with packed brown sugar.
- **Coconut Sugar Cookie:** Replace the butter with an equal amount of virgin coconut oil. If desired, add 1 tbsp (15 mL) flaked or shredded coconut, finely chopped, with the flour.

> ### Prep Ahead Option
> Measure the butter into the mug; cover and refrigerate. Whisk the egg yolk in a small airtight container; cover and refrigerate. Measure the sugar and vanilla into a small airtight container; cover and store at room temperature. Measure the flour and salt into a small airtight container; cover and store at room temperature until ready to use.

Shortbread Cookie

Begin brewing the Earl Grey and Darjeeling — with a few easy steps, you'll have a single serving of one of the very best tea accompaniments.

Tip

Don't cut back on the sugar in the recipe; in addition to adding sweetness, it helps keep the cookie tender.

♦ **12- to 16-oz (375 to 500 mL) mug**

3 tbsp	butter	45 mL
1/3 cup	all-purpose flour	75 mL
3 tbsp	granulated sugar	45 mL
1/8 tsp	salt	0.5 mL

1. In the mug, microwave butter on High for 15 to 30 seconds or until melted. Stir in flour, sugar and salt until well blended. Gently press into bottom of mug, smoothing the top.

2. Microwave on High for 45 to 60 seconds or until center is just set. Let cool entirely in mug before eating.

Variations

- **Brown Sugar Shortbread Cookie:** Use packed brown sugar in place of the granulated sugar.
- **Rosemary Lemon Shortbread Cookie:** Add 1/2 tsp (2 mL) finely grated lemon zest and a pinch of crumbled dried rosemary with the flour.
- **Gluten-Free Shortbread Cookie:** Replace the all-purpose flour with an all-purpose gluten-free flour blend.

Prep Ahead Option

Measure the butter into the mug; cover and refrigerate. Measure the sugar, flour and salt into a small airtight container; cover and store at room temperature until ready to use.

Peanut Butter Cookie

There's a time for discovering new flavors and a time for championing old favorites. When you're in the mood for the latter, make this peanut butter cookie.

Tips

For a subtle tropical twist, use an equal amount of coconut oil in place of the butter.

Don't be tempted to use a whole egg or an egg white in place of the egg yolk; the recipe will not turn out properly.

Any other creamy nut or seed butter (almond, cashew, sunflower seed) can be used in place of the peanut butter.

♦ **12- to 16-oz (375 to 500 mL) mug**

1 tbsp	butter	15 mL
1 tbsp	creamy peanut butter	15 mL
1	large egg yolk	1
2 tbsp	packed brown sugar	30 mL
1/4 tsp	vanilla extract (optional)	1 mL
3 tbsp	all-purpose flour	45 mL
1/8 tsp	salt	0.5 mL

1. In the mug, microwave butter and peanut butter on High for 20 to 30 seconds or until melted. Using a fork, whisk in egg yolk, brown sugar and vanilla. Still using the fork, stir in flour and salt until very well blended. Smooth top with your fingertips or the back of a spoon.

2. Microwave on High for 35 to 45 seconds (checking at 35) or until center is just set. Let cool slightly or entirely in mug. Eat directly from mug.

Variation

- **Gluten-Free Peanut Butter Cookie:** Replace the all-purpose flour with an all-purpose gluten-free flour blend.

Prep Ahead Option

Measure the butter and peanut butter into the mug; cover and refrigerate. Whisk the egg yolk in a small airtight container; cover and refrigerate. Measure the brown sugar and vanilla into a small airtight container; cover and store at room temperature. Measure the flour and salt into a small airtight container; cover and store at room temperature until ready to use.

Oatmeal Raisin Cookie

Oatmeal raisin cookies are a nostalgic choice anytime, and this single-serve interpretation is no exception.

Tips

Don't be tempted to use a whole egg or an egg white in place of the egg yolk; the recipe will not turn out properly.

An equal amount of maple syrup, brown rice syrup, corn syrup or agave nectar can be used in place of the honey.

Whole wheat flour can be used in place of the all-purpose flour.

Any other dried fruit (chopped if large) can be used in place of the raisins.

♦ **12- to 16-oz (375 to 500 mL) mug**

1 tbsp	butter	15 mL
1	large egg yolk	1
1 tbsp	packed brown sugar	15 mL
1 tbsp	liquid honey	15 mL
1/4 tsp	vanilla extract	1 mL
3 tbsp	all-purpose flour	45 mL
3 tbsp	large-flake (old-fashioned) or quick-cooking rolled oats	45 mL
2 tbsp	raisins	30 mL
1/8 tsp	ground cinnamon	0.5 mL
1/8 tsp	salt	0.5 mL

1. In the mug, microwave butter on High for 15 to 30 seconds or until melted. Using a fork, whisk in egg yolk, brown sugar, honey and vanilla. Still using the fork, stir in flour, oats, raisins, cinnamon and salt until very well blended. Smooth top with your fingertips or the back of a spoon.

2. Microwave on High for 40 to 60 seconds (checking at 40) or until center is just set. Let cool slightly or entirely in mug. Eat directly from mug.

Variations

- **Gluten-Free Oatmeal Cookie:** Use certified gluten-free oats and replace the all-purpose flour with an all-purpose gluten-free flour blend.

- **Cherry Almond Oatmeal Cookie:** Omit the cinnamon. Replace the raisins with dried cherries, and use 1/8 tsp (0.5 mL) almond extract in place of the vanilla.

Prep Ahead Option

Measure the butter into the mug; cover and refrigerate. Whisk the egg yolk in a small airtight container; cover and refrigerate. Measure the brown sugar, honey and vanilla into a small airtight container; cover and store at room temperature. Measure the flour, oats, raisins, cinnamon and salt into a small airtight container; cover and store at room temperature until ready to use.

Magic Cookie Layered Mug Bar

Call it a hello dolly, 7-layer bar or magic cookie bar — whatever the name, this incredible cookie tastes just as sweet. Now you can enjoy one in a matter of minutes, just for you. It's guaranteed to magically disappear.

Tip

To crush the graham cracker, break it into pieces and place in a small sealable plastic bag. Seal, then use a rolling pin or another heavy object to crush the cracker.

♦ 12- to 16-oz (375 to 500 mL) mug, sprayed with nonstick cooking spray

1 tbsp	butter	15 mL
2	square graham crackers, crushed (about $1/4$ cup/60 mL crumbs)	2
$1/3$ cup	semisweet chocolate chips, divided	75 mL
2 tbsp	sweetened flaked or shredded coconut, divided	30 mL
2 tbsp	chopped nuts (such as pecans, walnuts and/or peanuts), divided	30 mL
$1/4$ cup	sweetened condensed milk (not evaporated)	60 mL

1. In the mug, microwave butter on High for 15 to 30 seconds or until melted. Stir in graham cracker crumbs. Spoon half the crumb mixture into a small bowl or cup.

2. To the mug, add half the chocolate chips, half the coconut and half the nuts. Repeat the layers, starting with the reserved crumb mixture. Pour condensed milk over top.

3. Microwave on High for 60 to 75 seconds or until chocolate is melted. Refrigerate for 10 to 15 minutes before eating.

Variations

- **Butterscotch Magic Cookie Layered Mug Bar:** Use butterscotch baking chips in place of the chocolate chips.

- **Double Chocolate Magic Cookie Layered Mug Bar:** Use a chocolate graham cracker sheet in place of the regular graham cracker sheet.

- **White Magic Cookie Layered Mug Bar:** Use white chocolate chips in place of the semisweet chocolate chips.

Prep Ahead Option
Prepare through step 2; cover and refrigerate until ready to cook.

Chocolate Chip Butterscotch Blondie

The brownie has legions of loyal fans, but butterscotch blondies have a multitude of equally steadfast enthusiasts. If you count yourself among the devoted, you will love this ready-in-minutes mug version.

Tip

Don't be tempted to use a whole egg or an egg white in place of the egg yolk; the recipe will not turn out properly.

♦ 12- to 16-oz (375 to 500 mL) mug, sprayed with nonstick cooking spray

1 tbsp	butter	15 mL
1	large egg yolk	1
2 tbsp	packed brown sugar	30 mL
1/4 tsp	vanilla extract	1 mL
3 1/2 tbsp	all-purpose flour	52 mL
2 tbsp	semisweet chocolate chips	30 mL
1/8 tsp	salt	0.5 mL

1. In the mug, microwave butter on High for 15 to 30 seconds or until melted. Using a fork, whisk in egg yolk, brown sugar and vanilla. Still using the fork, stir in flour, chocolate chips and salt until very well blended. Smooth top with your fingertips or the back of a spoon.

2. Microwave on High for 40 to 60 seconds (checking at 40) or until center is just set. Let cool slightly or entirely in mug. Eat directly from mug.

Variations

- **Gluten-Free Butterscotch Blondie:** Replace the all-purpose flour with an all-purpose gluten-free flour blend. Use certified gluten-free chocolate chips.

- **Double Butterscotch Blondie:** Use butterscotch baking chips in place of the semisweet chocolate chips.

- **English Toffee Blondie:** Use chopped chocolate-covered English toffee candy bar in place of the chocolate chips.

Prep Ahead Option

Measure the butter into the mug; cover and refrigerate. Whisk the egg yolk in a small airtight container; cover and refrigerate. Measure the brown sugar and vanilla into a small airtight container; cover and store at room temperature. Measure the flour, chocolate chips and salt into a small airtight container; cover and store at room temperature until ready to use.

Vanilla Cake

For an anytime cake — including a last-minute celebration-for-one — this basic vanilla cake is hard to beat. It's easy to gussy up any which way, with spices, mix-ins or a swath of frosting. Or keep it simple; it's perfectly wonderful straight up.

Tips

To measure the egg, whisk 1 large egg in a small airtight container. Measure 2 tbsp (30 mL) into the mug as directed. Cover and refrigerate the remaining egg (about 2 tbsp/30 mL) for up to 2 days.

One small egg can be used in place of the 2 tbsp (30 mL) beaten egg.

♦ **12- to 16-oz (375 to 500 mL) mug, sprayed with nonstick cooking spray**

1 tbsp	butter	15 mL
2 tbsp	granulated sugar	30 mL
2 tbsp	beaten egg	30 mL
1 tbsp	milk	15 mL
1/4 tsp	vanilla extract	1 mL
3 tbsp	all-purpose flour	45 mL
1/8 tsp	baking powder	0.5 mL
1/8 tsp	salt	0.5 mL

1. In the mug, microwave butter on High for 15 to 30 seconds or until melted. Using a fork, whisk in sugar, egg, milk and vanilla. Still using the fork, beat in flour, baking powder and salt until very well blended.

2. Microwave on High for 75 to 90 seconds (checking at 75) or until risen and center is just set. Let cool slightly or entirely in mug. Eat directly from mug or gently remove to a small plate.

Variations

- **Gluten-Free Vanilla Cake:** Replace the all-purpose flour with an all-purpose gluten-free flour blend. Make sure the baking powder is gluten-free.

- **Coconut Cake:** Replace the butter with an equal amount of virgin coconut oil. If desired, add 1 tbsp (15 mL) flaked or shredded coconut, finely chopped, to the batter.

- **Chocolate Chip Cookie Cake:** Replace the granulated sugar with packed brown sugar. Add 1 1/2 tbsp (22 mL) miniature semisweet chocolate chips to the batter.

Prep Ahead Option

Measure the butter into the mug; cover and refrigerate. Measure the sugar, egg, milk and vanilla into a small airtight container; cover and refrigerate. Measure the flour, baking powder and salt into a small airtight container; cover and store at room temperature until ready to use.

Double Lemon Cake

Heaps of citrus zing, minimal ingredients, delicious, ready in minutes — what more could you want from a lemon cake?

Tips

Using oil, instead of butter, in this recipe helps to keep the cake extra-moist.

You can use 1/8 tsp (0.5 mL) lemon extract in place of the lemon zest.

Prep Ahead Option

Combine the flour, baking powder and salt in the mug; cover and store at room temperature. Whisk the egg in a small airtight container, then add sugar, oil, lemon zest and lemon juice; cover and refrigerate. Prepare the icing in a small airtight container; cover and refrigerate until ready to use.

♦ **16-oz (500 mL) mug, sprayed with nonstick cooking spray**

Cake

3 tbsp	all-purpose flour	45 mL
1/4 tsp	baking powder	1 mL
1/8 tsp	salt	0.5 mL
1	large egg	1
3 tbsp	granulated sugar	45 mL
2 tbsp	vegetable oil	30 mL
1 tsp	finely grated lemon zest	5 mL
1 1/2 tbsp	freshly squeezed lemon juice	22 mL

Icing

1/3 cup	confectioners' (icing) sugar	75 mL
1 1/2 tsp	freshly squeezed lemon juice	7 mL

1. *Cake:* In the mug, combine flour, baking powder and salt. Using a fork, beat in egg, sugar, oil, lemon zest and lemon juice until very well blended.

2. Microwave on High for 1 1/2 to 2 minutes (checking at 1 1/2) or until risen and center is just set. Let cool slightly or entirely in mug. Eat directly from mug or gently remove to a small plate.

3. *Icing:* In a small bowl or cup, use a fork to stir confectioners' sugar and lemon juice until smooth. Drizzle over cake.

Variations

- **Gluten-Free Lemon Cake:** Replace the all-purpose flour with an all-purpose gluten-free flour blend. Make sure the baking powder and confectioners' sugar are gluten-free.
- **Ginger Lime Cake:** Add 1/4 tsp (1 mL) ground ginger with the flour. Use lime zest and juice in place of the lemon zest and juice.
- **Fresh Orange Cake:** Use orange zest and juice in place of the lemon zest and juice.

Banana Toffee Cake

This sinfully delicious combination of banana and chocolate-covered toffee creates a mouthwatering cake.

Tips

To measure the egg, whisk 1 large egg in a small airtight container. Measure 2 tbsp (30 mL) into the mug as directed. Cover and refrigerate the remaining egg (about 2 tbsp/30 mL) for up to 2 days.

One small egg can be used in place of the 2 tbsp (30 mL) beaten egg.

Consider sprinkling the top of the batter with 1 tbsp (15 mL) chopped pecans or walnuts.

To make your own pumpkin pie spice, combine $\frac{1}{8}$ tsp (0.5 mL) each ground cinnamon, ground ginger and ground allspice, plus a very small pinch of ground cloves.

♦ **16-oz (500 mL) mug, sprayed with nonstick cooking spray**

$\frac{1}{4}$ cup	all-purpose flour	60 mL
$\frac{1}{8}$ tsp	baking powder	0.5 mL
$\frac{1}{8}$ tsp	salt	0.5 mL
2 tbsp	packed brown sugar	30 mL
$\frac{1}{3}$ cup	mashed very ripe banana	75 mL
2 tbsp	beaten egg	30 mL
1 tbsp	vegetable oil	15 mL
1 tbsp	milk	15 mL
3 tbsp	chopped chocolate-covered toffee candy bar	45 mL

1. In the mug, combine flour, baking powder and salt. Stir in brown sugar, banana, egg, oil and milk until very well blended. Stir in toffee.

2. Microwave on High for $1\frac{1}{2}$ to 2 minutes (checking at $1\frac{1}{2}$) or until risen and center is just set. Let cool slightly or entirely in mug. Eat directly from mug or gently remove to a small plate.

Variations

- **Gluten-Free Banana Toffee Cake:** Replace the all-purpose flour with an all-purpose gluten-free flour blend. Make sure the baking powder and candy bar are gluten-free.

- **Banana Split Cake:** Omit the toffee. Use granulated sugar in place of the brown sugar, and add 2 tbsp (30 mL) miniature semisweet chocolate chips, 1 tbsp (15 mL) dried cranberries and 1 tbsp (15 mL) chopped nuts (pecans, walnuts, peanuts) to the batter.

- **Spiced Banana Cake:** Omit the toffee. Add $\frac{1}{2}$ tsp (2 mL) pumpkin pie spice with the flour.

Prep Ahead Option

Combine the flour, baking powder and salt in the mug; cover and store at room temperature. Measure the brown sugar, banana, egg, oil and milk into a small airtight container; cover and refrigerate. Measure the toffee into a small airtight container; cover and store at room temperature until ready to use.

Salted Caramel Cake

Tuck a good book under your arm, pour a glass of milk and head to your favorite easy chair with mug in hand. Don't forget a napkin, as this caramel cake is definitely on the (deliciously) gooey side.

Tips

To measure the egg, whisk 1 large egg in a small airtight container. Measure 2 tbsp (30 mL) into the mug as directed. Cover and refrigerate the remaining egg (about 2 tbsp/30 mL) for up to 2 days.

One small egg can be used in place of the 2 tbsp (30 mL) beaten egg.

If you happen to have it, use sea salt flakes for the salt in this recipe.

♦ **16-oz (500 mL) mug, sprayed with nonstick cooking spray**

1 tbsp	water	15 mL
1 tbsp	butter	15 mL
2 tbsp	packed dark brown sugar	30 mL
2 tbsp	beaten egg	30 mL
1/4 tsp	vanilla extract	1 mL
3 tbsp	all-purpose flour	45 mL
1/8 tsp	baking powder	0.5 mL
1/4 tsp	salt	1 mL
2	soft caramel candies or chocolate-covered caramel candies	2

1. In the mug, microwave water and butter on High for 30 seconds or until mixture is hot and butter is melted. Let stand for 1 minute.

2. Using a fork, whisk in brown sugar, egg and vanilla. Still using the fork, beat in flour, baking powder and salt until very well blended. Microwave on High for 45 seconds.

3. Place candies in center of mug and push them gently into the cake. Microwave on High for 45 to 60 seconds or until firm to the touch and risen. Let cool slightly or entirely in mug. Eat directly from mug.

Variation

• **Gluten-Free Salted Caramel Cake:** Replace the all-purpose flour with an all-purpose gluten-free flour blend. Make sure the baking powder and candies are gluten-free.

Prep Ahead Option

Measure the water and butter into the mug; cover and refrigerate. Measure the brown sugar, egg and vanilla into a small airtight container; cover and refrigerate. Measure the flour, baking powder and salt into a small airtight container; cover and store at room temperature. Place candies in a small airtight container; cover and store at room temperature until ready to use.

Chocolate Cake

Everyone needs a great chocolate cake recipe, including one that can be made in a flash with the aid of the microwave. Up the chocolate ante with a smattering of chocolate chips in the batter.

Tips

To measure the egg, whisk 1 large egg in a small airtight container. Measure 2 tbsp (30 mL) into the mug as directed. Cover and refrigerate the remaining egg (about 2 tbsp/30 mL) for up to 2 days.

One small egg can be used in place of the 2 tbsp (30 mL) beaten egg.

Miniature chocolate chips distribute themselves more readily than regular chocolate chips. If you only have the latter, give them a brisk chop before adding them to the batter.

♦ **12- to 16-oz (375 to 500 mL) mug, sprayed with nonstick cooking spray**

2 tbsp	all-purpose flour	30 mL
1 tbsp	unsweetened cocoa powder	15 mL
1/8 tsp	baking powder	0.5 mL
1/8 tsp	salt	0.5 mL
2 tbsp	granulated sugar	30 mL
2 tbsp	beaten egg	30 mL
1 1/2 tbsp	vegetable oil	22 mL
1 1/2 tbsp	milk	22 mL
1 tbsp	miniature semisweet chocolate chips (optional)	15 mL

1. In the mug, combine flour, cocoa powder, baking powder and salt. Stir in sugar, egg, oil and milk until very well blended. Stir in chocolate chips (if using).

2. Microwave on High for 75 to 90 seconds (checking at 75) or until risen and center is just set. Let cool slightly or entirely in mug. Eat directly from mug or gently remove to a small plate.

Variation

- **Gluten-Free Chocolate Cake:** Replace the all-purpose flour with an all-purpose gluten-free flour blend. Make sure the baking powder and chocolate chips are gluten-free.

> **Prep Ahead Option**
> Combine the flour, cocoa powder, baking powder and salt in the mug; cover and store at room temperature. Measure the sugar, egg, oil and milk into a small airtight container; cover and refrigerate until ready to use.

Chocolate Hazelnut Cake

Chocolate hazelnut spread is already dessert in a jar, but you can transform it into chocolate hazelnut cake in a mug with next to no effort.

Tip

For the best flavor, opt for natural unsweetened cocoa powder (as opposed to Dutch process cocoa powder).

♦ **16-oz (500 mL) mug, sprayed with nonstick cooking spray**

2 tbsp	all-purpose flour	30 mL
1½ tbsp	unsweetened cocoa powder	22 mL
¼ tsp	baking powder	1 mL
Pinch	salt	Pinch
1	large egg	1
1 tbsp	granulated sugar	15 mL
2 tbsp	chocolate hazelnut spread	30 mL

1. In the mug, combine flour, cocoa powder, baking powder and salt. Using a fork, beat in egg, sugar and chocolate hazelnut spread until very well blended.

2. Microwave on High for 75 to 90 seconds (checking at 75) or until risen and center is just set. Let cool slightly or entirely in mug. Eat directly from mug or gently remove to a small plate.

Variations

- **Gluten-Free Chocolate Hazelnut Cake:** Replace the all-purpose flour with an all-purpose gluten-free flour blend. Make sure the baking powder is gluten-free.

- **Chocolate and Peanut Butter Cake:** Replace the chocolate hazelnut spread with an equal amount of creamy peanut butter. Replace the granulated sugar with 1½ tbsp (22 mL) packed brown sugar.

Prep Ahead Option

Combine the flour, cocoa powder, baking powder and salt in the mug; cover and store at room temperature. Whisk the egg in a small airtight container, then add sugar and chocolate hazelnut spread; cover and refrigerate until ready to use.

Red Velvet Cake
with Cream Cheese Frosting

Red velvet cake is a traditional Southern cake made flavorful with a hint of cocoa powder, tinted a deep, gorgeous red, and then slathered with cream cheese. If you're ready to dig in, you can, in about 15 minutes flat.

Tips

To measure the egg, whisk 1 large egg in a small airtight container. Measure 2 tbsp (30 mL) into the mug as directed. Cover and refrigerate the remaining egg (about 2 tbsp/30 mL) for up to 2 days.

One small egg can be used in place of the 2 tbsp (30 mL) beaten egg.

Prep Ahead Option

Combine the flour, cocoa powder, baking powder and salt in the mug; cover and store at room temperature. Measure the sugar, egg, oil, milk, food coloring and vinegar into a small airtight container; cover and refrigerate. Prepare frosting in a small airtight container; cover and refrigerate until ready to use.

♦ **16-oz (500 mL) mug, sprayed with nonstick cooking spray**

Cake

2 tbsp	all-purpose flour	30 mL
1 tbsp	unsweetened cocoa powder	15 mL
1/8 tsp	baking powder	0.5 mL
1/8 tsp	salt	0.5 mL
2 tbsp	granulated sugar	30 mL
2 tbsp	beaten egg	30 mL
1 1/2 tbsp	vegetable oil	22 mL
1 1/2 tbsp	milk	22 mL
1/2 tsp	red liquid food coloring	1 mL
1/8 tsp	white or cider vinegar	0.5 mL

Frosting

2 tsp	confectioners' (icing) sugar	10 mL
2 tbsp	whipped or soft tub cream cheese	30 mL

1. *Cake:* In the mug, combine flour, cocoa powder, baking powder and salt. Stir in sugar, egg, oil, milk, food coloring and vinegar until very well blended.

2. Microwave on High for 75 to 90 seconds (checking at 75) or until risen and center is just set. Let cool slightly or entirely in mug. Eat directly from mug or gently remove to a small plate.

3. *Frosting:* In a small bowl or cup, use a fork to stir sugar and cream cheese until well blended. Gently spread over cooled cake.

Variation

• **Gluten-Free Red Velvet Cake:** Replace the all-purpose flour with an all-purpose gluten-free flour blend. Make sure the baking powder and confectioners' sugar are gluten-free.

S'mores Cake

A mug and a microwave make campfire s'mores — in cake form — an anytime, always yummy treat from your kitchen.

Tip

There's no need to clean the mug between step 1 and step 2.

♦ **16-oz (500 mL) mug, sprayed with nonstick cooking spray**

3 tbsp	butter, divided	45 mL
2 tbsp	graham cracker crumbs	30 mL
4 tbsp	semisweet chocolate chips, divided	60 mL
1	large egg	1
1/4 cup	all-purpose flour	60 mL
2 tbsp	granulated sugar	30 mL
2 tbsp	unsweetened cocoa powder	30 mL
1/8 tsp	baking powder	0.5 mL
1/8 tsp	salt	0.5 mL
1/4 cup	miniature marshmallows	60 mL

1. In the mug, microwave 1 tbsp (15 mL) butter on High for 15 to 30 seconds or until melted. Stir in graham cracker crumbs until coated. Transfer to a small bowl or cup.

2. In the mug, microwave 3 tbsp (45 mL) chocolate chips and remaining butter on High for 25 to 30 seconds or until chocolate is melted. Stir until blended and smooth.

3. Using a fork, beat in egg, flour, sugar, cocoa powder, baking powder and salt until blended and smooth. Sprinkle with reserved crumb mixture, remaining chocolate chips and marshmallows. Stir slightly to partially blend in with cake mixture.

4. Microwave on High for 75 to 90 seconds or until puffed and center is just set. Let cool slightly or entirely in mug. Eat directly from mug or gently remove to a small plate.

Prep Ahead Option

Measure 1 tbsp (15 mL) butter into the mug; cover and refrigerate. Measure the graham cracker crumbs into a small airtight container; cover and store at room temperature. Measure 3 tbsp (45 mL) chocolate chips and remaining butter into a small airtight container; cover and refrigerate. Whisk the egg in a small airtight container; cover and refrigerate. Measure the flour, sugar, cocoa powder, baking powder and salt into a small airtight container; cover and store at room temperature. Measure remaining chocolate chips and marshmallows into a small airtight container; cover and store at room temperature until ready to use.

Gingerbread

As the weather grows colder and the holidays approach, there's no better time to make this mug cake. It fills the kitchen with the scent of all good things to come.

Tips

To measure the egg, whisk 1 large egg in a small airtight container. Measure 2 tbsp (30 mL) into the mug as directed. Cover and refrigerate the remaining egg (about 2 tbsp/30 mL) for up to 2 days.

One small egg can be used in place of the 2 tbsp (30 mL) beaten egg.

♦ **16-oz (500 mL) mug, sprayed with nonstick cooking spray**

3 tbsp	all-purpose flour	45 mL
½ tsp	pumpkin pie spice	2 mL
¼ tsp	ground ginger	1 mL
¼ tsp	baking powder	1 mL
⅛ tsp	salt	0.5 mL
2 tbsp	packed dark brown sugar	30 mL
2 tbsp	beaten egg	30 mL
1½ tbsp	vegetable oil	22 mL
1 tbsp	milk	15 mL

1. In the mug, combine flour, pumpkin pie spice, ginger, baking powder and salt. Stir in brown sugar, egg, oil and milk until very well blended.

2. Microwave on High for 75 to 90 seconds (checking at 75) or until risen and center is just set. Let cool slightly or entirely in mug. Eat directly from mug or gently remove to a small plate.

Variation

• **Gluten-Free Gingerbread:** Replace the all-purpose flour with an all-purpose gluten-free flour blend. Make sure the baking powder is gluten-free.

Prep Ahead Option

Combine the flour, pumpkin pie spice, ginger, baking powder and salt in the mug; cover and store at room temperature. Measure the brown sugar, egg, oil and milk into a small airtight container; cover and refrigerate until ready to use.

Brown Sugar Sweet Potato Cake

Even if you're a diehard chocolate fan, you'll fall (hard) for this moist autumnal cake.

Tips

To make your own pumpkin pie spice, combine $\frac{1}{8}$ tsp (0.5 mL) each ground cinnamon, ground ginger, and ground allspice, plus a very small pinch of ground cloves.

To measure the egg, whisk 1 large egg in a small airtight container. Measure 2 tbsp (30 mL) into the mug as directed. Cover and refrigerate the remaining egg (about 2 tbsp/30 mL) for up to 2 days.

One small egg can be used in place of the 2 tbsp (30 mL) beaten egg.

Try sprinkling the top of the batter with 1 tbsp (15 mL) chopped pecans or walnuts.

♦ **16-oz (500 mL) mug, sprayed with nonstick cooking spray**

$\frac{1}{4}$ cup	all-purpose flour	60 mL
$\frac{1}{4}$ tsp	pumpkin pie spice	1 mL
$\frac{1}{8}$ tsp	baking powder	0.5 mL
$\frac{1}{8}$ tsp	salt	0.5 mL
2 tbsp	packed dark brown sugar	30 mL
3 tbsp	sweet potato baby food purée	45 mL
2 tbsp	beaten egg	30 mL
1 tbsp	vegetable oil	15 mL

1. In the mug, combine flour, pumpkin pie spice, baking powder and salt. Stir in brown sugar, sweet potato purée, egg and oil until very well blended.

2. Microwave on High for 75 to 90 seconds (checking at 75) or until risen and center is just set. Let cool slightly or entirely in mug. Eat directly from mug or gently remove to a small plate.

Variations

- **Gluten-Free Brown Sugar Sweet Potato Cake:** Replace the all-purpose flour with an all-purpose gluten-free flour blend. Make sure the baking powder is gluten-free.

- **Brown Sugar Pumpkin Cake:** Use an equal amount of unsweetened pumpkin purée (not pie filling) in place of the sweet potato purée.

Prep Ahead Option

Combine the flour, pumpkin pie spice, baking powder and salt in the mug; cover and store at room temperature. Measure the brown sugar, sweet potato purée, egg and oil into a small airtight container; cover and refrigerate until ready to use.

Ricotta Cake

For anyone who loves Italian desserts made with ricotta, this easy-to-make mug will be a sweet indulgence.

Tip

You can use 1/4 tsp (1 mL) vanilla extract or finely grated lemon or orange zest in place of the almond extract.

♦ **12- to 16-oz (375 to 500 mL) mug**

1 tbsp	butter	15 mL
1	large egg	1
2 tbsp	granulated sugar	30 mL
1/3 cup	ricotta cheese	75 mL
1/8 tsp	almond extract	0.5 mL
2 tbsp	all-purpose flour	30 mL
1/8 tsp	baking powder	0.5 mL
1/8 tsp	salt	0.5 mL

1. In the mug, microwave butter on High for 15 to 30 seconds or until melted. Using a fork, whisk in egg, sugar, ricotta and almond extract. Still using the fork, beat in flour, baking powder and salt until very well blended.

2. Microwave on High for 75 to 90 seconds (checking at 75) or until risen and center is just set. Let cool slightly or entirely in mug. Eat directly from mug.

Variations

- **Gluten-Free Ricotta Cake:** Replace the all-purpose flour with an all-purpose gluten-free flour blend. Make sure the baking powder is gluten-free.

- **Cannoli Cake:** Add 1 tbsp (15 mL) miniature semisweet chocolate chips and 1 tbsp (15 mL) chopped lightly salted roasted pistachios to the batter.

Prep Ahead Option

Measure the butter into the mug; cover and refrigerate. Whisk the egg in a small airtight container, then add sugar, ricotta and almond extract; cover and refrigerate. Measure the flour, baking powder and salt into a small airtight container; cover and store at room temperature until ready to use.

Lemon Cream Pie

Lemon cream pie in a mug? Oh yes. This is the kind of recipe lemon lovers dream about: so simple, so bright with citrus flavor and so quick to assemble that you can savor it soon after you decide to make it.

Tip

To crush the cookies, place them in a small sealable plastic bag. Seal, then use a rolling pin or another heavy object to crush the cookies.

Prep Ahead Option

Measure the white chocolate chips into the mug; cover and store at room temperature. Measure the lemon zest and lemon juice into a small airtight container; cover and refrigerate. Measure the butter into a small airtight container; cover and refrigerate. Crush the cookies and store in the bag at room temperature until ready to use.

♦ **12- to 16-oz (375 to 500 mL) mug**

¼ cup	white chocolate chips	60 mL
1	container (5 to 6 oz/142 to 170 mL) lemon-, honey- or vanilla-flavored Greek yogurt	1
1 tsp	finely grated lemon zest	5 mL
1½ tbsp	freshly squeezed lemon juice	22 mL
1 tbsp	butter	15 mL
2	crème-filled vanilla sandwich cookies, crushed	2

1. In the mug, microwave white chocolate chips on High for 30 seconds. Stir. Microwave on High for 15 seconds. Stir until melted and smooth. If chocolate is not melted, microwave on High for another 15 seconds. Stir.

2. Remove lid from yogurt. Stir white chocolate, lemon zest and lemon juice into the yogurt until blended and smooth.

3. Add butter to mug (do not clean out traces of white chocolate). Microwave on High for 15 to 30 seconds or until melted. Stir until blended, then stir in cookies until combined. Gently press cookie mixture into bottom of mug.

4. Spoon yogurt mixture over cookie mixture. Refrigerate for at least 30 minutes or until filling is set. Eat directly from mug.

Variations

- **Peanut Butter Cream Pie:** Use honey- or vanilla-flavored yogurt. Omit the lemon zest and lemon juice. Add 1½ tbsp (22 mL) creamy peanut butter to the white chocolate chips during the last 15 seconds of cooking in step 1.

- **Lime Cream Pie:** Use lime zest and juice in place of the lemon zest and juice.

Chocolate Cream Pie

This shouldn't be so easy. This shouldn't be so decadent. But oh, how it is.

Tips

For the right consistency in the finished dessert, be sure to use Greek yogurt, not regular yogurt.

To crush the cookies, place them in a small sealable plastic bag. Seal, then use a rolling pin or another heavy object to crush the cookies.

♦ **12- to 16-oz (375 to 500 mL) mug**

¼ cup	semisweet chocolate chips	60 mL
1	container (5 to 6 oz/142 to 170 mL) vanilla-flavored Greek yogurt	1
1 tbsp	butter	15 mL
2	crème-filled chocolate sandwich cookies, crushed	2

1. In the mug, microwave chocolate chips on High for 30 seconds. Stir. Microwave on High for 15 seconds. Stir until melted and smooth. If chocolate is not melted, microwave on High for another 15 seconds. Stir.

2. Remove lid from yogurt. Stir chocolate into the yogurt until blended and smooth.

3. Add butter to mug (do not clean out traces of chocolate). Microwave on High for 15 to 30 seconds or until melted. Stir until blended, then stir in cookies until combined. Gently press cookie mixture into bottom of mug.

4. Spoon yogurt mixture over cookie mixture. Refrigerate for at least 30 minutes or until filling is set. Eat directly from mug.

Variations

- **Mocha Cream Pie:** Add ¾ tsp (3 mL) instant coffee granules, dissolved in 1 tsp (5 mL) warm water, to the yogurt in step 2.

- **White Chocolate Cream Pie:** Use white chocolate chips in place of the semisweet chocolate chips, and use crème-filled vanilla sandwich cookies in place of the chocolate sandwich cookies.

- **Butterscotch Cream Pie:** Use butterscotch baking chips in place of the chocolate chips, and use crème-filled vanilla sandwich cookies in place of the chocolate sandwich cookies.

Prep Ahead Option

Measure the chocolate chips into the mug; cover and store at room temperature. Measure the butter into a small airtight container; cover and refrigerate. Crush the cookies and store in the bag at room temperature until ready to use.

Pumpkin Pie

This extra-easy take on everybody's Thanksgiving favorite makes any weeknight meal feel like a celebration.

Tips

To crush the graham cracker, break it into pieces and place in a small sealable plastic bag. Seal, then use a rolling pin or another heavy object to crush the cracker.

Use any variety of crisp cookies you like, such as gingersnaps or chocolate cookies, in place of the graham cracker. You will need about 1/4 cup (60 mL) crumbs.

♦ **16-oz (500 mL) mug**

2 tbsp	butter, divided	30 mL
2	square graham crackers, crushed (about 1/4 cup/60 mL crumbs)	2
1	large egg	1
1/2 cup	pumpkin purée (not pie filling)	125 mL
1 1/2 tbsp	packed brown sugar	22 mL
1/2 tsp	pumpkin pie spice	2 mL
Pinch	salt	Pinch
1/4 tsp	vanilla extract	1 mL

1. In the mug, microwave butter on High for 15 to 30 seconds or until melted. Pour half the butter into a small bowl. Stir graham cracker crumbs into butter remaining in mug. Gently press into bottom of mug.

2. To the small bowl, add egg, pumpkin, brown sugar, pumpkin pie spice, salt and vanilla; beat with a fork until blended and smooth. Pour over crust.

3. Microwave on High for 45 to 75 seconds or until center is set. Let cool slightly or entirely in mug. Eat directly from mug.

Variation

- **No-Crust Pumpkin Pie:** Omit the crust. Melt 1 tbsp (15 mL) butter in the mug and beat in remaining ingredients.

Prep Ahead Option

Measure the butter into the mug; cover and refrigerate. Crush the graham cracker and store in the bag at room temperature. Measure the egg, pumpkin, brown sugar, pumpkin pie spice, salt and vanilla into a small airtight container; cover and refrigerate until ready to use.

Cinnamon Apple Crisp

Tender apples plus a cinnamon–brown sugar topping, minus the long prep and cook times, equals old-fashioned crisp bliss in modern form.

Tip

There's no need to clean the mug between step 1 and step 2.

♦ **16-oz (500 mL) mug**

Topping

1½ tbsp	butter	22 mL
3 tbsp	all-purpose flour	45 mL
2 tbsp	packed brown sugar	30 mL
¼ tsp	ground cinnamon	1 mL
Pinch	salt	Pinch

Filling

1	medium sweet-tart cooking apple (such as Braeburn or Gala), peeled and diced	1
2 tsp	granulated sugar	10 mL
Pinch	ground cinnamon	Pinch
1 tsp	butter	5 mL

1. *Topping:* In the mug, microwave butter on High for 15 to 30 seconds or until melted. Stir in flour, brown sugar, cinnamon and salt until blended. Transfer to a small bowl.

2. *Filling:* In the mug, combine apple, sugar, cinnamon and butter, tossing to coat. Microwave on High for 7 minutes or until apples are tender. Stir.

3. Sprinkle with topping. Microwave on High for 1 to 2 minutes or until topping is just set. Let stand for 15 minutes at room temperature, or refrigerate for 5 minutes, before eating.

Variations

- **Gluten-Free Apple Crisp:** Replace the all-purpose flour with an all-purpose gluten-free flour blend.
- **Ginger Pear Crisp:** Use 1 medium firm-ripe pear, peeled and diced, in place of the apple. Replace the cinnamon with an equal amount of ground ginger.

Prep Ahead Option

Measure the butter into the mug; cover and refrigerate. Measure the flour, brown sugar, cinnamon and salt into a small airtight container; cover and store at room temperature. Measure the apple, sugar, cinnamon and butter into a small airtight container; cover and refrigerate until ready to use.

Blackberry Crumble

Think summer, then think luscious, comfort-food dessert. Did a crumble come to mind? Let this easy dessert, plump with berries and crowned with buttery brown sugar–oat crumbs, warm you any season of the year.

Tips

Frozen or fresh blueberries, raspberries or mixed berries can be used in place of the blackberries.

There's no need to clean the mug between step 1 and step 2.

Prep Ahead Option

Measure the butter into the mug; cover and refrigerate. Measure the flour, oats, brown sugar and salt into a small airtight container; cover and store at room temperature. Measure the cornstarch and water into a small airtight container; cover and refrigerate. Measure the blackberries, sugar and butter into a small airtight container; cover and refrigerate until ready to use.

♦ **16-oz (500 mL) mug**

Topping

1 tbsp	butter	15 mL
2 tbsp	all-purpose flour	30 mL
1½ tbsp	quick-cooking or large-flake (old-fashioned) rolled oats	22 mL
1 tbsp	packed brown sugar	30 mL
Pinch	salt	Pinch

Filling

1 tsp	cornstarch	5 mL
1 tsp	water	5 mL
1⅓ cups	frozen or fresh blackberries	325 mL
2 tbsp	granulated sugar	30 mL
1 tbsp	butter	15 mL

1. *Topping:* In the mug, microwave butter on High for 15 to 30 seconds or until melted. Stir in flour, oats, brown sugar and salt until blended. Transfer to a small bowl.

2. *Filling:* In the mug, stir cornstarch and water until blended and smooth. Add blackberries, sugar and butter, tossing to coat. Microwave on High for 90 seconds if using frozen berries (60 seconds if using fresh berries). Mash slightly with a fork. Microwave on High for 45 to 75 seconds or until hot and bubbling. Stir.

3. Sprinkle with topping. Microwave on High for 60 to 90 seconds or until topping is just set. Let stand for 15 minutes at room temperature, or refrigerate for 5 minutes, before eating.

Variation

- **Gluten-Free Blackberry Crumble:** Use certified gluten-free oats and replace the all-purpose flour with an all-purpose gluten-free flour blend.

Bananas Faster Foster

The duo of brown sugar and butter is my sweet tooth nirvana, which explains why I'm such a bananas Foster fan. My mug version makes it easier than ever to savor my bliss.

Tip

Wait to peel and slice the banana until just before using. If prepared too far in advance, it will turn brown and become slightly mushy.

♦ **16-oz (500 mL) mug**

1 tbsp	packed dark brown sugar	15 mL
Pinch	ground nutmeg	Pinch
2 tsp	butter or virgin coconut oil	10 mL
2 tsp	dark rum, brandy or apple juice	10 mL
1 tsp	lemon juice	5 mL
1	large firm-ripe banana, cut into 1/2-inch (1 cm) thick slices	1

Suggested Accompaniments

Vanilla ice cream, vanilla frozen yogurt or non-dairy vanilla frozen dessert; vanilla-flavored Greek yogurt; whipped cream

1. In the mug, combine brown sugar, nutmeg, butter, rum and lemon juice. Microwave on High for 1 minute or until hot and bubbly.

2. Add banana, gently tossing to coat. Microwave on High for 45 to 75 seconds or until heated through. Let stand for 1 minute. Serve with any of the suggested accompaniments, as desired.

> **Prep Ahead Option**
> Combine the brown sugar, nutmeg, butter, rum and lemon juice in the mug; cover and refrigerate until ready to use.

Banana Pudding

How does such a simple dessert — classic banana pudding layered with fruit and vanilla cookies — have such wide appeal? My guess is that, like many favorite things, the familiar comforts are what we like best.

Tips

Wait to peel and dice the banana until just before using. If prepared too far in advance, it will turn brown and become slightly mushy.

This makes a generous serving. It's great for sharing, or for enjoying after a light meal.

◆ **16-oz (500 mL) mug**

1	single-serve container (4 oz/114 mL) vanilla pudding	1
1	container (5- to 6-oz/142 to 170 mL) vanilla-flavored Greek yogurt, divided	1
½	large firm-ripe banana, diced	½
⅓ cup	coarsely broken vanilla wafers	75 mL

1. In the mug, combine pudding and half the yogurt until well blended. Stir in banana and wafers. Smooth the top with the back of the spoon. Spoon in the remaining yogurt, smoothing top.

2. Refrigerate for at least 30 minutes before eating.

Variation

- **Peanut Butter Banana Pudding:** Before beginning step 1, in the mug, microwave 1½ tbsp (22 mL) creamy peanut butter on High for 15 to 30 seconds or until melted. Stir in pudding and half the yogurt and continue with step 1.

> **Prep Ahead Option**
>
> Prepare through step 2; cover and refrigerate for up to 4 hours before serving.

Vanilla Pudding

All you need to make this creamy pudding (besides the mug and the microwave) is a handful of ingredients and a fondness for vanilla.

Tips

An equal amount of arrowroot can be used in place of the cornstarch.

Any variety of milk (dairy or non-dairy) can be used. Keep in mind that pudding made with nonfat or lower-fat milk will have a lighter texture than one made with milk with a higher fat content.

♦ **12- to 16-oz (375 to 500 mL) mug**

♦ **Square of plastic wrap or parchment paper**

2 tbsp	granulated sugar	30 mL
1 tbsp	cornstarch	15 mL
2/3 cup	milk	150 mL
1 tbsp	butter	15 mL
1/2 tsp	vanilla extract	2 mL

1. In the mug, use a fork to whisk sugar and cornstarch. Whisk in milk a little at a time (to avoid clumps) until blended and smooth. Add butter.

2. Microwave on High for 60 seconds. Stir until blended. Microwave on High for 10 to 30 seconds, stopping to stir every 10 seconds, until shiny and thick. Stir in vanilla.

3. Place plastic wrap directly on the surface of the pudding (to prevent a skin from forming). Refrigerate for at least 30 minutes (until warm) or until completely cold.

Variations

• **White Chocolate Pudding:** Reduce the sugar to 1 tbsp (15 mL) and omit the butter. Add 2 tbsp (30 mL) white chocolate chips with the vanilla and whisk with a fork until chips are melted and mixture is smooth.

• **Butterscotch Pudding:** Replace the granulated sugar with packed brown sugar.

• **Rich Vanilla Pudding:** Replace the milk with an equal amount of half-and-half (10%) cream.

Prep Ahead Option

Whisk the sugar and cornstarch in the mug; cover and store at room temperature. Measure the milk, butter and vanilla into separate small airtight containers; cover and refrigerate until ready to use.

Chocolate Pudding

Surrender to the sublime. Chocoholics will be hard-pressed to find an easier (or more frugal!) chocolate fix when cravings strike.

Tips

An equal amount of arrowroot can be used in place of the cornstarch.

Any variety of milk (dairy or non-dairy) can be used. Keep in mind that pudding made with nonfat or lower-fat milk will have a lighter texture than one made with milk with a higher fat content.

♦ 12- to 16-oz (375 to 500 mL) mug

♦ Square of plastic wrap or parchment paper

2 tbsp	granulated sugar	30 mL
1½ tbsp	unsweetened cocoa powder	22 mL
1½ tsp	cornstarch	7 mL
½ cup	milk	125 mL
1 tbsp	butter	15 mL
½ tsp	vanilla extract	2 mL

1. In the mug, use a fork to whisk sugar, cocoa powder and cornstarch. Whisk in milk a little at a time (to avoid clumps) until blended and smooth. Add butter.

2. Microwave on High for 60 seconds. Stir until blended. Microwave on High for 10 to 30 seconds, stopping to stir every 10 seconds, until shiny and thick. Stir in vanilla.

3. Place plastic wrap directly on the surface of the pudding (to prevent a skin from forming). Refrigerate for at least 30 minutes (until warm) or until completely cold.

Variations

- **Extra-Rich Chocolate Pudding:** Add 1 tbsp (15 mL) semisweet chocolate chips with the vanilla and whisk with a fork until chips are melted and mixture is smooth.

- **Mocha Pudding:** Add ¾ tsp (3 mL) instant coffee granules, dissolved in 1 tsp (5 mL) warm water, with the vanilla.

Prep Ahead Option

Whisk the sugar, cocoa powder and cornstarch in the mug; cover and store at room temperature. Measure the milk, butter and vanilla into separate small airtight containers; cover and refrigerate until ready to use.

Rice Pudding

Cinnamon-scented, vanilla-enriched, raisin-freckled rice pudding in a matter of minutes? Hello, delicious.

Tips

An equal amount of packed brown sugar, liquid honey, agave nectar or pure maple syrup can be used in place of the granulated sugar.

Any variety of milk (dairy or non-dairy) can be used. Keep in mind that pudding made with nonfat or lower-fat milk will have a lighter texture than one made with milk with a higher fat content.

♦ **16-oz (500 mL) mug**

1	large egg	1
2 tbsp	granulated sugar	30 mL
1/8 tsp	salt	0.5 mL
1/8 tsp	ground cinnamon	0.5 mL
1/3 cup	milk	75 mL
1/4 tsp	vanilla extract	1 mL
1 cup	cooked instant brown rice (or other leftover cooked rice)	250 mL
2 tbsp	raisins or dried cranberries (optional)	30 mL

1. In the mug, use a fork to whisk egg, sugar, salt, cinnamon, milk and vanilla until very well blended. Stir in rice and raisins (if using) until blended.

2. Microwave on High for $1^1/_2$ to 2 minutes (checking at $1^1/_2$) or until firm to the touch and liquid is absorbed.

Variations

- **Quinoa Pudding:** Use an equal amount of cooked quinoa in place of the rice.
- **Chocolate Rice Pudding:** Omit the cinnamon and add $1^1/_2$ tbsp (22 mL) unsweetened cocoa powder with the sugar. Replace the raisins with 1 tbsp (15 mL) semisweet chocolate chips.

Prep Ahead Option

Prepare through step 1; cover and refrigerate until ready to use.

Bread Pudding

Leave the labor-intensive recipes for bread pudding on the shelf and whip up a batch for one in no time, without any fuss. You can vary this basic recipe in countless ways to suit your taste and mood — it's almost impossible to go wrong.

Tips

Add up to 2 tbsp (30 mL) raisins or chopped dried fruit with the bread cubes.

An equal amount of small plain croutons can be used in place of the bread cubes.

♦ **16-oz (500 mL) mug**

1	large egg	1
2$\frac{1}{2}$ tbsp	granulated sugar	37 mL
$\frac{1}{8}$ tsp	salt	0.5 mL
$\frac{1}{8}$ tsp	ground nutmeg or cinnamon	0.5 mL
$\frac{1}{2}$ cup	milk	125 mL
$\frac{1}{4}$ tsp	vanilla extract	1 mL
1 cup	bread cubes (preferably stale)	250 mL

1. In the mug, use a fork to whisk egg, sugar, salt, nutmeg, milk and vanilla until very well blended. Add bread cubes, stirring and pressing them down into the custard to absorb the liquid. Let stand for at least 15 minutes (so the bread absorbs the liquid). Press bread down with a fork to compact.

2. Microwave on High for 1$\frac{1}{2}$ to 2$\frac{1}{2}$ minutes (checking at 1$\frac{1}{2}$) or until firm to the touch and liquid is absorbed.

Variations

- **Chocolate Chip Bread Pudding:** Add 2 tbsp (30 mL) miniature semisweet chocolate chips with the bread cubes.

- **Raisin Spice Bread Pudding:** Replace the nutmeg with $\frac{1}{4}$ tsp (1 mL) ground cinnamon, and add 2 tbsp (30 mL) raisins with the bread cubes.

- **Maple Bread Pudding:** Replace the sugar with an equal amount of pure maple syrup. Use cinnamon instead of nutmeg.

- **Pumpkin Bread Pudding:** Reduce the milk to $\frac{1}{3}$ cup (75 mL) and add 2 tbsp (30 mL) pumpkin purée (not pie filling) with the milk. Replace the granulated sugar with packed brown sugar. Replace the nutmeg with $\frac{1}{4}$ tsp (1 mL) pumpkin pie spice.

Prep Ahead Option

Whisk the egg, sugar, salt, nutmeg, milk and vanilla in the mug; cover and refrigerate. Measure the bread cubes into a small airtight container; cover and store at room temperature until ready to use.

Egg Custard

If you love crème brûlée, you'll love this easy egg custard, too (they're close cousins).

Tips

For even more flavor, add a pinch of ground nutmeg or cinnamon with the salt.

If your microwave offers you only Low, Medium-Low, Medium, Medium-High and High power options, and does not allow you to choose a percentage of power to cook on, adjust the recipe as follows: Microwave on Medium-Low for 5 minutes. Microwave on Low for $1\frac{1}{2}$ to 2 minutes or until custard is just set as described in step 2.

♦ **12- to 16-oz (375 to 500 mL) mug**

1 tbsp	granulated sugar	15 mL
1 tsp	cornstarch	5 mL
$\frac{1}{3}$ cup	half-and-half (10%) cream	75 mL
1	large egg	1
$\frac{1}{4}$ tsp	vanilla extract	1 mL
Pinch	salt	Pinch

1. In the mug, use a fork to combine sugar, cornstarch and cream until cornstarch is dissolved. Whisk in egg, vanilla and salt until blended.

2. Microwave on 20% power for 6 to $6\frac{1}{2}$ minutes (checking at 6) or until puffed and center is just barely set (it should still jiggle slightly). Let cool for at least 5 minutes, cool entirely or refrigerate until cold.

Variations

- **Cappuccino Custard:** Add 1 tsp (5 mL) instant coffee granules with the sugar.
- **Cocoa Custard:** Add 1 tbsp (15 mL) unsweetened cocoa powder with the salt.
- **Butterscotch Custard:** Replace the granulated sugar with an equal amount of packed light brown sugar. Add 1 tsp (5 mL) butter to the cream mixture.
- **Caramel Custard:** Replace the granulated sugar with an equal amount of prepared caramel sauce. Drizzle the cooled custard with 1 to 2 tsp (5 to 10 mL) caramel sauce.

> **Prep Ahead Option**
> Prepare through step 1; cover and refrigerate until ready to heat.

Pumpkin Custard

Any day is occasion to give thanks with this gently sweet, spiced pumpkin custard. If you long for a bit of crunch, use a gingersnap cookie or two to scoop up the custard (munching as you go), or crumble the cookies over the custard before eating.

Tips

For even more flavor, add $\frac{1}{4}$ tsp (1 mL) vanilla extract.

Try topping the custard with a dollop of vanilla-flavored yogurt or a drizzle of pure maple syrup or liquid honey.

If your microwave offers you only Low, Medium-Low, Medium, Medium-High and High power options, and does not allow you to choose a percentage of power to cook on, adjust the recipe as follows: Microwave on Medium-Low for 6 minutes. Microwave on Low for 2 to $2\frac{1}{2}$ minutes or until center is just set.

♦ **12- to 16-oz (375 to 500 mL) mug**

1 tbsp	granulated sugar	15 mL
1 tsp	cornstarch	5 mL
$\frac{1}{8}$ tsp	pumpkin pie spice or ground cinnamon	0.5 mL
Pinch	salt	Pinch
$\frac{1}{4}$ cup	half-and-half (10%) cream	60 mL
1	large egg	1
2 tbsp	pumpkin purée (not pie filling)	30 mL

1. In the mug, use a fork to combine sugar, cornstarch, pumpkin pie spice and salt. Whisk in cream until cornstarch is dissolved. Whisk in egg and pumpkin until blended and smooth.

2. Microwave on 20% power for $7\frac{1}{2}$ to 8 minutes (checking at $7\frac{1}{2}$) or until center is just set. Let cool slightly or entirely in mug.

Variation

- **Sugar-Free Pumpkin Custard:** Substitute 2 packets (about $\frac{1}{2}$ tsp/2 mL) of powdered stevia or stevia-blend sweetener for the granulated sugar.

Prep Ahead Option

Prepare through step 1; cover and refrigerate until ready to heat.

Brownie Batter Dip

This luscious dip is a cross between brownie batter and chocolate cheesecake. In other words, irresistible.

Tips

The cream cheese you choose can be light or regular.

You can use 3 tbsp (45 mL) soft tub-style cream cheese in place of the brick-style cream cheese.

♦ **12- to 16-oz (375 to 500 mL) mug**

3 tbsp	brick-style cream cheese (1½ oz/45 g), cut into small pieces	45 mL
1 tbsp	butter, cut into small pieces	15 mL
¼ cup	confectioners' (icing) sugar	60 mL
2 tbsp	unsweetened cocoa powder	30 mL
2 tsp	milk	10 mL
¼ tsp	vanilla extract	1 mL
2 tsp	miniature semisweet chocolate chips (optional)	10 mL

Suggested Accompaniments

Pretzels; fresh fruit (apple slices, strawberries, banana slices); graham crackers or animal crackers

1. In the mug, microwave cream cheese and butter on High for 10 seconds or until softened. Stir until blended.

2. Stir in confectioners' sugar, cocoa powder, milk and vanilla until blended and smooth. Sprinkle with chocolate chips, if desired. Serve with any of the suggested accompaniments, as desired.

Variations

- **Mocha Brownie Batter Dip:** Add 1 tsp (5 mL) instant coffee granules with the cocoa powder.

- **Coconut Brownie Batter Dip:** Use an equal amount of virgin coconut oil in place of the butter. If desired, sprinkle the finished dip with 1 tbsp (15 mL) sweetened or unsweetened flaked coconut.

Prep Ahead Option

Measure the cream cheese and butter into the mug; cover and refrigerate. Measure the confectioners' sugar and cocoa powder into a small airtight container; cover and store at room temperature. Measure the milk and vanilla into a small airtight container; cover and refrigerate until ready to use.

S'mores Dip

Chocolate and marshmallows are a favorite combination, and nowhere are they better — or easier — than in this indulgent s'mores dip.

Tips

You can use 20 miniature marshmallows in place of the marshmallow crème. Use 5 marshmallows in step 1. Sprinkle the remaining marshmallows on top of the chocolate mixture in step 2.

Marshmallow crème is vegan, so to make this dip entirely vegan, simply use non-dairy (vegan) chocolate chips and non-dairy milk.

♦ **12- to 16-oz (375 to 500 mL) mug**

¼ cup	semisweet chocolate chips	60 mL
4 tbsp	marshmallow crème, divided	60 mL
1 tbsp	milk	15 mL

Suggested Accompaniments

Graham cracker sticks or pieces; fresh fruit (apple slices, strawberries, pear slices, grapes)

1. In the mug, combine chocolate chips, 1 tbsp (15 mL) marshmallow crème and milk. Microwave on High for 30 seconds. Stir. Microwave on High for 15 seconds. Stir until melted and smooth. If chocolate is not melted, microwave on High for another 15 seconds. Stir.

2. Spoon remaining marshmallow crème into mug. Let stand for 30 seconds, then gently swirl into the chocolate mixture with a spoon. Serve with any of the suggested accompaniments, as desired.

Variations

- **White Chocolate S'mores Dip:** Use white chocolate chips in place of the semisweet chocolate chips.
- **Peanut Butter Cup S'mores Dip:** Add 1 tbsp (15 mL) creamy peanut butter with the chocolate chips.

> **Prep Ahead Option**
>
> Combine the chocolate chips, 1 tbsp (15 mL) marshmallow crème and milk in the mug; cover and refrigerate. Measure the remaining marshmallow crème into a small airtight container; cover and store at room temperature until ready to use.

Index

Library and Archives Canada Cataloguing in Publication

Saulsbury, Camilla V., author
250 best meals in a mug : delicious homemade microwave
meals in minutes / Camilla V. Saulsbury.

Includes index.
ISBN 978-0-7788-0474-1 (bound)

1. Microwave cooking. 2. Quick and easy cooking. 3. Cookbooks
I. Title. II. Title: Two hundred fifty best meals in a mug.

TX832.S29 2014   641.5'882   C2013-908145-3